Research Methods in Public Administration and Public Management

Research in public administration and public management has distinctive features that influence the choices and application of research methods. Periods of change and upheaval in the public sector provide ample opportunities and cases for research, but the standard methodologies for researching the social sciences can be difficult to follow in the complex world of the public sector. In a dynamic political environment, the focus lies on solving social problems whilst also using methodological principles needed for doing scientifically sound research.

This textbook represents a comprehensive guide to doing and using research in public management and administration. It is impressively succinct but covering a wide variety of research strategies including: action research, hypotheses, sampling, case selection, questionnaires, interviewing, desk research, prescription and research ethics. This textbook does not bog the nascent researcher down in the theory but does provide numerous international examples and practical exercises to illuminate the research journey. Sandra van Thiel guides us through the theory, operationalization and research design process, before explaining the tools required to carry out impactful research.

This concise textbook will be core reading for those studying research methods and/or carrying out research on public management and administration.

Sandra van Thiel is a Professor of Public Management at Radboud University, Nijmegen, The Netherlands. From 2006–12 she was Associate Professor Public Administration, Erasmus University, Rotterdam, and she has been a guest lecturer at Vaasa University, Finland and the Catholic University at Leuven, Belgium. She has published, edited and lectured extensively on Public Management and Public Administration, both in her native The Netherlands and internationally.

ROUTLEDGE MASTERS IN PUBLIC MANAGEMENT
Edited by Stephen P. Osborne, Owen Hughes, Walter Kickert

Routledge Masters in Public Management series is an integrated set of texts. It is intended to form the backbone for the holistic study of the theory and practice of public management, as part of:

■ a taught Master's, MBA or MPA course at a university or college,
■ a work based, in-service programme of education and training, or
■ a programme of self-guided study.

Each volume stands alone in its treatment of its topic, whether it be strategic management, marketing or procurement, and is co-authored by leading specialists in their field. However, all volumes in the series share both a common pedagogy and a common approach to the structure of the text. Key features of all volumes in the series include:

■ a critical approach to combining theory with practice which educates its reader, rather than solely teaching him/her a set of skills,
■ clear learning objectives for each chapter,
■ the use of figures, tables and boxes to highlight key ideas, concepts and skills,
■ an annotated bibliography, guiding students in their further reading, and
■ a dedicated case study in the topic of each volume, to serve as a focus for discussion and learning.

Managing Change and Innovation in Public Service Organizations
Stephen P. Osborne and Kerry Brown

Risk and Crisis Management in the Public Sector
Lynn T. Drennan and Allan McConnell

Contracting for Public Services
Carsten Greve

Performance Management in the Public Sector
Wouter van Dooren, Geert Bouckaert and John Halligan

Financial Management and Accounting in the Public Sector
Gary Bandy

Strategic Leadership in the Public Sector
Paul Joyce

Managing Local Governments
Designing management control systems that deliver value
Emanuele Padovani and David W. Young

Marketing Management and Communications in the Public Sector
Martial Pasquier and Jean-Patrick Villeneuve

Ethics and Management in the Public Sector
Alan Lawton, Karin Lasthuizen and Julie Rayner

Making and Managing Public Policy
Karen Johnston Miller and Duncan McTavish

Research Methods in Public Administration and Public Management
An introduction
Sandra van Thiel

'This invaluable book provides a wealth of practical advice and methodological insights. It draws from Professor van Thiel's extensive experience as a leading public administration scholar, and someone who is equally at home in undertaking research for theory testing, issue exploration, or policy development. The book contains numerous worked examples, case studies and a glossary, making it the ideal companion for the public administration researcher at whatever stage in their career.'
Professor Chris Skelcher, *University of Birmingham, UK*

'Writing methodology books in such a messy field as public administration is difficult. Writing them for beginners is doubly difficult. Sandra van Thiel has overcome these difficulties to give us a book that is concise, accessible and comprehensive. She has also managed to treat the methodology wars within the field in a very even-handed way: even where I disagreed with her I found her account balanced and fair. Highly recommended.'
Christopher Pollitt, Emeritus Professor,
Public Management Institute, Catholic University of Leuven, Belgium

'This book is long overdue. Studying and doing research in Public Administration and Public Management has become ever more popular in recent years. In doing that we utilize all modern research methodologies of the social sciences, as we should! But at the same time research in these areas poses unique problems and challenges. At last we finally have our own textbook which explicates these problems and demonstrates how to handle them, using inspiring examples of "best practice" in public administration research.'
Prof. Dr. Werner Jann, *Chair for Political Science, Administration and Organization, Faculty for Economics and Social Sciences, Potsdam University, Germany*

'Sandra van Thiel has produced the solution for a problem faced by students and supervisors of research in public administration: how to make a rigorous exposition of research methods relevant to the investigation of problems in public policy and management. Embedded in the problems faced by public and related organisations, Research Methods in Public Administration and Public Management is a thorough, clear and focused exposition which will enable its readers to choose the right research strategy and carry out relevant and useful research.'
Norman Flynn, *Centre for Financial and Management Studies, SOAS, University of London, UK*

'Many scholars would argue that research in all the social sciences is essentially the same. Sandra Van Thiel demonstrates rather conclusively that there are special issues of research in public administration, and that our methods need to be considered in light of those issues. This is an extremely useful text for students embarking on investigating the workings of the public sector.'
B. Guy Peters, *University of Pittsburgh, USA*

Research Methods in Public Administration and Public Management

An introduction

Sandra van Thiel

Routledge
Taylor & Francis Group

LONDON AND NEW YORK

First published 2007
by Coutinho Publisher in Dutch
by Routledge 2014 in English
2 Park Square, Milton Park, Abingdon, Oxon OX14 4RN

and by Routledge
711 Third Avenue, New York, NY 10017

Routledge is an imprint of the Taylor & Francis Group, an informa business

British Library Cataloguing in Publication Data
A catalogue record for this book is available from the British Library

Library of Congress Cataloging in Publication Data
Thiel, Sandra van.
 Research in public administration and public management: an introduction/
Sandra Van Thiel.
  pages cm. – (Routledge masters in public management ; 11)
Includes bibliographical references and index.
 1. Public administration–Research. I. Title.
 JF1338.A2T477 2014
 351.072–dc23

                    2013027804

ISBN: 978-0-415-65581-1 (hbk)
ISBN: 978-0-415-65582-8 (pbk)
ISBN: 978-0-203-07852-5 (ebk)

Typeset in Bembo
by Taylor & Francis Books

Contents

List of illustrations   ix
Acknowledgements   xi

1   Research in public administration   1
   1.1 The unique features of research in Public
       Administration   1
   1.2 Research in Public Administration and policy   5
   1.3 Aim and outline of the rest of the book   10

2   The research problem   12
   2.1 Choosing and formulating a research problem   12
   2.2 The research aim   15
   2.3 The research question   17

3   Theoretical framework   24
   3.1 The empirical cycle   24
   3.2 What is theory?   28
   3.3 Philosophies of science   31
   3.4 The role of theory in Public Administration research   36

4   Operationalization   43
   4.1 Operationalization in three steps   43
   4.2 Sampling   45
   4.3 Reliability and validity   48
   4.4 Validity and reliability: sources of interference   51

5   Research design   54
   5.1 The different elements of the research design   54
   5.2 Choosing a research strategy, method and technique   57

6   The experiment   61
   6.1 The classic experiment   61
   6.2 Simulations and gaming   64

6.3 The field experiment   67
6.4 Reliability and validity in experiments   68
6.5 Observation   70

7 The survey   74
7.1 The survey: characteristics and types   74
7.2 The written questionnaire   75
7.3 The reliability and validity of questionnaires   82

8 The case study   86
8.1 Case study research   86
8.2 The selection of cases   89
8.3 The reliability and validity of case studies   92
8.4 The interview   93

9 Desk research   102
9.1 Using or re-using existing data   102
9.2 Three methods for gathering and analysing
    existing data   107

10 Analysing quantitative data   118
10.1 Quantitative data   118
10.2 Collecting and ordering the data   119
10.3 Analysis   126
10.4 Descriptive statistics   127
10.5 Inferential statistics   128
10.6 Reliability and validity when analysing
     quantitative data   135

11 Analysing qualitative data   138
11.1 Qualitative data   138
11.2 Collecting and ordering the data   142
11.3 Analysing the data   143
11.4 The reliability and validity of qualitative
     data analysis   150

12 Reporting results   153
12.1 Forums   153
12.2 Reporting formats   155
12.3 The purpose of reporting research results   158
12.4 Writing down the results   159
12.5 Prescription   164

Bibliography   169
Glossary   175
Index   190

Illustrations

FIGURES

3.1	Schematic outline of the empirical cycle	25
6.1	Schematic outline of the classic experiment	62
10.1	Normal distribution	124
10.2	Example of a scattergram	131
11.1	Example of a taxonomic scheme of codes	148

TABLES

2.1	Research aims	15
2.2	Research questions	18
3.1	Philosophies of science in Public Administration research	36
4.1	Sampling	46
5.1	Characteristics of the four main research strategies	58
5.2	Characteristics of diverse research methods	59
10.1	Example of a code book	121
10.2	Example of a data matrix	122
10.3	Example of a cross-tabulation	127

BOXES

1.1	Examples of prevalent topics in Public Administration and Public Management research	2
1.2	Reconstruction of programme theories	6
1.3	Evaluation and evidence-based policymaking	8
2.1	Action research	16
2.2	Example: formulating sub-questions	20
2.3	Hypotheses	22
3.1	Falsification and verification	26
3.2	The regulative cycle	28

3.3	Example: schematic representations of theoretical model	30
3.4	Examples of the use of theory in Public Administration research	37
3.5	Literature skills	39
4.1	Scales of measurement	44
4.2	Validating or standardizing measurement instruments	50
4.3	Triangulation	52
5.1	The time dimension in research	56
6.1	Exogenous variables and intervening variables	63
6.2	Designing a simulation game	65
6.3	Examples of policy experiments	67
6.4	Example of observation study	71
7.1	Examples of research with questionnaires	76
7.2	Scales	79
8.1	Examples of case study research in Public Administration	87
8.2	Choices involved in designing a case study	91
8.3	The interview manual	96
8.4	The Delphi method	97
9.1	Example: existing data sources for research on healthcare	103
9.2	Types of textual analysis	108
9.3	Examples of the application of content analysis in Public Administration	111
9.4	Examples of secondary analysis in Public Administration	112
9.5	Examples of meta-analysis in Public Administration and Public Management research	114
10.1	Reporting on results	129
10.2	Examples of studies in Public Administration and Public Management using quantitative data	134
11.1	Forms of qualitative research	139
11.2	Examples of qualitative research in Public Administration and Public Management	141
11.3	Coding an interview: example	144
11.4	Fuzzy set qualitative comparative analysis (QCA)	149
12.1	Selection of international, refereed journals in Public Administration and Public Management	157
12.2	Guidelines for writing a press release	157
12.3	Model for reporting research results	161
12.4	Unwelcome tidings	166

Acknowledgements

Teaching students of public administration – whether it be at the undergraduate, Master's or PhD level – about research methods is a challenging but rewarding task. Courses in research methods are usually not the most popular with students, either because the subject seems unimportant with a view to future jobs in the public sector, or because people feel fazed by statistics. In actual fact, however, doing research is far more about logic than statistics. To demonstrate this, I decided to write an introduction to research methods in Public Administration (PA) and Public Management (PM) that offers lots of practical guidance and examples.

In 2007, I made the deliberate choice to write this book in Dutch, intending to make the text easily accessible to a wide variety of students, including post-graduates. Moreover, I wanted to provide an introduction into Dutch PA and PM research, and show its diversity as regards topics, methods and findings. After its initial publication, the book soon became popular with lecturers all over the country, being used for teaching at different institutes for higher education as well as universities. Student evaluations were positive, too, leading to a second edition in 2010, which made some minor adjustments, and provided additional exam questions for online self-testing.

Over the years, many foreign colleagues enquired about my book, yet I always had to disappoint them when they asked whether they could use it for their own tuition. A call issued by Stephen Osborne (on behalf of Taylor & Francis) for manuscripts on research methods in Public Administration and Public Management opened the prospect of getting my book translated and published for the international market. I would sincerely like to thank Stephen Osborne, Taylor & Francis, David Varley and Rosemary Baron for giving me this great opportunity, and I am grateful for their sustained cooperation. I also hope that the present volume will inspire a new group of lecturers who teach research methods, and that students will enjoy the material it offers.

This book could not have been realized without the assistance of Rina F. de Vries, who translated the original text for me, remaining faithful to the spirit in which I first wrote the Dutch version. Needless to say, any remaining mistakes are entirely mine. The Dutch publishing company Coutinho N.V. rendered ample aid with the business side of things; special thanks go to Wouter Nalis and Marie-Lou Huijts.

Regarding contents, I am indebted to Jan Hakvoort and Harm 't Hart, whose thoughts and teaching on research methods contributed to my own ideas on the subject; indirectly, they gave shape to this volume as well. Other colleagues who helped me to sharpen my mind – either because we agreed on matters or because we disagreed – are Markus Haverland, Merlijn van Hulst and Berry Tholen. I trust that they can find traces of the many discussions we had on various subjects throughout the text. Andrej Zaslove deserves my thanks for being my first proofreader.

Finally, as always, I would like to express my gratitude to Jeroen, without whom I would not be able to do research, to write and teach, all at the same time, in the first place.

Sandra van Thiel
Nijmegen, 30 June 2013

Chapter 1

Research in public administration

Public Administration is the study of the management, operation, and functioning of government bodies and organizations in the public sector. As such, it is not unique: other disciplines study this subject as well. Public Administration (PA) distinguishes itself, though, by analysing the public sector from several angles in an integrated manner. In other words, it is interdisciplinary in character, employing knowledge from various disciplines in an integrated manner – or at least it is a multidisciplinary form of research, which applies the insights from different disciplines to one and the same subject.

Public Administration builds on four parent disciplines, namely law, economics, political science and sociology. Not only does it make use of the theories in these fields, but it applies the associated methods and techniques. However, the distinctive features of Public Administration mean that researchers use these methods and techniques in their own particular way. A separate textbook on research in Public Administration is therefore indispensable (see Burnham, Gilland, Grant, & Layton-Henry, 2008, and Pierce, 2008, for comparable introductions into political science research).

What are these unique features of Public Administration research? This forms the subject of the present chapter.

1.1 THE UNIQUE FEATURES OF RESEARCH IN PUBLIC ADMINISTRATION

Apart from its interdisciplinary approach, Public Administration research has three other distinctive features. These unique features all influence the way in which research is conducted.

The first distinctive feature has to do with the central object of research in Public Administration, which is the public sector. In the past few decades, the definition of what is generally regarded as the public sector has grown ever wider. Indeed, the public sector has evolved into much more than just 'the government' in a narrow sense, such as politicians and civil servants. In particular since the early 1980s, the sector of semi-government has increased rapidly in size; examples of new elements that have developed are independent executive agencies, private non-profit organizations – such as charities and non-governmental organizations (NGOs) – and state-owned enterprises (Pollitt & Talbot, 2004; OECD, 2002). In addition, citizens, interest groups, civil societies and companies are ever more actively involved in policy development and decision making. As a consequence of all this, Public Administration and Public Management research concerns itself with an ever wider array of subjects, which can range from things like the construction of a new railway line to local policies on the sales of soft drugs, political leadership, the voting behaviour of citizens, departmental reshuffles, assigning funds for scientific research, international security policy, or the privatization of a national airport (see Box 1.1 for more examples).

BOX 1.1 EXAMPLES OF PREVALENT TOPICS IN PUBLIC ADMINISTRATION AND PUBLIC MANAGEMENT RESEARCH

■ *New Public Management* (NPM) comprises a range of reform measures that were first introduced into the public sector in the 1980s. NPM encompasses business management techniques such as performance measurement, benchmarking, one-stop shops, vouchers, structural disaggregation of government units (into semi-autonomous agencies, or even privatization of state-owned enterprises), and much more. Numerous publications deal with the reasons why governments have adopted such reform measures, how they have been implemented, and what results have been achieved. For a seminal article, see Hood (1991). These days, the debate often focuses on the question whether NPM is still alive and kicking (Lapsley, 2008), or whether we have entered the post-NPM era (Christensen & Laegreid, 2008).

■ *Co-production* refers to the fact that policies cannot be developed and decided upon by politicians or civil servants alone; citizens need to cooperate as well. For example, the redevelopment of dis-advantaged neighbourhoods has a bigger chance of success if local inhabitants support the policy measures to be taken: support can be created by involving citizens in the decision-making process. Co-production goes beyond consultation, as it requires active citizen involvement from the earliest stages of policy making. The questions of how government officials can achieve true co-production and what the consequences are for democratic accountability processes usually occupy a central place in publications that deal with this topic (see, amongst others, work by Pestoff for more information)

■ How and why the current *financial crisis* developed is another hot topic, in particular when it comes to the role that central govern-ments may have played in bringing it about. Could the government have prevented the crisis, for example, by stricter regulation and monitoring (consider, for example, the role of the central banks)?

National governments have responded differently to the economic downturn, sometimes introducing budget cuts, sometimes making certain investments or carrying out takeovers in the form of, for example, the nationalization of banks. As the crisis continues to unfold, however, new research into such questions needs to be carried out. (For an overview and analysis of government action in the early years of the crisis, see Taylor, 2009.)

- *Leadership* in the public sector, by politicians and top civil servants, is a subject that has been studied extensively (see, for example, the work carried out by Downs in the 1960s). There are numerous theories on leadership, with each theory describing a different leadership style. Recently, the research done by Bass (1990) on transformational leadership has received much attention: transformational leaders have a clear vision of what needs to be done, which they can communicate well. Moreover, transformational leaders exhibit a high level of trust in their employees. By empowering employees to act and decide autonomously, such leaders promote self-actualization (a term developed by Maslow) in their employees.

- As a consequence of the processes of *globalization*, there are ever more governmental actors involved in the development and implementation of policies. See, for example, the transposition of European Union (EU) directives into national legislation, the rise of international markets or cross-border forms of cooperation, besides other phenomena such as traditional military cooperation, within the North Atlantic Treaty Organization (NATO) and the United Nations (UN). *Multi-level governance* (see, for instance, the work carried out by Marks and Hooghe) and *Europeanization* (see the research by Majone, Knill, or Scharpf) are but a few of the strands of literature that deal with the consequences of globalization, and the effects it has on central (and local) governments.

- *Crisis management* has become a growing industry; consequently, it is an ever more important topic in Public Administration and Public Management research. Crisis management is often strongly related to problems of *security*, which these days concern not just military issues, but also include other security threats, such as environmental (e.g. CO_2) and health problems (e.g. SARS – Severe acute respiratory syndrome). Numerous publications are available on this subject, as well as a number of specialized journals for studies on crisis management and international security issues.

As will be clear from this list, many research subjects in Public Administration are unique. For example, there is only one central bank, one system for national elections (e.g. proportional representation), and one president or prime minister. What is more, when it comes to certain other subjects, such as regional governments, coalition parties and universities, the number of cases often tends to be small. On the one hand, this will make research easier; it is clear which organizations or respondents have to be included in a study. On the other hand, drawing firm conclusions will be difficult, as material for comparison is not available, which may hamper the generalization of research results to other situations or translating them into theory (see Chapter 4 on validity). Because of this, researchers in Public Administration and Public Management often have to use special methods that allow for drawing scientifically sound inferences on the basis of subjects that are singular, unique or rare. The case study is a typical example of a method frequently applied in Public Administration research (see Chapter 8).

That research in Public Administration often involves but a limited number of cases does not necessarily mean that the amount of data to be processed is always small. Quite the contrary, in fact: many subjects of study will turn out to be extremely complex and substantive. Consider, for example, a study on decision making. In principle, a decision can be reduced to a simple 'yes' or 'no', yet in practice the situation is frequently complicated. Usually several different actors are involved in the decision-making process, such as politicians, civil servants, interest groups, companies and international organizations. Each of these parties will have their own interests and beliefs, which all have to be incorporated into the decision finally made. Indeed, research on decision making often comprises a large amount of information on numerous actors, who interact with each other for a prolonged period of time, in order to reach a shared decision in the end (Klijn & Koppenjan, 2004). This means that a unique case can generate a sizeable body of data.

The second unique feature of research in Public Administration has to do with its applied nature. Public Administration is still a relatively young discipline, and research typically concentrates on finding solutions to topical issues in the public sector (Ricucci, 2010). Stated differently, Public Administration researchers usually do not study subjects in a laboratory setting; rather they tend to concern themselves with problems situated in everyday reality (Robson, 2002). Moreover, they are frequently hired by organizations or policymakers to address a certain problem or give specific advice. When researchers convert the knowledge they have acquired into recommendations or suggested solutions (see Chapter 12), they move from an empirical method to a more normative one. Legal research is a typical example of this: on the basis of the analysis of legal rules, advice is given on how to proceed. However, as we shall see in Chapter 3, not all researchers find making recommendations or giving advice an equally useful or worthy purpose.

The applied nature of PA research points to a third important characteristic of Public Administration – namely, its limited body of knowledge. As it is the case, Public Administration has produced but few big theories of its own. Of course, exceptions can be mentioned, for example public service motivation (Perry & Wise, 1990), network theory (Kickert, Klijn, & Koppenjan, 1997), and New Public Governance (Osborne, 2009). Having said this, most theories used by researchers in Public Administration originate in the parent disciplines (for an overview, see the various handbooks, such as Dryzek, Honig, & Phillips, 2006; Moran, Rein, & Goodin, 2006; and Ferlie, Lynn, & Pollitt, 2007).

This lack of an own body of theory can partly be explained by Public Administration being such a young discipline (Ricucci, 2010). What is more, research tends to follow the changes and developments taking place in the public sector: such trends often set the research agenda. Political and social problems can prompt new subjects of study, too. Think, for example, of the rise of New Public Management, the response to acts of terrorism after 9/11 and, more recently, the effects of the financial crisis (compare Box 1.1). All in all, therefore, Public Administration focuses more on finding solutions to everyday problems rather than developing new or big theories. If we add the fact that many of its study subjects are unique – which makes generalized, theoretical advancement difficult at any rate – it will be clear that research in Public Administration is more often practical in nature than theory-oriented.

Taken together, the distinctive features of Public Administration lead to a predominant use of methods which are suitable for studying a small number of cases, and which allow for a direct application of results to everyday practice. This does not preclude research also being conducted into historical subjects (over time), however, or the application of statistical techniques in large-scale studies. Likewise, fundamental research – which focuses purely on the development of new theories – is frequently carried out, as we shall see later on. Still, the features described above typify the nature of mainstream research in Public Administration (Pollitt, 2006; Perry, 2012).

1.2 RESEARCH IN PUBLIC ADMINISTRATION AND POLICY

As we have seen, research in Public Administration aims to study and find solutions to topical issues and problems in the public sector. Such issues and problems can concern a broad range of subjects, such as the success or failure of social integration, improving government efficiency, determining the right composition of a government coalition, predicting the consequences of population ageing, or making decisions on awarding contracts for the construction of new roads or housing estates. What these subjects have in common is that they all revolve around public policy, whether it concerns the development and design of new policies, the implementation of existing ones, or the evaluation of the effects of policies applied in the past.

Public Administration conducts both research *into* policy and *for* policy, and it studies all aspects *of* the policy cycle, from the very beginning of setting the policy agenda to the possible termination of a policy. Roughly speaking, we can distinguish between: 1 research in which public policy is the *subject* of study; 2 research that has a certain policy as its *outcome*; and 3 research that *feeds into* the policymaking process (Pawson & Tilley, 2004; Parsons, 1995). Often these different research aims interconnect, and a certain study fulfils several different purposes. In Chapter 12 I shall elaborate on this point, and also discuss the fact that the findings of policy-oriented research are not always acknowledged or applied in practice. Regrettably, recommendations made by researchers in Public Administration are frequently mothballed.

Policy as a subject of research

In research where public policy forms the subject of study, policies are usually regarded as instruments or methods to achieve certain goals (Parsons, 1995, p. xv). The policy content is less relevant in this case. Different types of policy spring to mind here: laws and regulations, subsidies, contracts, but also matters such as the best way of structurally designing a public-private partnership, or even the application of management techniques by organizations in order to reach a certain policy objective.

Research in Public Administration that concentrates on the subject of public policy aims to contribute to a better insight into and a more efficient use of policies: the intention is to improve policy in an instrumental sense. Often-cited examples of this type of research are the development of decision-making models (for example, the 'garbage can model'), the design of manuals for policy design or memos, and the reconstruction of programme theories (see Box 1.2; compare Parsons (1995, p. 440) on forensic analysis). Research results can ultimately be used to create new policies, take decisions, or evaluate policy effects, although this need not be a primary objective.

BOX 1.2 RECONSTRUCTION OF PROGRAMME THEORIES

A policy programme is often defined as a plan to solve a particular problem; it describes a policy, social or organizational problem, as well as the means that will be deployed to solve this problem. A reconstruction of the underlying assumptions of the policy plan enables researchers to assess the consistency and validity of the policymakers' logic; such studies often form part of the evaluation of the effectiveness of the proposed measures. Programme assumptions can be based on knowledge derived from scientific theories or on advice given by academic researchers, but they are not scientific elements in themselves. A reconstruction of the assumptions underlying a policy plan consists of taking the following steps (Leeuw, 2003):

1 Gather information on the statements policymakers make about the background against which the policy is set. Such information comprises, for example, the minutes and reports of meetings, memoranda and official advisory reports.
2 Sift through the data for information on problem perception, such as explanations given about why the suggested policy would form a solution to the problem. The researcher must also try and identify

---

which *actors* and *factors* play a role in the policy sector and policy process. If this information is lacking, additional data can be obtained by conducting interviews.

3 Describe as precisely as possible the underlying assumptions of the policy (in the form of 'if-then' statements). Three main types of relation can be distinguished, namely:

■ Causal relations, which specify the causes and consequences of the problem, and the policy suggested to tackle it;

■ Final relations, which specify the intended application of means, and the methods by which certain targets are to be reached; and

■ Normative relations, which describe the underlying political beliefs, and specify any desirable or undesirable outcomes.

4 Make a systematic inventory of the logical order or formal system of the different relations, and the way in which they interact. For example, the researcher can draw up a tree diagram or an arrow graph.

5 Use the rules of argumentation theory to identify and fill in any missing links in the system of relations. For example, the researcher can check for:

■ The accuracy with which certain concepts are described;

■ The empirical foundations on which the different assumptions rest;

■ Whether or not certain assumptions conflict with each other.

6 Evaluate the aggregate of assumptions on their practical feasibility in the implementation stage. Amongst others, attention will have to be paid to:

■ Whether the assumptions made by policymakers also describe how a policy can be actually implemented;

■ Whether the plan specifies what can and what cannot be achieved;

■ Whether limiting constraints such as social acceptance, costs and the timing of the policy process have been taken into account.

7 On the basis of the assessments made, the researcher can draw conclusions on the possible effectiveness, validity and quality of the policy theory. If called for, the process can be rounded off by formulating some recommendations.

Research that feeds into policy

As explained above, if public policy forms the central subject of study, the contents of the policy in question will be of little relevance as compared to method. If, however, research results are meant to be used for the development of new policies, such substantive features become of paramount importance.

After all, the study to be carried out is meant to make a contribution in this respect, and give an outline of what the new policy will have to comprise. Typical examples of such policy-supporting research are the following:

- Research on trends, that is, signalling and analysing economic, social and cultural developments. This also involves predicting the possible consequences of certain trends by sketching scenarios. A scenario is a description given by the researcher of situations that may develop if a particular policy choice is made;
- Cost-benefit analysis, in which the costs and benefits of public policy are assessed, either before developing a policy (*ex ante*), or after the decision to implement the policy has been taken (*ex post*). Non-monetary costs and gains can also be incorporated into this type of analysis (compare with the scenarios mentioned above); and
- Evaluation research (see Box 1.3 for an overview of different types of evaluation).

Public Administration researchers are not the only scientists who do research on behalf of policymakers. As the literature and newspapers show, there are many examples of sociologists, political scientists and economists making prognoses or advising the government on where public policy in a certain realm should be heading. Besides academic researchers, there are various other organizations that occupy themselves with studying things such as socio-economic trends, the effects of public policy, and policy efficiency. Examples are national audit offices, think tanks, statistical government bureaux, central banks, and international organizations like the World Bank and International Monetary Fund (IMF).

BOX 1.3 EVALUATION AND EVIDENCE-BASED POLICYMAKING

Evaluation is part of the policy cycle: an assessment is made of whether the implementation of a policy has led to the goals initially specified. Research can be done, for example, on whether a certain policy measure or subsidy has reached the intended target group, if the policy implementation has been successful, services and products have been delivered, the costs outweigh the benefits and so forth. The evaluation of public policy has grown in importance in recent decades. Power (1994) even speaks of an 'audit explosion'.

This increase in attention for policy evaluation can be ascribed to the growing focus on results and efficiency as part of the NPM reforms. These days, the impact of a policy is often an important source of information for the development of new policies. Based on the *evidence* on the effects (or lack thereof) of policies that have already been implemented, new policy proposals can be expected to ensure effectiveness (or greater effectiveness) and will therefore receive wide support

---

in the political and societal realm. Just as in a field like medicine, only effective policies will be applied to new situations – hence the term 'evidence-based policymaking'.

Evaluative research comes in different shapes, which can be specified in terms of three dimensions:

- Researchers can do a formative evaluation, and concentrate on how processes develop. They can also perform a summative evaluation, which is geared at investigating how the targets specified can be achieved. In the first type of evaluation, the focus lies on studying the way in which a policy measure has been developed. Attention is paid to the decision-making process, and to what problems, if any, have arisen during the implementation and execution phase. Summative evaluation, on the other hand, is target-oriented, and concentrates mainly on the effectiveness of a policy. It can also be directed at studying efficiency, or at giving an indication of the balance between costs and benefits.
- Evaluative research can vary according to when exactly the evaluation takes place: before (*ex ante*) or after (*ex post*) a policy is introduced. An *ex ante* evaluative study, conducted during the stage of policy design, can contribute to making a proper assessment of expected costs and benefits, sometimes leading to an adjustment of plans; this means that it may influence the ultimate design or the very decision to implement a certain policy. *Ex post* evaluations can be used to support the decision to continue on the policy course set out, or to make certain adaptations on the way, or even to terminate a policy measure.
- Lastly, evaluative research can serve different purposes. It can be normative in character, in the sense of rendering a conclusion on whether a certain policy has been the right line to follow. Other studies serve a strictly empirical purpose, and confine themselves to gathering knowledge or giving a purely factual account of policy developments and results.

These three dimensions are not mutually exclusive, by the way: different combinations and forms of research can occur. To give an example, environmental impact studies often take place prior to policy implementation (*ex ante*): they give an assessment of the likely consequences of the policy for the environment (summative), with the aim of aiding policymakers in making the right decision (normative). Another example is research on the social support that a policy is likely to gain. The latter form of research would be of a formative, normative type.

(For more information see: Pawson & Tilley, 2004; Rossi, Lipsey, & Freeman, 2004.)

Policy as the outcome of research

Policymakers regularly call in the aid of researchers to try to find a solution to a certain policy problem. If the aim of such research is that of developing new policy instruments (laws, subsidies) or management techniques (finance, ICT, personnel), or to decide on which procedure to follow (operating through networks, decentralization or free market processes), policy is, in effect, the outcome of research. Again, this type of research is not the exclusive domain of Public Administration. For example, legal professionals can be asked for help as well, say, to give advice on formulating new bills of law. PA researchers can also participate in advisory committees for new policy proposals, although it has to be added that this field of study is often dominated by management consultants. Lastly, many policymakers employ their own researchers or enlist the services of independent advisory bodies. Such advisory bodies usually also employ Public Administration researchers.

1.3 AIM AND OUTLINE OF THE REST OF THE BOOK

This book offers an introduction to research in Public Administration and Public Management for those who are as yet unfamiliar with the subject. In the first instance, the text is meant for undergraduate students of Public Administration and Public Management. However, it also offers guidelines for researchers and students who are active in other disciplines, such as legal scholars, sociologists, or political scientists.

As I intend this book to be a practical guide to doing research in a scientifically sound manner, I have divided its contents along the lines of the different phases of the research process. All research starts with formulating a research problem. In Chapter 2 I explain how researchers can improve the feasibility of a study by formulating a clearly outlined and sufficiently detailed research problem. By deciding on the main aim of one's study, and preparing well-circumscribed research questions, the foundations are laid for the rest of the research. Indeed, the way in which the research problem is laid out influences all subsequent steps of the research.

The phase of deciding which theory to use is described in Chapter 3. In Chapters 4 and 5, the next steps in the research process are outlined. When the research problem has been formulated and a relevant theoretical framework has been chosen, it becomes clear what the main subject of study is (Chapter 4) and which research methods will be most suitable (Chapter 5). In Chapter 6–9, I discuss the diverse research methods that are available to the Public Administration researcher.

Once information has been gathered, the phase of data analysis begins. Again, there are various techniques to choose from. The ultimate choice depends on the nature of the data, as is explained in Chapters 10 and 11. In Chapter 12 I describe how, on the basis of the analysis, a researcher can draw certain conclusions. The final step of the research consists of formulating recommendations and reporting the research results to, amongst others, policymakers.

Every chapter has a similar set-up. First, I describe in general terms what a particular phase of research entails. I illustrate this by giving some examples of studies in Public Administration and Public Management, which show how the research phase in question works out in practice. Text boxes provide information on special topics or techniques. Each chapter concludes with a list of recommended literature for those interested in reading more on the subjects discussed in the chapter. I also give special exercises for students, which are designed to practise applying what has been explained in the text. Finally, there is a Glossary of the main terms and definitions used.

FURTHER READING

Pawson, R., & Tilley, N. (2004). *Realistic Evaluation*. London: SAGE.
Raadschelders, J.C.N. (2011). *Public Administration: the interdisciplinary study of government*. UK: Oxford University Press.

EXERCISES

1 Select ten recent issues of two or more journals of Public Administration or Public Management, and make an inventory of the most popular research topics (tip: you need not read the entire articles – usually, reading an abstract will suffice). Can you find similar-sounding topics and, if so, are these topics concentrated in just one journal, or do different journals all show the same emphasis?
2 Select a recent report from the national audit office in your home country (tip: most audit offices publish their reports online). Does the report contain any policy recommendations and, if so, can you find out how the government concerned responded to these recommendations?
3 Select a White Paper or policy memorandum on a topic of your choice (for the purpose of this exercise, make sure that the document you use is between five and ten pages long). Reconstruct the underlying programme theory, as described in Box 1.2. Formulate recommendations on how the authors (policymakers) could make their line of argumentation clearer.

Chapter 2

The research problem

Opinions vary on what precisely constitutes a research problem. Most definitions share the idea, however, that the research problem describes: 1 the main subject or central question of study; and 2 what kind of answer or conclusion is sought. With respect to the latter, research can serve different purposes: it can aim to arrive at a description, an explanation, or a solution to a certain problem. The research problem therefore not only outlines the *subject* of study (the research question), but also what *purpose* the study is intended to serve (the research aim). In the research *design*, the researcher describes the way in which the study will actually be carried out (see Chapter 5).

2.1 CHOOSING AND FORMULATING A RESEARCH PROBLEM

The research problem lays the foundations for the rest of the research; it brings into focus what exactly will be studied and how. These initial choices influence all subsequent steps, such as the decision of which theoretical framework to apply, what methods and techniques to use for gathering and analysing the data, and what kind of conclusions can be drawn from the study. Formulating the research problem is a serious act of commitment, which has to properly founded and validated. Of course, this does not mean to say that adaptations cannot be made at a later stage. As the research is being carried out, it may turn out that the problem as originally formulated has to be revised in some way or other – for example, because the intended study is practically unfeasible, or there is less or more information available than initially thought. Such adjustments to the original design, too, must be well justified and carefully documented.

The process of arriving at a clearly delineated research problem is sometimes called 'problematizing'. Although in everyday speech the word 'problem' has negative connotations, denoting trouble or some kind of difficulty, in the scientific community it is merely used as a neutral term, designating a subject of study. A problem is a puzzle, a question, which need not always be some kind of stumbling block that has to be overcome. For example, reconstructing a plane crash can render insight into what has happened and why, but it does not provide any means of avoiding the calamity (it cannot, because the accident has already happened). In cases such as these, we employ the term 'knowledge problem'. Having said all this, it is certainly true that Public Administration is often applied in nature, concentrating on practical issues for which a certain solution is sought. To illustrate, reconstructing the plane crash can result in recommendations on how to prevent similar disasters in future or render suggestions for improving crisis management.

Problematizing requires preparatory research being done first (compare Verschuren & Doorewaard, 2010). By gathering information on a particular subject, the researcher can determine which aspects or dimensions will be suitable for study, and how relevant the research will be. Carrying out preparatory research involves tasks such as perusing scientific journals, consulting experts and others involved (such as sponsors), making an inventory of previously conducted studies, and so forth.

In the preparatory research stage, the researcher tries to ascertain what the central problem is (a knowledge problem or a practical issue), what sub-problems it consists of, what is already known on the subject, and what contribution the study could or should make. The information gained in this manner is used to select a relevant and feasible research problem. In principle, the thirst for knowledge is unquenchable and the number of questions we can ask is endless; however, it is important to choose just one research question and one research aim – if only to ensure that the study will be feasible and have sufficient focus.

Which particular research question and research aim are ultimately chosen depends on the following:

■ The researcher's interests and background knowledge. Everyone has their own personal preferences and experiences, which will guide the choice of an interesting research problem. A concomitant risk of such partialities and unique individual knowledge is that a researcher may also turn out to be biased. For example, many people – including researchers – take the word 'government' to mean the national government rather than, say, the local council.

■ The existing body of scientific knowledge. The scientific relevance of a study varies with the extent to which it will contribute to existing knowledge. Studying a subject about which only little is known (virgin territory) or about which the evidence is contradictory (puzzles) will make the biggest contribution to the body of scientific knowledge: this kind of research is scientifically most relevant. By reviewing the literature during the preparatory stage, the researcher gains insight into what is already known on a subject (for practical tips on this, see McMenamin, 2006).

■ The sponsor's preferences. If a study is commissioned and subsidized by a sponsor, the researcher has to ensure that the research problem forms a satisfactory (and scientifically sound) translation of the sponsor's wishes and aims. This can turn out to be rather difficult in practice. Sponsors often lack the background knowledge to phrase their questions correctly; also, policymakers are hardly ever interested in theoretical depth. Moreover, political volatility can cause the interest in a subject to wane whilst the research is still in the process of being carried out (see also Chapter 12). For more information and tips on how to convert a sponsor's requests into a scientifically sound research problem, see Verschuren and Doorewaard (2010).

■ Practical issues. A study has to be feasible and workable. Practical matters such as the scope of the study, time and money constraints, the access needed to sources of information or people, and the expertise and creativity of the researcher are all crucial – though not always decisive – points, worthy of careful consideration.

As stated, a research problem must be well founded and properly formulated. In the research problem, the researcher describes what choices have been made on the basis of the preparatory research. When it comes to research in Public Administration and Public Management, it is important not just to give an indication of the scientific relevance of the study, but also of its public or societal relevance. What will the contribution of the study be to solving topical social issues or policy questions?

Mistakes often made

During the process of choosing and formulating a research problem, certain mistakes are sometimes made. Often the relation between the main research aim and central question remains unclear, because one of them has not been properly specified, or the two are incongruous with each other. Frequently, too, the research problem has not been delineated precisely enough. This can show, for example, in the researcher planning to study too many different things at once, or a focus on detail (symptoms) rather than on the real, underlying problem (the disease). To illustrate the latter, government policy is usually implemented by a chain of organizations. Consider the stance taken by the government on crime, for example: this will have a bearing on the police investigating criminal offences and arresting people, on the public prosecution bringing action against the accused and, finally, on a judge passing sentence. A study of the effects of government policy can concentrate on just a part or link of such a chain; however, this also means that the conclusions drawn on the effects of government policy will be limited to that particular link. For example, a study of police performance does not allow for inferences to be drawn about the functioning of the court. For all such reasons, it is vital to outline as precisely as possible what will form part of the study, and what will be left out, and why – with the annotation that the research has to be socially and scientifically relevant as well.

A mistake often made in applied research (and so particularly relevant to the field of Public Administration) is that the research problem does not give an adequate translation of the sponsor's requests. The researcher has to bear in mind that the sponsor is struggling with a practical problem, for which a realistic solution is sought. The scientific interests and expertise of the researcher can be an aid in finding such a solution, but only if the final results of the study can be applied in an everyday context. This means that a balance must be struck between theory and practice. After all, a treatise on the inadvertent effects of performance rating in the police force is of little help to a chief officer hoping to learn how performance indicators can be developed or improved.

2.2 THE RESEARCH AIM

Research can fulfil several aims. Applied research is meant to solve a practical issue or problem, described by the sponsor who commissioned the study. Fundamental research, on the other hand, is geared in the first instance towards acquiring scientific knowledge. It is important for the researcher to give a precise indication of what purpose the study is meant to serve. Merely 'doing research' is not an aim in itself; neither is 'finding out what happened'. Such descriptions are not nearly detailed enough, and give no information on the contribution the study is expected to make.

Table 2.1 provides an overview of possible research aims. As the accompanying descriptions show, we can distinguish a hierarchy of aims. For example, the more knowledge already exists on a subject, the less relevant exploratory and descriptive research will be. Similarly, research aims such as diagnosis, design and evaluation can only be achieved if the problem under study has already been described and explained. I shall return to these points during the discussion on sub-questions (see below).

Table 2.1 Research aims

Aim	Description
Exploration	Research that *investigates* a subject about which little or no knowledge is available. Exploratory research results in detailed *empirical* descriptions. Exploration is also used in studies of how actors assign meaning, such as the way in which certain concepts are applied in practice.
Description	Research in which events or the characteristics of a certain subject are *described*. A description can be empirical (for example, events arranged in chronological order). However, *ordering* can also take place in terms of theoretical concepts, such as actors or factors. Descriptive research should not be confused with the reporting of results.
Explanation	Research in which the *causes* of a certain problem are sought or studied. Explanatory research can apply existing theories in the search for causes. Another option is to develop a new theory, based on the empirical findings (for more on this subject, see Chapter 3).

▨ **Table 2.1** (continued)

Aim	Description
Testing	Research in which – on the basis of theoretical knowledge – preliminary expectations (*hypotheses*) are formed regarding the problem under study. As a rule, such expectations concern problem characteristics or possible causes. In an empirical study, the researcher tries to ascertain whether these expectations meet reality. See also Box 2.3 on hypotheses.
Diagnosis	Research that is mainly applied in character. The researcher tries to establish what the problem is, and which factors or actors contribute to this problem in a positive or negative sense. The diagnosis helps to gain insight into possible keystones of a solution to the problem.
Design	Research that results in suggested solutions to a practical problem, or recommendations on how to improve a situation (*prescription*). A Public Administration design can vary from a new management model to a set of guidelines or a draft policy text, depending on the problem studied.
Evaluation	Research aimed at gauging whether a certain policy or arrangement has helped to realize the specified targets. The evaluation can concern policy development and implementation, or the desired effects (see Box 1.3). Evaluative research usually results in a normative judgement. If this is requested, recommendations can be made for improvement (prescription).

Do note that comparative research – that is, research comparing countries, policy sectors, organizations, or different groups of people with each other – is a means to an end: comparison helps to describe, explain, evaluate and so on. Comparison is not a separate research aim in itself.

The aim of a piece of research relates directly to its main research question; every research aim corresponds with a certain type of question (see below). The feasibility of a study is greatly enhanced if the researcher formulates a distinct, discrete research aim: the research problem comprises just one single aim, which applies to the entire study. It has to be added, though, that there are types of research that have several different aims (see Box 2.1 on action research).

BOX 2.1 ACTION RESEARCH

In action research, researchers are actively involved in the situation under study. Usually, the researcher is trying to devise a way to improve the situation, either because they work or live in this situation (or organization) themselves, or because they strive to create a better world – hoping, for example, to improve the position of disadvantaged social groups or other minorities.

What this basically means is that in action research, the researcher forms part of the research situation, and participates in events. Sometimes, too, researchers constitute their own subject, for example, because they want to assess and improve their own performance. Think of teachers' training courses, healthcare evaluations, and so on.

Action research comprises several phases, each of which has its own particular research aim:

1   *describing* and establishing what the initial problematic situation is, and outlining the study that will be conducted;
2   arriving at a *diagnosis* by gathering and analysing information;
3   *designing* a plan for improving the situation;
4   supervising the implementation of the plan (intervention); and
5   monitoring and *evaluating* progress, and making recommendations for further progress.

(For more information on action research, see Stringer, 1996.)

2.3 THE RESEARCH QUESTION

The research question does not just specify the subject under study, but also delineates the research in other respects. Amongst other things, the research question denotes the units of observation – that is, which persons, documents, organizations or countries will actually be examined or questioned. The researcher also has to give an indication of the time and place to which the study pertains. Such limits to the research territory always have to be borne in mind, as they influence the scope of the validity of one's conclusions (see Chapter 4 for more explanation). For example, results found in one situation will not necessarily be valid in another. Finally, in the research question a first indication can be given of which theories – if any – will be used. The application of such theories has to concur with the research aim and the intended use of theory (see Chapter 3 for further explanation).

Formulating the research question

The research question is directly related to the research aim: every specific type of research aim corresponds with a certain type of question. Exploratory and descriptive questions, for example, are often of the 'which' or 'what' variety. Questions geared at design or evaluation usually begin with phrases such as 'how' or 'in what manner'. Table 2.2 gives some examples to illustrate that different research aims concur with different types of question.

As the examples in Table 2.2 show, research questions can be formulated in many different ways. A single subject can inspire a wide array of questions,

Table 2.2 *Research questions*

Aim	Question
Exploration	Exploratory questions are open-ended, and presuppose there is as yet no knowledge on the subject of study. For example: *in what way* do public organizations A and B use indicators for measuring personnel performance?
Description	Descriptive questions often focus on characteristics of the subject of study. For example: *which* indicators do public organizations A and B use to measure personnel performance? A description can also be given in terms of theoretical notions. For example: what sort of input and output indicators do public organizations A and B use to measure personnel performance?
Explanation	Explanatory questions often start with the word 'why'. The researcher aims to establish the causes and circumstances that have led to certain behaviours or policy measures. For example: *under which conditions* does the use of performance indicators by public organizations A and B lead to a more productive personnel performance?
Testing	Testing questions are usually of the yes/no variety. Based on the theory, the researcher formulates certain expectations, which are subsequently translated into questions. For example: does the use of performance indicators by public organizations A and B lead to a more productive performance *if* employees have been actively involved in developing these indicators? Or (to see whether this is a proportionate effect): is it true that the more closely involved employees are in the initial stages, the more productive their performance will ultimately be?
Diagnosis	Diagnostic questions try to identify practical problems or stumbling blocks. For example: which organizational and financial *problems* do public organizations A and B encounter when trying to introduce indicators for measuring personnel performance? Diagnostic questions are often geared at ascertaining the success or failure of policies or organizational changes.
Design	Design questions are geared at finding a solution to a certain problem. They usually refer to measures for improvement, or norms such as 'better' or 'more efficiently'. For example: how can public organizations A and B introduce performance indicators without meeting with resistance from their personnel?
Evaluation	Evaluative questions often probe into the process and results of changes that have been made (interventions). For example: has the introduction of performance indicators by public organizations A and B led to more productive personnel performance?

which often diverge from each other in subtle but significant respects. Just one word can make a world of difference as to which question exactly the researcher is trying to answer. Formulating a clearly defined, proper research question takes a lot of practice and constant revision, and even experienced researchers often have to go back and make adjustments to their original wording. This brings me to the criteria for formulating a good research question.

Criteria for formulating a good research question

A research question has to be workable. After all, it is no use asking a question that cannot be answered. A good and proper research question should therefore be (compare Verschuren & Doorewaard, 2010):

- Relevant – in a societal or a scientific sense (or both; see also above);
- Precise, meaning that it is singular (do not ask more than one main question), and well delineated in terms of the units of observation, time and place;
- Purposeful – that is, geared at arriving at a certain kind of answer (as specified in the accompanying research aim);
- Congruous with the theory and methodology: the study has to be relevant in the sense of linking up with existing knowledge. Also, the research question has to give a clear indication of how the knowledge that is being sought can best be acquired and analysed;
- Internally logical and consistent. The research question usually consists of a main or overarching question and a set of sub-questions. Sub-questions reflect the intermediate steps that the researcher has to take in order to reach the ultimate target of answering the main research question.

Regarding its *format*, it is important to put the research question explicitly in the text, usually in the introductory section to a report or article. Finally, a questioning form is to be preferred, so do use a question mark.

Sub-questions

Usually, the main research question cannot be answered in one go. For this reason, it is often necessary to formulate several sub-questions, each of which applies to a particular part of the study. *The sum of the answers to all sub-questions taken together forms the answer to the main research question.*

Arriving at relevant sub-questions requires logical thought and reasoning. How many and what kind of sub-questions can be derived depends entirely on the nature of the main research question, and general guidelines cannot be given. Having said this, there are two important rules of thumb (compare Verschuren & Doorewaard, 2010). First, the number of sub-questions increases with the amount of characteristics, conditions, actors, or norms specified in the main research question and, also, with the various relations between these that can be distinguished. Second, the higher up in the hierarchy of research aims the researcher wants to go (for example, explaining something rather than just giving a description), the more sub-questions will be needed. In Box 2.2, an example is given of how these rules of thumb work out in practice.

19

BOX 2.2 EXAMPLE: FORMULATING SUB-QUESTIONS

In Table 2.2, the following example was given of an explanatory main research question: Under which conditions does the use of performance indicators by public organizations A and B lead to a more productive personnel performance?

We can distinguish three key subjects here: 1 the conditions for more efficient performance; 2 the use of performance indicators; and 3 the public organizations A and B. This means that a minimum of three sub-questions is needed.

The first sub-question will concentrate on the use of performance indicators by public organizations A and B. This is a descriptive question, meant to investigate whether the two public organizations make use of performance indicators, and how these indicators are applied. The second sub-question concerns personnel performance in the two public organizations. This question must at least describe personnel performance in a way that shows how this can be influenced by using performance indicators. For example, performance can be compared over time (before and after indicators were introduced), or between organizations that do use performance indicators and organizations that do not. As to the third sub-question, it will centre on the general (theoretical) conditions under which performance indicators lead to a more productive personnel performance. Finally, to establish whether such theoretical conditions apply in organizations A and B, a fourth sub-question is needed. The answers to all four sub-questions taken together enable us to answer the main research question, which makes the main research question and the set of sub-questions internally consistent.

All in all, the research question will now read as follows:

Main, overarching question:

Under which conditions does the use of performance indicators by public organizations A and B lead to more productive personnel performance?

Sub-questions:

1 How do public organizations A and B use performance indicators to measure personnel performance?
2 Is personnel performance more productive in public organizations that do use performance indicators, as compared to organizations that do not use such indicators?
3 Which conditions enable (or disable) the use of performance indicators that lead to more productive personnel performance?

> 4   Are the conditions under which performance indicators lead to a more productive personnel performance actually met by public organizations A and B?
>
> This example also shows that some sub-questions will have to be answered by means of empirical research, whilst other sub-questions demand a theoretical answer. Sometimes, too, a question can or has to be answered in both an empirical and a theoretical sense. Moreover, the logic of the research problem, reflected in the order of the sub-questions, is not the same as the logic of the study (as we will see in Chapter 3: in deductive research theory comes before empirical research); likewise, it need not follow the structural logic of the research report (compare Chapter 12).

Mistakes in the research question

Formulating the main research question and the accompanying sub-questions is not an exact science, and often mistakes creep in. The most commonly made mistakes are (Verschuren & Doorewaard, 2010):

- Insufficiently precise wording. Central concepts must be defined in plain and unambiguous language: if different interpretations are possible, it will be unclear what exactly the research is about (this is called insufficient conceptualization). For example, a research question in which the term 'the government' is used is not precise and exact enough: does the researcher mean the national government, a certain ministry, a municipal council, or a semi-public body?
- Wrong level of abstraction. Sometimes a study tries to answer a broadly phrased question by presenting knowledge about one particular example. In such cases, it is advisable to narrow down the main research question. For example, in a study on the civil service ethos of municipality X, the research question should be targeted at X, and not municipal councils in general, as this would refer to too high a level of abstraction. After all, the extent to which X can be said to be representative of other municipalities may be doubtful (see also Chapter 4). Frequently, too, the level of abstraction is too low, with sub-questions bearing more the character of items for an interview or a questionnaire. Such 'observation questions' have to be formulated at a later stage, after operationalization has taken place (see Chapter 4).
- Incompleteness. A research question has to be well delineated in terms of subject, place and time. For testing questions this is even of paramount importance, because a point of reference is needed for testing. For example, asking after an increase in election turnout is of little use if it is unclear

which elections exactly are meant, and against which base year the increase will be measured.

■ Incorrect suppositions, or even prejudice, about the relationship between central concepts or about the notions employed. Suggestive and coloured language should be avoided at all times, as it reduces objectivity and therefore the credibility of the study. Prejudiced statements, such as 'bureaucracy is by definition a bad thing' or 'citizen involvement in decision making only slows the process down', are not just vague and incorrect, but can also harm the chances of successfully carrying out the study and finding a good solution to a social problem.

BOX 2.3 HYPOTHESES

Instead of phrasing a testing research question, it is also possible to formulate a hypothesis. A hypothesis is a testable proposition (so not a question, but a statement). The research findings can either support the hypothesis or cause it to be rejected.

A hypothesis is derived from theory, and consists of the following four elements: (1) the circumstances or conditions under which (2) a certain factor, called the independent variable, creates a certain change or effect by way of (3) a certain mechanism in the (4) dependent variable. In Chapter 3, the process of deducing a hypothesis and its constituent elements from the theory is explained further.

Examples of possible hypotheses are the following:

■ The more women there are employed in high political functions, the more often the issue of female emancipation will be placed on the political agenda.
■ The higher the number of floating voters, the more frequently election programmes will be consulted.

A good hypothesis is one-directional, explicit in terms of the predicted effect, and does not allow for ambiguity. Instead of a hypothesis, the researcher can also formulate *expectations* or make *predictions*, which are not subject to such strict requirements.

FURTHER READING

Verschuren, P., & Doorewaard, H. (2010). *Designing a Research Project*. Schiedam: Boom Juridische Uitgevers.

EXERCISES

1   Consider the following (main) research questions, and give the accompanying research aim. Justify your answer with appropriate arguments. If you think that a certain research question is inadequately formulated, explain why this would be so, and suggest a better wording.

   a. How is the Ministry of Environment organized?
   b. Under which circumstances will the Ministry of Environment have to make changes to its organizational structure?
   c. How does the body of senior civil servants at the Ministry of Environment deal with the internally conflicting interests of economy and ecology?
   d. Does the Ministry of Environment still have a future?

2   Formulate a hypothesis about the effect of the participation of leaders of national political parties in local election campaigns on the turnout in local elections. Explain how you have arrived at your hypothesis (see also Box 2.3).

3   How many and which sub-questions will result from the following testing main research question: 'Which theoretical model can best explain the decision-making process on the privatization of the national airport: the barrier model or the flow model?' Specify the way in which you have derived the sub-questions.

Chapter 3

Theoretical framework

Scientific research distinguishes itself from ordinary research by its systematic and structured approach, adhering to certain norms and ideas. These norms and ideas regulate the scientific research process, which is why they are called regulative ideas (Swanborn, 1996).

In this chapter, I shall discuss the role and place of theory in scientific research. Research can build on existing theories; however, it can also result in the development of new theories, depending on the phase of the empirical cycle with which a study is concerned.

3.1 THE EMPIRICAL CYCLE

Figure 3.1 shows the empirical cycle as outlined by De Groot (1969). Scientific research always takes a certain problem as its starting point. As explained in Chapter 2, this can be either a knowledge problem or a practical issue.

In the induction phase (on the right-hand side of the diagram), the researcher observes the empirical world. He or she describes the problem to be studied and tries to diagnose its characteristic features or causes in the situation in which the problem occurs. As this suggests, inductive research is usually of the exploratory or descriptive type. Such research is especially relevant if there is little existing knowledge on a subject – for example, because it concerns a topical issue or has never been studied before. The literature review conducted during the preparatory research stage will have provided information on how much is already known on a subject (see Chapter 2).

To give an example of the use of inductive research, consider a researcher being interested in the phenomenon of people's petitions. In several countries, including the UK and the USA, every citizen is allowed to start a petition on a particular topic, and call upon the government to create new legislation, or in some countries hold a referendum. The petition has to be supported by a large number of signatures, usually from registered voters. In most countries, this is a fairly recently introduced measure, which enables citizens to exert direct influence on political decision making. However, being such a recent phenomenon, people's petitions are also a relatively novel subject of study, which means that research will necessarily be of the exploratory kind.

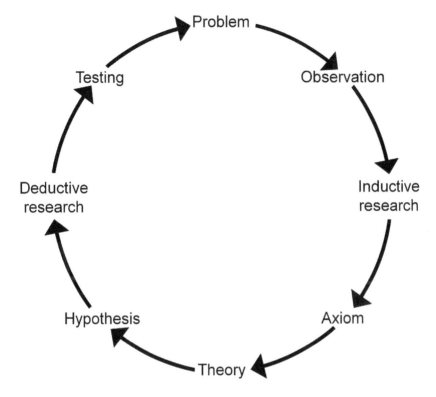

Figure 3.1
Schematic outline of the empirical cycle

On the basis of the data gathered during the empirical phase, a model can be constructed. A model is a simplified image of reality, which shows how the problem that is being studied has arisen and what its characteristic features are. These characteristics can help the researcher to arrive at possible explanations (and so gather new knowledge or develop new theories), or find a solution to the problem. With respect to the example of people's petitions, inductive research might result in a description of what kind of citizen usually decides to undertake action, what issues exactly stimulate people to become politically active, or what hurdles they encounter in practice.

In the model constructed, the empirical information that has been gathered is generalized; that is, it is put in a broader perspective than just the specific case that has been studied. For example, what has been concluded with respect to one or two people's petitions is translated into something that holds for other or even all such petitions. Deriving general statements from a particular empirical situation is called formulating axioms. Axioms are the building blocks of models and theories, which specify the suppositions made on possible relations between the characteristics of the units of observation that are studied – for

25

example, what kind of citizen is likely to launch a petition, or which impediments may arise. The phase of induction ends with building a model or theory.

In the deduction phase (on the left-hand side of the diagram), an explanation is sought for the research problem by using existing theories. On the basis of a theory, a model of the research situation is constructed. Just as in the induction phase, the model gives a general explanation or description of what may be at issue in the specific case to be studied. Contrary to induction, though, deductive research can only be done when theory or knowledge on the subject is already available. The aim is to investigate whether the explanation suggested by the theory holds true. This is achieved by formulating and testing hypotheses (see Box 2.3) on the possible causes of the problem under study. Sometimes different theories offer alternative explanations, and various hypotheses can be tested on their validity (see Box 3.1).

With respect to the example of people's petitions, as yet only little is known on this particular subject. However, theories are available on the more general phenomenon of political participation: these theories can be used to formulate hypotheses on what kind of citizen is likely to develop a petition, or which political issues are likely to arouse most interest. During the phase of empirical research, the researcher can test whether these expectations or predictions meet with reality.

By testing the theoretically derived expectations, more knowledge is gathered on the research problem. Also, it will become clear to what extent our current knowledge is lacking, and whether the theory applied provides a sound explanation for the research problem. If it fails to do so, a new knowledge problem has been shown to exist, which can be studied in turn. This completes the empirical cycle.

BOX 3.1 FALSIFICATION AND VERIFICATION

Scientific knowledge is always uncertain. Every piece of research tries to add to the existing body of scientific knowledge, or fill in the gaps that still exist. This process of adding to the body of knowledge is called the accumulation of knowledge. For the accumulation of knowledge, it is important to make clear agreements on the *validity* of knowledge: when do research results constitute a valid contribution to the existing body of scientific knowledge? The work of Popper (2002 [1953]) is especially relevant here.

Popper introduced the criterion of falsifiability into science by rejecting induction as a leading principle for research. In an inductive study, the researcher aims for verification, the aim being to seek empirical evidence for the suppositions made. As Popper explained in his seminal article, such an approach has two major drawbacks. First, it can lead to selectivity, because the researcher will (perhaps unconsciously) tend to focus on those observations that confirm the expectations formulated earlier. In other words, the knowledge gained by induction may not be objective, or can even be unreliable. Second, when it comes to the crunch, true induction would require the researcher to study *all* possible situations before drawing any hard and fast conclusions. Such a task is practically impossible, and also extremely inefficient.

To avoid these pitfalls, Popper suggested the alternative method of trying to find evidence disproving a certain theoretical supposition. If such contradictory evidence is not found, the basic premise or explanation offered for the research problem cannot be refuted, and must be considered valid. This approach has also been described as that of using a null hypothesis and an alternative hypothesis. As long as the null hypothesis (H_0) has not been rejected, it will remain true. If, on the contrary, the null hypothesis *is* refuted, the alternative hypothesis (H_a) becomes the most likely premise, until H_a is rejected as well. Step by step, the process builds up to the explanation that is the most valid.

Although the approach suggested by Popper does indeed seem more efficient (after all, only one counterexample needs to be found to refute a hypothesis), several objections can be raised against the falsification principle. First, counterevidence does not always lead to refutation of a theory (Kuhn, 1996 [1962]). Quite the contrary, in fact: often counterevidence is taken as proof that the researcher has not tested the theory in the right manner. Also, counterevidence can lead to a theory being adapted instead of rejected. The argument for making such adaptations is that we cannot discard all possible theories until nothing is left, and also that one exception to the rule does not mean that the general rule is entirely unsound. Having said this, falsifiability is still one of the leading principles in the social sciences (see, for example, King, Keohane, & Verba, 1994, p. 100).

The induction and deduction phases create a logical sequence, and together they form a complete research *cycle*. In practice, though, most scientific studies will confine themselves to just one of the two phases, depending on the amount of knowledge already available. As we have seen in Chapter 1, in Public Administration, research often concentrates on unique cases or topical issues, which means that there is usually only little knowledge available and no general models exist as yet. For this reason, research in Public Administration is often inductive in character. Moreover, most studies in Public Administration are of the applied variety, seeking to find solutions to practical problems rather than being geared at theory building (see Box 3.2). If deductive research is being done, theories from the parent disciplines can be used.

BOX 3.2 THE REGULATIVE CYCLE

Most research in Public Administration and Public Management is applied in nature, aiming to find a solution to a practical problem. Constructing and testing generally valid models has less priority in such a case. Practical research can even be said to have a logic of its own: it tries to diagnose, design and evaluate. Van Strien (1997) calls this the regulative cycle, in echo of the empirical cycle. The regulative cycle consists of the following phases (compare action research in Box 2.1):

Research problem → diagnosis → plan → intervention → evaluation

In the regulative cycle, the researcher employs scientific methods and modes of thought, but with a different purpose than in the empirical cycle. The main aim is to improve or change an existing situation which has been diagnosed earlier. A sort of mini theory (plan) is developed or applied, which only holds for the particular case that is being studied. Also, normative ideas will play an important role. After all, the researcher is trying to arrive at recommendations (prescription) about how changes or improvements can be made (intervention). Commissioned research by sponsors often follows the logic of the regulative cycle.

To summarize this section, inductive research leads to the development of new theories, whereas deductive research makes use of existing theories. Axioms and hypotheses form each other's counterpart; both are premises or predictions, but they originate from different sources. Axioms are founded on empirical knowledge; hypotheses are derived from theory. We now need to consider what exactly theory is.

3.2 WHAT IS THEORY?

In everyday speech, the word 'theory' refers to a set of ideas that describe how something (such as an object, situation or event) is constructed or has come into being. A scientific theory does exactly the same, with the difference that it is more structured in its set-up and design. To be precise, a scientific theory is an interconnected, coherent system of premises which aims to describe, explain or predict certain phenomena (compare, for example, Kuhn, 1996 [1962]).

There are three different types of premises, the first of which are assumptions or postulates. Assumptions form the point of departure for a piece of research. Their validity is not called into question, and they do not constitute a subject of study themselves. For example, neo-institutional economics postulates rational choice as a basic model for human behaviour, which means that people's actions are thought to be directed towards attaining certain goals. Human behaviour is purposive and therefore predictable: 'in circumstances like these, people will choose to act in such a way.'

The model forms the heart of the theory (second element). A model specifies concepts, variables, conditions and mechanisms. As stated before, a model is a simplified version of reality, which shows, first of all, what kind of phenomenon is being studied. In Public Administration, research problems are usually not of the tangible kind, and research often concentrates on concepts or mental constructs. Examples of such concepts are ministerial accountability, interactive decision making and discretionary authority. Concepts or constructs have to be defined in a way that delineates what exactly the research is about and also what is being excluded.

As a next step, the concept is translated to the empirical situation on which the study concentrates. In Chapter 4, ample attention will be paid to this translation process, which is called 'operationalization'. At this point, the main thing to know is that operationalization results in identifying the variables that will be included in the study. A variable is a feature or aspect of the unit of observation in which the concept being studied expresses itself. For example, the variable 'organizational culture' can express itself in corporate clothing, manners of conduct, values, stories, etc. Such aspects can take on different values or scores: corporate clothing can be obligatory or not, whether and how anniversaries are celebrated in the office, and so on.

In causal models, which mean to give an explanation of a certain phenomenon, a distinction is made between the dependent variable (DV) and the independent variable (IV). The aim is to describe how the dependent variable is influenced by the independent variable. The circumstances in which an effect will actually take place are called conditions: these, too, form part of the model. Conditions can either enable or constrain an effect. To illustrate, consider a researcher interested in finding out whether population ageing (IV) will lead to a higher demand for healthcare (DV). The effect of population ageing on the demand for healthcare will be greater if the average life expectancy increases: the longer people live, the longer they will need healthcare.

Finally, the mechanism of the model is the way in which the independent variable affects the dependent variable. The mechanism shows how, under certain conditions, variables correlate. For example, if people develop ever more serious health problems as they grow older (mechanism), and the average life expectancy rises (condition), an increase in the population of elderly people (IV) will lead to an increase in the demand for healthcare (DV).

The research model is often presented by means of a diagram or scheme, such as a formula or an arrow diagram (see Box 3.3). This offers a clear and simple structure to see the different relations postulated between the variables.

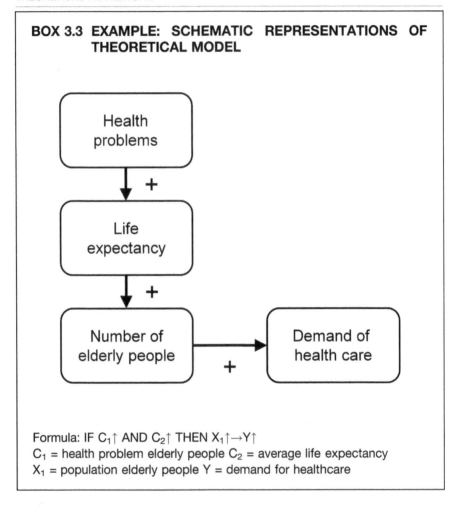

BOX 3.3 EXAMPLE: SCHEMATIC REPRESENTATIONS OF THEORETICAL MODEL

Formula: IF $C_1\uparrow$ AND $C_2\uparrow$ THEN $X_1\uparrow\rightarrow Y\uparrow$
C_1 = health problem elderly people C_2 = average life expectancy
X_1 = population elderly people Y = demand for healthcare

A third and final category of theoretical premises are hypotheses or predictions. On the basis of the assumptions made and the model constructed, the researcher can formulate testable predictions of what causes and effects will be seen. In Box 2.3, it was explained how hypotheses can be constructed. Hypotheses show that if certain assumptions are made, the model leads to predictions about the effect of the independent variable on the dependent variable. Predictions bear the character of laws: 'if X then Y', or 'the more A, the less B.'

A *complete* theory comprises all three elements mentioned – although sometimes the different component parts are considered theories in themselves, especially when a theory is still in the process of being developed. Opinion is divided on how comprehensive a theory should be, and what its function and place should be in research. The answer to these questions depends on a researcher's scientific views or philosophy of science.

3.3 PHILOSOPHIES OF SCIENCE

A philosophy of science refers to the views that a researcher has of:

- What science is;
- In what way scientific research should ideally be conducted; and
- What contribution science can make to society – or what its relationship with society is or should be.

Researchers' views on these matters are partly influenced by their personal beliefs. Other factors of influence are their scientific schooling and the prevailing set of concepts and thought patterns – which are collectively known as the 'paradigm' – in their own discipline, or in science in general. The term paradigm (Kuhn, 1996 [1962]) refers to a theoretical tradition or accepted method in a certain discipline, which guides a coherent research agenda and is coupled to a certain scientific approach. A paradigm is shared and supported by a large number of researchers: a so-called 'school of thought'. Over time, views can change and paradigms can shift, due to, for example, new theoretical or methodological insights. Famous examples of paradigm shifts are the discovery that the Earth is round instead of flat, and relativity theory: in both instances, major changes resulted in the reigning philosophy of science. An example of a paradigm shift in Public Administration is the insight that policy processes often do not follow a rational sequence, but tend to have a chaotic or cyclical character instead (Parsons, 1995, p. 67–77). Another example is the change in theoretical thinking about organizations, which, after the discovery of the Hawthorne effect (by, amongst others, Elton Mayo), shifted from the notions applied by the Scientific School of Management (Taylorism) to the insights of Human Relations-oriented school.

A researcher does not always consciously choose a particular philosophy of science: being familiar with a certain approach can play a role as well, as do personal habit and style. During the period of scientific schooling, the researcher internalizes a particular view of science and scientific methodology. Still, conscious choice or not, the philosophy of science applied by researchers greatly influences which subjects they will study and how the research is conducted. For example, certain approaches assign great value to fundamental research and testing, whilst other approaches see applied research as the singular most important task of science (compare Wildavsky, 1979).

Different philosophies of science can be distinguished, which either alternate over time or co-exist at a certain point. In this chapter, the currently most influential schools of thought in Public Administration (compare Ricucci, 2010) will be discussed: 1 the empirical-analytical or positivist approach; and 2 the interpretative approach. I shall describe these two approaches in terms of four basic scientific-philosophical principles (compare Marsh & Furlong, 2002):

- Their ontological position. Ontology is a branch of metaphysics which concerns itself with the nature or 'being' of what is studied; it poses the question if reality truly does exist. This harps back to the old problem of whether certain phenomena can be said to be real or tangible, or whether they only exist as ideas in our heads. Studies in Public Administration often focus on concepts, the immaterial properties of which can make doing research relatively complicated.

- Their epistemological position. Epistemology is the branch of knowledge that studies the nature of knowledge. It concerns itself with the question whether we can actually know reality and, in particular, whether there is just one reality that is the same to each and every living person. If the latter were true, we should be able to study phenomena in an objective manner, and research findings would be understood by everyone in the exact same way.

- Their model of man. In the social sciences, people occupy a central position, as units of observation, as the cause of a certain phenomenon, and as the ones undergoing the consequences of a certain phenomenon. With respect to theory and doing research, the most important aspect of the model of man applied is whether human beings are thought to have free will – which can make their decisions difficult or even impossible to foresee – or whether their actions are entirely predictable, because they follow from certain deterministic principles. The underlying concept of human behaviour and its causes is usually reflected in the theoretical assumptions made, as we discussed earlier in reference to theoretical models.

- Their methodological position. In the natural sciences, physical laws are studied. Likewise, social science tries to formulate the laws that describe man and human behaviour. However, people differ from natural phenomena such as, say, gravity: after all, a human being is a conscious entity with a mind that can learn things. Because of this, certain scientists consider the approach generally followed in the natural sciences unsuitable for doing research in the humanities.

The empirical-analytical approach

The empirical-analytical approach advocates doing research in a way that emulates the approach generally followed in the natural sciences. The aim is to test theoretical rules or laws – preferably in the form of hypotheses, derived by way of deduction – in order to find a causal explanation for empirically observed phenomena. Falsification (see Box 3.1) is the leading principle here. Being generally deductive in its method and theory driven, empirical-analytical research is sometimes also referred to as fundamental research.

The basic premise on which such research rests is that scientific knowledge can be and should be acquired in an objective manner, by means of empirical observation and systematic research. This conception of science is sometimes also called positivism. The situation under study is regarded from a distance: researchers do not participate in the research situation, contrary to approaches such as action research.

It has to be added, though, that there are empirical-analytical scientists who take an intermediate view on whether research can really generate objective data. Some researchers prefer the term 'inter-subjective knowledge', so to indicate that in practice the validity of knowledge or the interpretation of observations will depend on certain agreements or rules (De Groot, 1969). An example of such a rule is the principle of methodological individualism. Often conclusions about large units of observation, such as organizations or countries, are drawn on the basis of material that has been gathered at the level of individual people (for obvious reasons, a country or a ministry cannot be interviewed). In situations like these, researchers can decide beforehand how the individual data had best be aggregated. For example, they can agree that the data will not be simply added up, but will be weighed in proportion to certain characteristics of the individuals studied, such as function or position, or educational background.

Empirical-analytical researchers often have a preference for quantitative research (see Chapter 5). This fits in with the natural science ideal, as it allows the researcher to exert strict control over the design and execution of a study, reducing risks of bias and subjectivity. Applying such methods also means that a study has to meet stringent scientific criteria, especially as regards validity and reliability (see Chapter 4).

All in all, therefore, we can say that empirical-analytical researchers strive to gather and interpret knowledge about real life in as objective a manner as possible. Not only do they think this is feasible, but they believe that their approach is the best and most scientific way: only by proceeding in an empirical-analytical way can a discipline be regarded as scientifically 'grown-up' (*normal science*; see Ricucci, 2010). It should be pointed out, though, that there are certain limitations to the knowledge gathered in this manner. For example, statements can only be made on units and variables that have been actually studied. Having said as much, it still remains true that by taking an empirical-analytical approach, a researcher can fairly confidently generalize results on a limited number of variables to larger units (groups, organizations, or people).

The empirical-analytical approach has been subject to a great deal of criticism, in particular with respect to the following three points. First of all, critics have pointed out that the approach is not as objective as its proponents often tend to claim. The prescriptive character of empirical-analytical research, especially its rules on how research should be conducted, testifies to implicit value judgements, both on what constitutes proper scientific research and the function of science in society. Second, the natural science ideal is not considered to be applicable to research in the social sciences by the critics. Because people are capable of reflective thought and self-evaluation, their behaviour is not as predictable as physical phenomena are. Also, people can learn from past experience, which makes meeting the scientific criterion of being able to replicate a study a tricky issue. In other words, the deterministic model of man that occupies such a central place in the empirical-analytical approach often does not seem realistic. As a third shortcoming, critics have mentioned the one-way causality of the theoretical models that are usually applied. It is customary in such models for the independent variable to have an effect on the dependent variable, not vice versa. Yet in practice the influence could well run both ways, and limiting one's view to IV → DV models might not do full justice to reality.

Besides such general points, we can mention several other reasons why the empirical-analytical approach is often not suitable for research in a specialized field such as Public Administration. As mentioned earlier, Public Administration has few theories of its own, which makes it rather difficult to apply the deductive method. Moreover, the often applied and normative nature of research in Public Administration conflicts with the idea of gathering knowledge in an objective or inter-subjective manner. Indeed, most empirical-analytical researchers reject the idea of prescription (compare Chapter 12). In spite of all this, there are plenty of researchers in Public Administration who do prefer to take an empirical-analytical perspective.

The interpretative approach

Researchers who take an interpretative approach to science assume that there is not just one empirical world, but everyone (individuals or groups of people) has their own perspective or personal view of reality. As will be clear, such a model of man differs significantly from that applied by empirical-analytical scientists. In the interpretative approach, when two people are subjected to one and the same event, the way they experience things can differ significantly. Reports on the event in question will often diverge on several points: think, for example, of the discrepancies between eyewitness accounts in police investigations. This basic assumption of reality being subjective has far-reaching implications for the way in which research is conducted.

With respect to the phenomena they study, interpretative researchers try and reach a certain level of understanding or (in German) *Verstehen*. They begin by studying people's perceptions: how certain events are experienced, and what kind of meaning or interpretation is assigned to these events. In order to arrive at a clear understanding of people's perceptions, a holistic approach is followed, which means that events are studied in their totality. As a rule, a study concentrates on only one event or situation; however, all the different elements of the event or situation are taken into consideration. Whether or not these findings can be generalized depends on the number of units of study. Usually the research involves only a few units of study, although it does generate a lot of detail on a wide array of variables. This makes testing theoretical laws or hypotheses difficult. Still, theory often does play an important role in inductive research. For example, existing theory can form a basic guideline: the researcher can apply a model and use it to determine which variables, conditions and mechanisms to watch out for in the unique context (compare with the regulative cycle discussed in Box 3.2). Also, induction can generate new theories on the basis of the singular case that is being studied (see Chapters 4 and 8 on theoretical generalization). Stated differently, interpretative research can be both inductive and deductive in character; however, the emphasis on uniqueness and subjectivity will usually lead the researcher to favour an inductive approach.

A final point to be mentioned is that in interpretative research people's actions and interactions are studied in their own unique context. Different labels are used to refer to this context. Terms frequently applied are: social network, configuration, system, or institutional context. These labels correspond with the different schools of thought in interpretative research, such as social-constructivism and institutionalism. Usually the context is examined by means of qualitative methods, of which the case study is the most famous example (see Chapter 8). A case study allows the researcher to gather and analyse data on complex and non-numeric variables (such as perceptions), and later arrive at an interpretation of these (see also Chapter 11).

Interpretative research has received its own portion of criticism. First of all, critics have stressed the risk of a double hermeneutics. The interpretative researcher studies the perceptions of the people included in a study, which makes it difficult to determine whether the knowledge acquired will be generally valid. Another related objection is that if reality is indeed always subjective, researchers can do no more than give their own interpretation of it: they will always be telling their own story. Some interpretative researchers, such as post-modernists, allege that the function of science is indeed just that: telling stories (Ricucci, 2010). However, as critics have pointed out, such a view of science seems to undermine the very basis for its existence, for how can one distinguish between the researcher's own story and that of other scientists or people, such as journalists or politicians?

With respect to the smaller field of research in Public Administration, another point of criticism can be raised. The interpretative approach takes the uniqueness of individuals, events and contexts as given: however, this uniqueness hampers theory development and testing, which in turn complicates the building of a body of knowledge. Some critics find this undesirable, saying that it damages the scientific character of Public Administration research (compare Ricucci, 2010).

Table 3.1 summarizes the two approaches. The four basic scientific-philosophical principles mentioned earlier have been used for comparison.

In the discussion so far, the contrast between the two main approaches to science in Public Administration has been phrased in somewhat stronger terms than apply in actual practice. In fact, many researchers will place themselves somewhere in between these extremes (see, for example, realism as defined by Robson, 2002, and Marsh & Furlong, 2002). Sometimes, too, different labels – such as 'positivism' for the empirical-analytical approach – or different forms of categorization or contrasts are applied. Being such a young discipline, Public Administration is characterized by a plurality of scientific approaches (Ricucci, 2010).

Table 3.1 *Philosophies of science in Public Administration research*

	Empirical-analytical	Interpretative
Ontology	There is such a thing as an objective reality, which is tangible (and can be measured)	All reality is subjective, or a matter of perspective
Epistemology	Knowledge is objective, or at least inter-subjective	All knowledge is interpretation
Model of man	Deterministic: behaviour is predictable	Voluntaristic: free will
Natural science ideal	Yes	No
Typical characteristics of research	Geared at answering the research problem and generalizing. Operationalization of theory: testing and explaining (deduction, falsification). Quantitative data	Identification with unique subject of study (*Verstehen*). Meaning and relations (holistic): description and understanding (usually induction). Qualitative data

Finally, it should be noted that different philosophies of science often react to one another, and that the distinction between the various approaches tends to be hazy rather than absolute. It does remain important, though, to realize that a researcher's scientific approach is of great influence: both on the way in which research is carried out (which can show in a certain bias), and on the way in which the research of others is judged or used (with the risk of tendentiousness). Moreover, some basic knowledge on the different philosophies of science helps to explain why often such hot debates arise between scientists on research, research methods, and the function of science in society (see also Chapter 12 on ethics).

3.4 THE ROLE OF THEORY IN PUBLIC ADMINISTRATION RESEARCH

As will be clear by now, theory can fulfil different functions in research, depending on whether a study is inductive or deductive. Indeed, the very choice for an inductive or deductive design will depend on how much theoretical knowledge is already available on a subject. In addition, the researcher's philosophy of science will play a role.

When it comes to doing research in Public Administration and Public Management, a choice can be made from a range of theories from the parent disciplines, although usually certain adjustments will have to be made. To illustrate, theories on organizations have been developed in sociology, organizational science and management studies. It has to be said, however, that scientists do not always agree on the validity of these models for research on *public* organizations. According to some authors, public organizations have certain distinctive features, which prohibit a straightforward application of generic theories (Rainey, 2009; Bozeman & Bretschneider, 1994; Allison, 1980). In addition, the fact that many research subjects in Public Administration are unique has as a consequence that general theories and models usually require some form of adaptation before they can actually be applied.

When and how exactly theory is used in Public Administration varies greatly. In deductive studies, theory precedes empirical research; in inductive studies, theories are only developed during or after the empirical phase. Box 3.4 offers some examples.

BOX 3.4 EXAMPLES OF THE USE OF THEORY IN PUBLIC ADMINISTRATION RESEARCH

■ One of the best-known examples of research in Public Administration is Allison's study of the Cuban Missile Crisis. The crisis first broke out in October 1962, when the USA discovered that the Soviet Union was placing intermediate-range missiles in Cuba. The US Armed Forces were raised to their highest state of readiness. After several days of intense debate within the upper layers of the US government, however, President Kennedy decided against launching a nuclear war, imposing a naval quarantine around Cuba instead. Allison reconstructed and explained this unique chain of events, applying three different theoretical frameworks to analyse the decision-making process during the Cuban Crisis: namely, rational choice, organizational science and political behaviour. The results of his analysis (Allison & Zelikow, 1999) show that the various perspectives applied all highlight different causes and consequences, and that a combination of all three frameworks renders a fuller, more complete analysis than each on its own.

■ In 1993, Putnam published his famous work on the functioning and performance of regional governments in Italy (title: *Making Democracy Work*). In this inductive and longitudinal study, Putnam describes the results of 20 years of research. As he 'shows, government efficiency does not result so much from economic circumstances or the managing skills of politicians and civil servants. Rather, trust in personal relationships, traditional methods and task division are decisive factors. From the material gathered – which includes documents and interviews – Putnam distilled 12 indicators for 'measuring' institutional performance. These indicators can be used to express government efficiency.

■ Hood (1994) used *grid-group* culture theory (GGC) to explain why government reorganizations take place: which forms of reorganization are most popular, why, and how successful are the changes made? GGC theory assumes that society – and by analogy political-administrative systems – can be viewed in terms of two dimensions. The *group* dimension concerns the degree to which individual behaviour is constrained by group relations; the *grid* dimension expresses the degree to which behaviour is determined by custom and rules. Taken together, the two dimensions (2 x 2) result in four different styles, labelled 'fatalistic', 'hierarchical', 'individualistic' and 'egalitarian'. Each style matches a certain way of handling government reorganizations, such as the implementation of New Public Management reforms. By means of GGC theory and deduction, Hood was able to formulate testable hypotheses.

■ A final example of the use of theory is Van Gunsteren's (1998) study on citizenship. By applying three existing theories – liberalism, communitarism and republicanism – Van Gunsteren has constructed different forms of citizenship. Neither of these forms seems to match current conceptions of citizenship, however, which is why he has suggested a fourth, new type, called neo-republican citizenship. Neo-republican citizenship combines diverse elements of the more traditional forms, of which Van Gunsteren gives several examples. His study is an example of deductive research in which theoretical models are tested and further developed.

Deductive research and theory

Once the research problem has been decided upon, a deductive study will concentrate on constructing the theoretical framework. In the theoretical framework, the researcher indicates what kind of answers the existing theory provides to the main research question and sub-questions.

(Note to the reader: this does not mean that specific theories should actually be mentioned in the research question. For example, the question 'Which factors influence the decision to vote for a certain political party?' can be answered by using different theories, such as rational choice theory or human capital theory. Although these terms can be used in the research question, it is not obligatory to do so. Only if it is the research aim to compare or test explanations offered by different theories is it necessary to name these theories explicitly in the research question. In our example, the research question could run as follows: 'Which theory, rational choice or human capital, provides the best explanation for the decision to vote for a certain political party?')

A theoretical framework is *not* a summary of all kinds of existing theories: such an overview is given in the literature review conducted during the preparatory research stage (see Chapter 2). Rather, the theoretical framework tries to suggest a specific answer to the main question raised by the study. In order to construct a theoretical framework, the researcher uses existing theories or parts thereof. If necessary, these are supplemented with new ideas, assumptions or hypotheses. A critical stance is required here, by the way: researchers can indicate shortcomings in existing theories or point out certain contradictions. Most importantly, the researcher has to develop his or her own argument, using different theoretical building blocks. Literature references should be given in line with style conventions to show on which body of knowledge the argument being built is founded (see also Box 3.5 on literature skills).

BOX 3.5 LITERATURE SKILLS

Several handbooks are available that discuss how to search for scientific literature on a particular subject. Here are a few extra tips:

■ Before you start, try and find what keywords come closest to describing the subject of study. Use both English words and keywords in your native language. Do not limit yourself to just one or two terms, but use several synonyms and combinations of keywords. Some digital databases – which comprise articles from scientific journals – have a thesaurus for finding suitable keywords. Search engines may also offer alternative phrasings.

■ Publications in scientific journals are the quickest way of gathering knowledge on a particular subject. Articles are more concise than entire books; review articles (compare Chapters 9 and 12), in particular, often contain a wealth of information.

■ Note that Internet search engines such as Google Scholar only provide access to texts that have been published online. To gain access to specialized journals in Public Administration, Public Management or other disciplines, you should use the databases at your library, such as ISI or Scopus. Governmental databases usually offer legal texts, parliamentary documents and official reports. Some scholars publish their ongoing research online, via SSRN or on their personal website. As more and more journals and universities subscribe to the principle of open access, a large and growing body of information is becoming rapidly available.

■ Begin your search with the most recent publications and work your way backwards through time. In more recent articles, an overview is usually given of earlier studies. Reading these references prevents repeating the search already carried out by others.

■ Use the list of references given in a good article, book or book chapter as a guide for finding important publications or authors on a subject. Like a true detective, track and trace all clues handed to you by the literature, but stop searching and reading when you reach the point of re-encountering what you have already got. The added value of continuing your search will be negligible by this time.

Different style guides are available that describe what literature references should look like: the APA, Chicago, Vancouver and Harvard manuals are but a few examples. In the book you are reading right now, the APA system has been applied (see: apastyle.apa.org). A style guide describes the way in which the literature should be referred to in the main text and how the list of references at the end of the text are laid out. Often slightly different formats apply for articles, books or reports. In addition, most word processors have an option for saving and editing literature references, such as EndNote; online free software, such as Zotero, is also available. By using such software, you can easily adapt your reference style to the standards required for publishing in a certain discipline or with a specific publisher or scientific journal (see also Chapter 12).

The theoretical framework provides guidance to the research. It shows what needs to be studied in order to gain an empirical as well as a theoretical answer to the chosen research question. As such, it can be compared to a navigation system. The framework specifies which route on the theoretical map the researcher has to take in order to arrive at the desired destination. The route itself consists of diverse assumptions and predictions, giving an indication of what constitutes the shortest and quickest route (the number of variables), warnings about any obstacles that may be encountered, advice on alternative routes in case of congestion (conditions, mechanisms), and suggestions for interesting outings on the way. The researcher follows the route set out by the theoretical framework, and tests if the explanation it offers provides a suitable answer to the research problem. In the final stages, an evaluation can be made of whether the chosen route was indeed the best course to follow and if results fit with reality.

Criteria for a sound theoretical framework

A sound, workable theoretical framework should satisfy at least four different criteria. The first of these is consistency, which means that the theoretical framework has to concord with the research problem (this is also called the 'fit'). In addition, the framework may not show any internal contradictions, especially as regards its basic assumptions. Conflicting predictions do not really pose a problem, though (see Box 3.1 on falsification). The second criterion is testability. In deductive studies, the theoretical framework ideally results in a set of hypotheses which can be tested in the empirical phase. A third, related criterion is the empirical accuracy of the hypotheses formulated. Greater empirical accuracy enhances the quality of the theoretical framework. The fourth criterion, simplicity, refers to the need for sparseness with respect to the number of variables, conditions and assumptions specified. *Science is the art of explaining a complicated concept in easy terms.* A feasible, straightforward model does not contain more variables and concepts than necessary to provide an adequate explanation for the phenomenon studied: the more complex the theoretical framework, the more difficult its practical implementation will be. This last criterion is also called parsimony. Some authors refer to the 'elegance' of a model: a simpler model is considered more elegant. In practice, the number of elements needed in the theoretical framework varies per subject, and no general rules can be given for this.

Inductive research and theory

In the empirical cycle, inductive research starts with making empirical observations. The observations made are subsequently translated into suppositions or axioms, which can serve as a basis for building a theory or model.

Starting with observation does not mean to say that inductive researchers proceed in a totally random, unguided manner. Usually, a certain view or expectation already exists with respect to the research line to be followed. These expectations are derived from logical and sound reasoning, earlier research, the findings of other researchers on comparable subjects, or information gained from those who will be involved in the study. Researchers will try and get as broad an overview as possible of the research situation (the holistic approach) by gathering as many data as they can.

During the course of research, the researcher will detect certain patterns, such as correlated events, which might provide an explanation for the phenomenon of interest. Such patterns can then be studied further on their consistency and validity. By proceeding in this way, the researcher actually begins building a theory whilst still being busy gathering the empirical data. The analytical process continues until after the study has been concluded, and the database is complete (see Chapter 11 for further explanation).

In inductive research, therefore, research results in a theoretical framework. Just as in deductive research, the demands of consistency, empirical accuracy and parsimony have to be met. The theoretical framework specified need not be testable, however, as testing will only take place during the next phase of the empirical cycle.

To conclude

The order in which the chapters of this book have been written follow a deductive approach. Having first concentrated on theory, I will now proceed to discuss more practical subjects, such as research design. In everyday practice, research in Public Administration and Public Management is sometimes deductive and sometimes inductive in nature (see the examples given in Box 3.4). The way in which the study material in this book has been arranged should not be taken as a dictate for doing research along deductive lines; the current set-up was merely chosen as a simple way of ordering the material for study.

Textbooks on research methods can be organized in different ways. Some authors opt for a contrast between qualitative and quantitative research (Pierce, 2008), whereas others stress the difference between fixed and flexible research designs (Robson, 2002). There are also authors who prefer to confine themselves to just one philosophy of science or scientific angle from which to approach the subject of doing research (compare Chapter 11). In this volume, the distinction between inductive and deductive research will be a running thread in all subsequent chapters. It has to be borne in mind, though, that both inductive and deductive forms of research are needed to make a complete empirical cycle.

FURTHER READING

Kuhn, Th. (1996 [1962]). *The Structure of Scientific Revolutions*. Chicago: University of Chicago Press.
Ricucci, N.M. (2010). *Public Administration: Traditions of Inquiry and Philosophies of Knowledge*. Washington, DC: Georgetown University Press.

EXERCISES

1   A paradigmatic choice need not always be a conscious choice. This also holds for other choices, such as choosing your favourite music. Consider your own music preference. What kind of music do you like best? How did you choose this particular style? Also, what does your favourite music mean with regard to other choices, like your lifestyle (clubbing, friends) or appearance (hairstyle, clothes)? How deeply does your choice of music penetrate the rest of your life? This exercise aims to show the profound influence that 'paradigmatic' choices can have.

2   Create a theoretical model of how you decided on your studies by following an inductive approach. Which suppositions (assumptions) played a role in the decision-making process (living at home, college reputation)? Which independent variables (actors and factors) exerted an influence? Try and create a model that reflects the process of decision making, and compare your model with that of other students who have done the same exercise.

3   Ask three people who have undergone the same event to tell about their experiences. Write three separate reports, and compare these with each other. (As an alternative: compare the lecture notes of three fellow students who have all attended the same lecture.) Which similarities and differences can be noticed, and how can you explain these? (See the sections on the interpretative approach.)

4   Wikipedia has not been authorized by scientists, which means it is not allowed as a source for literature reviews or theoretical frameworks. Scientists are permitted, however, to provide information to Wikipedia, and write articles for the site on the basis of their own research. Gather information from scientific articles on a subject in Public Administration of your choice, and write a text for Wikipedia using this background material. Do not forget to mention your sources!

Chapter 4
Operationalization

The transition from theory to empirical research is called operationalization. In the phase of operationalization, theoretical concepts are translated into entities that can be observed or measured in the real world. Making concepts 'measurable' does not always mean to say that they are converted into quantitative units or numbers. As we shall see, different scales or levels of measurement can be distinguished.

Operationalizing variables is an important step in deductive research, although it is relevant to inductive research as well, as will be explained in Chapter 11. The process of operationalization gives direction to the empirical part of a study: it shows exactly *what* will be studied or measured. *How* such measurements will actually take place is described in the research design (see Chapter 5).

4.1 OPERATIONALIZATION IN THREE STEPS

Opinions vary on how the process of operationalization should be carried out, but there are always three steps to take (compare Babbie, 1992).

The first of these is giving a definition of the theoretical concepts of central interest to the research. Formulating such definitions helps to delineate what exactly will be studied. As it is the case, theoretical concepts are often complex and multi-faceted. Also, they can be difficult to describe in concrete, tangible terms (see Chapter 3). Consider, for example, the concept of citizens' political involvement: this can denote the trust that citizens have in politics, or the feeling they have of being involved in the political process, there being no gap between citizens and politicians. However, the very same concept can also refer to the knowledge citizens have about political processes, or their playing an active political role. The researcher has to decide which of all these facets or elements will be included in the study – and so also which elements will be left out. The aim is to formulate an unambiguous, well-circumscribed definition.

The second step consists of determining the different ways in which the theoretical construct can express itself in the real world; in Chapter 3 such expressions were referred to as 'variables'. These variables will now be operationalized in terms of measurements or indicators. Often the same theoretical concept can be interpreted and delineated in several different ways. For example, citizens' political involvement can be measured by studying either their political knowledge or their trust in politics. Alternatively, one can choose other indicators, such as the interest citizens have in politics, their voting behaviour, or the degree to which they identify with a certain political party.

In Chapter 3, a distinction was made between the independent variable and the dependent variable (abbreviated as IV and DV). All these variables need to be operationalized.

The third and final step is to decide for each variable which values or scores it can assume (see also Box 4.1). The researcher must give an indication, too, of how the different variables relate to each other, and the way in which they relate to the original construct. For example, someone's knowledge on political developments can be measured by asking what they know about certain political figures or events (everything/nothing; a lot/a little). The relationship assumed here is that if citizens are more informed (IV↑), they will be more closely involved in politics (DV↑). Such relationships between variables can be presented schematically in the analytical framework, which can take the visual format of, for example, an arrow graph (see Box 3.3). The different values that a variable can assume will have an influence on what research methods will turn out to be suitable in the empirical phase (see Chapter 10 on statistical techniques).

BOX 4.1 SCALES OF MEASUREMENT

Variables can take on a range of values or scores; observing these values is called 'measuring' the variable. A variable can be measured on different levels or scales:

1   Nominal scale. If the values or scores of a variable cannot be arranged in any particular order, we call the variable nominal. Nominal-level variables are sometimes also called 'qualitative'. A well-known example is voting behaviour: for example, someone can be assigned a score of 1 for voting Conservative, a score of 2 for Labour, and 3 for Liberal Democrat. The order of these values is random, and has no numerical meaning. After all, three Conservative votes do not equal one vote for Liberal Democrat; neither is a vote for Labour more than a Conservative vote.

2   Ordinal scale. If the values of a variable can be arranged in a certain order, but without there being any clear idea of what the exact difference is between two different scores, we call the variable ordinal. At the ordinal level, values can only be ordered by the degree to which they differ: we can speak of little or much, values ranging from low to high, or less to more. For example, political parties are sometimes placed on a continuum that ranges from (extreme) left to (extreme) right.

3   Interval scale. In case of interval-level variables, the distance between consecutive scores is always the same, and the intervals between two scores have the same interpretation throughout. However, scores cannot really be used for absolute computations: a score of 2 will not be twice as much as a score of 1. This type of variable is rare. An example often cited is that of temperature. The difference between 10 and 15 degrees Celsius equals the difference between 20 and 25 degrees; however, 20 degrees is not twice as warm as 10. Also, 0 degrees Celsius does not mean an absence of temperature; 0 is simply the value assigned to a certain value on the scale.

4   Ratio scale. A ratio-level variable has fixed intervals between scores, and also a fixed zero point, which means that values can be compared with each other, with zero acting as a reference point. Election turnout is a good example of a ratio variable.

Often there are various options for making a variable 'measurable'. The researcher has to decide on the best option – both from a theoretical and a practical point of view – and determine if it is perhaps necessary to use a combination of different measuring methods. All such choices must be motivated in the research design (see Chapter 5). As this indicates, the research design (which describes *how* the study will be conducted) follows from the operationalizations (of *what* exactly will be studied). The process of operationalization should not be confused with other research activities, such as devising a questionnaire or preparing an interview. The main concern in this phase is to translate the theory into measurable variables, not the act of measurement itself.

4.2 SAMPLING

Apart from the question of *what* exactly will be studied, there is also the matter of *who* will form the units of study. It is hardly ever possible to include all potential units of study in the research, which means that a certain selection has to be made. Such a selection is called a sample. To give a full definition: a sample (n) is a selection from the total population (N) of possible units of study. The population of interest can consist of people, but can also consist of situations (organizations, cities, countries), cases (see Chapter 8) or sources (documents or databases: see Chapter 9). Only those units that are included in the sample will actually be studied; however, the research findings may be used to draw conclusions on the population as a whole (see below on external validity).

In very rare instances, the entire population is being studied. Examples of this are national censuses or population screening projects. Also, if the total research population is limited in size (for example, the aldermen on a council or the regions of a country), or if it consists of just one case, there will be no need to

Table 4.1 Sampling

Non-probability sampling	Probability sampling
Purposive sample: selection made by the researcher on theoretical grounds	**Random sample:** selection from a known population on the basis of chance
Snowball sample: selection via the units of study	**Stratified random sample:** selection from pre-defined strata (groups or sub-populations) on the basis of chance
Quota sample: selection made by the researcher on the basis of the number of units needed and features or characteristics of interest	**Cluster sample:** selection of a number of units on the basis of a shared feature or characteristic
Self-selection: by respondents through voluntary participation	**Two-step sample:** a combination of several different probability formats

Source: (Based on Black, 1999, p. 118)

draw a sample. As observed in Chapter 1, in Public Administration research often concentrates on unique or small numbers of cases, which means that sampling will be redundant.

Sampling procedures vary, as the overview in Table 4.1 shows. Basically, we can distinguish two different approaches: probability and non-probability sampling. Within these principal categories, diverse sub-forms can be seen; also, sometimes a combination of different sampling methods is used. The researcher has to justify the choice for a certain method in the so-called sampling framework, which is included in the research design (see Chapter 5).

Non-probability sampling

By drawing a non-probability sample, the researcher makes a purposive selection of certain units of study. Usually, such a format is applied if there are only a few units of study available (Miles and Huberman, 1994, p. 27–34). The selection ultimately made is founded on theoretically relevant criteria – after all, the sample is meant to be purposive, not haphazard. To illustrate the procedure of purposive sampling, and the choices that are sometimes involved, consider someone studying the governance culture in a certain municipality. In such a case, the researcher can decide to concentrate on politicians only, on the grounds that politicians are role models to the rest of the organization, and therefore prominent interpreters of governance culture. As an alternative, the researcher can decide to interview just civil servants, because civil servants often have a longer service record, which means that they will be more knowledgeable about governance culture. In both instances, the sample is purposive and reflects a conscious research decision.

A typical form of non-probability sampling is the so-called snowball sample. This method is often applied in research on subjects that are illegal or taboo.

Think, for example, of issues to do with failing ethics or integrity, such as corruption and fraud. When studying such a subject, the researcher will first try to find someone who is prepared to talk about the matter, the idea being that the informant might mention a second volunteer, and so forth. Non-probability samples are also frequently applied in preparatory research (conducted before the research problem is given its definite shape), or in pilots aimed at testing a certain research instrument (see, for example, Chapter 7).

The ideal size of a non-probability sample depends on the size of the research population as a whole. No firm rules or guidelines can be given here, although generally speaking, the larger the sample, the better.

Probability sampling

The second basic method is probability sampling. In this approach, the units of study are not chosen on the basis of theoretical criteria, but selected by chance or probability. For example, the researcher studying governance culture that we mentioned earlier can decide on a design in which every fifth or tenth person from the personnel register is interviewed. An advantage of this method is that if the sample is large enough, research results will apply to the entire population: according to the laws of probability, a sufficiently large sample is representative of the population as a whole (Black, 1999, p. 177). In other words, probability sampling facilitates the option to generalize one's findings. There are special formulae for calculating the ideal sample size; the usual rule of thumb is that the sample should comprise circa 20% of the entire population. When the population is sizeable (for example, all inhabitants of a country), a lower percentage suffices, as long as the sample remains representative.

Improving the representativeness of a sample

Besides randomization there are other ways of ensuring representativeness of both probability and non-probability samples. For example, a selection can be made on the basis of certain characteristics of the units of study, for example, gender (male versus female), size (small municipalities versus large ones), or type (policymakers versus those who implement a policy). A researcher can also aim for a certain absolute distribution of a characteristic (or quotas: for example, 50% male and 50% female), or a relative distribution that reflects the distribution of the characteristic in the population as a whole. This last approach is called stratification; a stratum (plural: strata) is a characteristic feature by means of which the population is divided into sub-groups.

Finally, other forms of selection can be thought of as well, for example the two-step sample. In a two-step sample, a select group of units of study is defined first (for example, all municipalities in a region or country), from which the researcher subsequently chooses a number of units that will actually be included in the sample (x municipalities). The choice in the second step will often be based on certain stratifying criteria (such as large municipalities versus small ones, or urban versus rural regions). Again, all such decisions have to be motivated in the sampling framework.

4.3 RELIABILITY AND VALIDITY

Reliability and validity are important criteria for sound scientific research, which is why I shall treat these subjects in fairly great detail here. In later chapters, where the focus shifts to specific research methods, I will discuss the risks and problems with respect to validity and reliability associated with the different methods.

Reliability

The reliability of a study is a function of: 1 the accuracy, and 2 the consistency with which the variables are measured. The more accurately and consistently the variables are measured, the more certain it is that results will not be coincidental, but paint a systematic and representative picture. In explanatory research, a high level of reliability means that the explanation offered is most certainly the right one; in descriptive research, it means that no distortion has taken place; whereas in a prescriptive study, it means that the results can be used to make firm and clear recommendations, which will be unquestionably effective (under the same conditions).

As stated, the first element of reliability is accuracy. Accuracy refers in particular to the measurement instruments that are used, such as questionnaires or observation schemes (see subsequent chapters). The variable to be measured should be captured as correctly and precisely as possible; also, a clear distinction must be made between the different values that a variable can assume. To illustrate, in order to measure political knowledge, it is not enough simply to ask if someone reads the paper. After all, the paper brings all kinds of other news as well (such as sports, culture, comic strips and recipes), and just asking if people read the paper does not distinguish sufficiently between those people with and those without political knowledge. A better and more reliable measurement instrument is to ask people whether they follow the political news or national affairs in the papers they read.

In research in the social sciences, the second element of reliability – consistency – is harder to achieve. Consistency revolves around the idea of repeatability: under similar circumstances the same measurement will lead to similar results. Repeatability enhances the reliability of a study, as it provides the certainty that the results that have been found are indeed right. In the social sciences, though, research often concentrates on people, either as units of study or as a source of information. As pointed out in Chapter 3, people can learn from past experience, which means that repeating a study will not always produce the same results. A good example is that of people who are training to take a certain exam; they will score higher each time they do a test exam. Having said as much, there are means and ways of attaining repeatability, and thus enhancing the reliability of a study. One method is to create a large enough sample, so that a study can be implemented in the exact same way with different groups of people, or in different situations. Also, researchers can repeat each other's studies. This last method, which is called replication, should be carefully documented: the researcher has to specify exactly which steps have been taken, so as to make clear that the procedure that has been followed matches those of earlier studies.

Lastly, the reliability of a study is increased by ensuring that one's measurement instruments are sound. The prudent researcher will gain advice from methodologists or experienced colleagues before deciding on the best way to proceed. Frequently, though, mistakes are made in the course of research, due to human error, inexperience, lack of expertise, or because of unforeseen events. The researcher can try and anticipate such setbacks by proper training beforehand. Another option is to discuss the choices made with other researchers – before, during and after one's study – so as to enhance what we call 'inter-researcher reliability'.

The suitability of various methods and techniques for studying certain subjects will be discussed later, in the chapters on specific research methods. At this point, I would merely like to stress that researchers in Public Administration have to bear the fact in mind that reliability is imperative for doing sound scientific research. Indeed, it is a vital criterion in all phases of study.

Validity

In the literature on methodology, different forms of validity are distinguished, with labels such as: predictive validity, face validity, ecological validity, content validity, construct validity, statistical validity, or congruent validity (see, among others, Cook and Campbell, 1979). In essence, all these terms concern variants of just two basic types of validity: namely, internal and external validity.

Internal validity refers to the cogency of the study itself: has the researcher really measured the effect they intended to measure? What matters here is: 1 whether a certain theoretical construct has been adequately operationalized; and 2 whether the presupposed (causal) relationship between the independent and the dependent variable actually does exist. As to the first point, the researcher has to ensure that the operationalizations chosen form an adequate translation of the theoretical construct. The measurement instrument has to be clearly defined and exclusive, which means that it cannot be used for measuring other constructs. If it could, confusion ('confounding') might result, and the validity of the research conclusions would be seriously affected. For example, the variable political knowledge is a valid indicator of political involvement, seeing that a certain interest and degree of involvement in politics is a prerequisite for acquiring political knowledge. In contrast, reading the paper is not a valid measure, because the paper offers various other articles which have nothing to do with politics.

External validity describes the extent to which a study can be generalized: do research results also hold for other persons, institutions, moments in time or locations? External validity is especially important for statistical research (see

which often uses sample results to arrive at statements on the
a whole. There are also other ways of generalizing findings,
e shall see in Chapter 8.

ntee sufficient validity, it is of crucial importance to develop a
of measurement instruments, which can be tested in a pilot.
re, the right sample must be selected. Another way of guarding
validity ⎯ to ask fellow researchers, methodologists and experts to comment on
the chosen operationalizations and sampling method. The researcher can also
use measurement instruments that have already been validated by others (see
Box 4.2). Finally, statistics offers an array of techniques to test whether a study
is sufficiently valid (see Chapter 10).

BOX 4.2 VALIDATING OR STANDARDIZING MEASUREMENT INSTRUMENTS

When measuring a certain construct, the researcher can choose to use a
tried and tested method, which has been frequently applied by others
before. There are several advantages to replicating earlier research,
besides the obvious practical gain that no new measurement instrument
needs to be developed. One such advantage is that replication contributes to the reliability of a study. Moreover, doing comparable studies
will facilitate the process of generalizing findings later (external validity).

If the same measurement instrument (such as a questionnaire or test)
is used by many different researchers, the possibility arises to validate or
standardize the measurement instrument. Validation or standardization
means that an average or mean score can be computed. A famous
example of a validated measurement instrument is the IQ test. Once the
IQ test had been used to measure the intelligence level of large groups
of people, it became possible to apply statistical tests to the results, and
calculate a mean intelligence score. During subsequent applications, the
score of individuals could be interpreted in terms of this mean. In other
words, an IQ test score now gives not just information on the intelligence of the individual that has been measured, but also provides an
indication of whether this individual is more or less intelligent than the
average person. The mean is the standard by which the individual score
is measured.

To standardize an instrument, it must first be applied on a wide scale,
preferably in different groups (such as young people and elderly people,
or voters and non-voters) or in different situations (such as countries or
administrative levels). Variegated samples like these may create the
problem of having to 'translate' questions: not just into different lan-
guages (in internationally comparative research), but also by adapting
them to fit the local context of the target group for which the

measurement instrument is to be used. Questions about the legal status of an organization, for example, will be answered differently depending on the administrative legal system in a country; the UK common law system has different typologies from the *Rechtsstaat* model in many other European states. In other words, the researcher has to be aware of the relevance of a certain topic in a particular country or setting, and allow for suitable answer categories.

An example of a measurement instrument in Public Administration that has been used in several countries over a long period of time is the World Values Survey. In this survey, an array of questions on value-related issues is presented to large groups of citizens. Subjects vary from religion to environmental sustainability, the importance attached to social relationships, the multi-cultural society, and politics. Because the survey covers such a wide and varied base, country and group scores can easily be compared (there is a reference point). The results of the survey and the measurement instrument itself have been made available on the Internet (www.world valuessurvey.org).

4.4 VALIDITY AND RELIABILITY: SOURCES OF INTERFERENCE

Reliability and validity are closely interconnected. *Research that lacks in reliability cannot have much validity.* (The reverse does not hold true, by the way: a measurement instrument can be accurately and consistently measuring the wrong thing.) Because of this narrow relation, reliability and validity are often mentioned in one and the same breath. However, as explained above, they pertain to different aspects of research.

In this section, I shall discuss several sources of interference that can impair the reliability and validity of a study. There are three main sources of interference: 1 caused by the research method or measurement instrument used – during both the phases of gathering and processing information; 2 interference caused by the researcher; and 3 interference caused by the units of study (data sources).

The researcher as a source of interference

In the end, researchers are 'only human', which means that their own particular biases and expectations can exert an influence on research and measurement as well. It is important to remain conscious of such private opinions and norms (see Chapter 3 on different philosophies of science). Moreover, just like any other human being, a researcher can make mistakes during the implementation of a study. Good schooling and inter-researcher assessment are therefore crucial.

Measurement instruments as a source of interference

The development of accurate and valid measurement instruments requires craftsmanship. However, researchers may make mistakes, both in the development stage as well as in the actual application of the instruments. For example, sometimes, when conducting an interview, a researcher decides to add or skip a certain question. In such a case, the information collected in the whole study does not consist of entirely comparable data, and it becomes uncertain whether the theoretical construct has been measured validly and reliably.

The units of study as a source of interference

If a study spans a long period of time, the risk will often arise that certain changes occur in the research situation as time progresses. In Public Administration, for example, elections or political incidents may cause certain units of study, such as politicians, to disappear entirely from view, which will make it difficult to arrive at valid statements. Regrettably, such risks are hard to control, because the researcher cannot exert any direct influence on such matters.

Also, in research where people are the main data source, possible informants may be either unwilling to participate in the study or give information that is unreliable. A well-known example is that of socially desirable answers; instead of stating their own opinion or telling the truth, people may try and meet the researcher's expectations, or reply in a way they think is politically correct. Another frequently observed phenomenon is 'response error', with people always answering in the affirmative – irrespective of the questions posed – or misunderstanding what exactly the researcher is aiming at (for example, by taking the questions too literally). In research in which people are being interviewed, such risks should always be taken into account. In Chapter 7, some ways of countering these effects will be discussed. Box 4.3 discusses triangulation, a well-known way to reduce threats to validity and reliability.

BOX 4.3 TRIANGULATION

A tested means of enhancing reliability and validity is triangulation. Originating as a term from trigonometry, in the social sciences the word triangulation is used to indicate that more than one method is employed in a study, with the aim of double (or triple) checking on the data collection and research results. Triangulation can be applied: 1 in the operationalization phase (several measurement instruments are developed for the same theoretical construct); 2 to data sources (for example, not just gathering information from people, but also from documents and earlier studies); 3 to researchers (for example, inter-researcher comparison); 4 to research methods (for example, conducting interviews as well as analysing documents).

By gleaning information from several sources, or analysing it in various different ways, the researcher will soon gain an idea of how reliable or valid the data really are. If results on one and the same subject are inconclusive, further research will be needed before any reliable and valid conclusions can be drawn (Miles and Huberman, 1994, p. 267). Triangulation is sometimes also referred to as applying a *mixed methods* design. It is most frequently used in qualitative research (compare Chapter 8 on case studies).

FURTHER READING

Babbie, E. (1992, 6th edition). *The Practice of Social Research*. Belmont, CA: Wadsworth Publishing Company.

Daniel, J. (2012). *Sampling Essentials: Practical Guidelines for Making Sampling Choices*. London: SAGE.

EXERCISES

1   Find commonly used definitions in the scientific literature for the following concepts: ministerial responsibility, democracy, state tradition, constitutional state, privatization. Operationalize the concepts, and indicate which variables, scores and levels of measurement apply to your operationalizations.

2   Look up the World Values Survey (see Box 4.2) on the Internet, and study the questions used in the survey. Retrace how the different variables have been operationalized and subsequently turned into survey items. Do you notice any difference between the survey items applied in different countries, for example, regarding language or contextual information (in the answer categories)?

3   Opinion polls are based on samples taken from the overall population. Find a recent poll (for example, a poll held during the latest elections, or one that was taken shortly after some critical political event), and try to ascertain how the sample was arrived at. Look at what kind of sampling procedure was used, and how representative the sample is (whether it forms a suitable basis for generalization).

Chapter 5

Research design

So far I have discussed the subjects of how to choose and formulate a research problem, and the role and development of the theoretical framework. I have also explained the way in which theoretical concepts are operationalized, and that different types of sample can be drawn. Taken together, these steps prepare the decision of *how* a study will be carried out, and which methods and techniques will be used in the empirical phase of research. In the research design, all such choices are documented and explained.

In this chapter, I shall discuss the various elements that make up the research design. I shall pay attention also to research strategies, methods and techniques. In Chapters 6–9, the focus will shift to specific research methods.

5.1 THE DIFFERENT ELEMENTS OF THE RESEARCH DESIGN

Regardless of the research aim, or whether an inductive or deductive approach is followed, the researcher always has to account for the choices made and the steps that are taken during a particular study (see Chapter 4 on reliability). Having said this, it is certainly true that the research aim does exert an influence on what exactly has to be recorded in the research design. In a deductive study, attention must be paid to the theoretical framework and the operationalizations; in inductive research, such matters receive less emphasis.

A research design consists of the following eight elements:

1   The research problem, which comprises the main aim of the study, its central or overarching question, and the various sub-questions that have been derived. Set out in an introduction, the research problem reflects the results from the preparatory research, the literature review and, if applicable, a sponsor's wishes or aims (see Chapter 2). It also gives an indication of the scientific and societal relevance of the study.

2   The theoretical framework. In *deductive* research, the research design specifies which theories will be applied, and why. Usually the theoretical framework will only be fully developed after the research design has been approved (by, for example, a sponsor or a research council in the case of grant applications). In the initial stages, only a first sketch is given of the

theoretical framework that the researcher has in mind: this includes the central variables, some preliminary operationalizations and sometimes a few hypotheses. In *inductive* research, the theoretical framework will only be defined after the empirical phase has been completed, and therefore does not form part of the research design. Even so, a first indication has to be given of the way in which the data will be used to develop new theories (see also point 4 below).

3   The sampling framework. This describes which units of study will be sampled, what selection procedure will be applied, and why a certain selection will be made (irrespective of whether it concerns a probability or a non-probability sample, see Chapter 4). In addition, the data sources that will be used must be specified. Data sources can be the same persons, organizations or documents as the units of study, yet this need not always be the case: information can be gained from third parties or external sources as well. For example, in a study on the management style of mayors, interviews may be held with mayors, but also with aldermen, civil servants, or citizens; in addition, newspaper articles can be used to glean extra information. In such a design, mayors form the basic units of study, but are not the sole data source.

4   The chosen research strategy, method(s) and technique(s). Often a scientific study can be implemented in different ways, as will be explained in the second half of this chapter. Here, it is merely important to note that the choices made with respect to the research strategy, methods and techniques have to be carefully documented and explained. Ideally, these choices reflect the nature of the subject of study, the scientific knowledge that is already available on the subject, and the research aim. The researcher's philosophy of science, experience and educational background may play a role as well (see below).

5   A specification of the measures that will be taken to ensure reliability and validity. When explaining why a certain strategy, method or technique has been chosen, a researcher also has to indicate what will be done to counter the influence of likely sources of interference with reliability and validity. In Chapters 6–9, I shall point out the risks involved in using certain research methods, and specify what remedies can be applied. It is vital to identify potential sources of interference before a study is actually implemented. If such problems are only detected afterwards, results will be invalidated, and the research will have been carried out for nothing.

6   The way in which the data will be analysed. After the data collection, the process of analysis begins. Usually a range of different analytical techniques can be applied, depending on the nature of the data (see Box 4.1 on scales of measurement). Also, there are diverse computer programs available for data analysis, as will be shown in Chapters 10–11. In inductive research, data analysis constitutes a crucial element of the research design. After all, the analysis is meant to result in new theoretical propositions (axioms), and the chosen method and technique will have to contribute to this aim.

The researcher must therefore clearly specify what procedure he or she intends to follow, and why this particular procedure is chosen. In Chapter 11, we shall see that the analytical method is further refined during the empirical phase.

7   An assessment of material costs, staffing and a time schedule, so as to give an indication of the practical feasibility of the study. This element of the research design is especially important when the study has been commissioned by a sponsor, or a certain deadline has to be met (see also Box 5.1 on time dimensions in a research design). In commissioned research, the cost assessment forms are in effect a quote for the sponsor.

8   A specification of the way in which the research results will be reported. In Chapter 12, I shall show that research results can be presented in various formats to the sponsor, or to a scientific or general audience. In the same chapter, I shall also explain that a researcher can formulate recommendations (called: prescription), a subject that is especially relevant to research in Public Administration and Public Management.

BOX 5.1   THE TIME DIMENSION IN RESEARCH

Time can be a variable in research, for example, when developments or changes in the units of study are monitored during a certain interval. In longitudinal research, several measurements are taken over a longer period of time. There are different ways to include a time dimension in research (see also Babbie, 1992, p. 99–102):

■   The simplest form is that of measuring a variable on both 'sides' of a particular event. For example, the researcher can measure voting behaviour before and after a certain political event. The interest lies in the difference between the two moments in time, and what influence (causality) the event has had. The classic experiment (see Chapter 6) is also of this type.

■   In cohort studies, the focus lies on units of study that form a homogenous group. All measurements pertain to a group of units who share a certain characteristic; an example is people who were all born in the same period or in the same year (a generation). The study is repeated on a regular basis, although a different sample from the same generation can be drawn every time that measurement takes place. To give an example, the cohort approach can be used to study changes in people's average voting behaviour as they grow older.

■   In panel studies, the researcher works with a fixed group of units. People are monitored over a longer period of time (for example, from youth till old age), to see whether certain characteristics (such as voting behaviour) change over time.

- In trend studies, the same measurement is repeated on several occasions, with units that share certain characteristics at the moments of measurement. In the example of voting behaviour, a trend study could involve comparing two different measurements, such as the voting behaviour of people in their fifties then (first measurement) and people in their fifties now (second measurement).
- In cross-sectional studies, just one measurement takes place, but a distinction is made between units of study in terms of time, such as lifetime or age. In this manner, sub-groups are created which are considered representative of a certain generation. The researcher can derive statements on developments or changes over time by comparing the current younger generation with the older group (both in the here and now).
- If the interest lies in past events, a retrospective design may be suitable. This can vary from searching the archives for information to asking people to tell about how certain things were in former days. The latter approach is not without risk, however: people's memories are not always reliable.

A deductive research format provides more guidance than an inductive design. In a deductive study, all steps that will be taken in the course of the study are decided upon beforehand. Likewise, it is clear from the start what the research aims to do: namely, testing a theoretical explanation. For this reason, a deductive study is often thought to be a more viable option. Inductive research offers no such guarantees. However, *this does not mean that either deductive research is to be preferred or better than inductive research, or inductive research is by definition less accurate and specific.* Science gains from both types of study (think of the empirical cycle discussed in Chapter 3). The choice as to which design is most suitable for a certain research problem depends on factors such as the state of scientific knowledge (theory), a researcher's experience and expertise, practical considerations (time and money), and a sponsor's wishes or aims.

5.2 CHOOSING A RESEARCH STRATEGY, METHOD AND TECHNIQUE

A central element of the research design is the choice of which strategy to follow and what methods and techniques to apply. Research strategy, method and technique are terms that are often confused with each other. Following 't Hart, Van Dijk, De Goede, Jansen, and Teunissen (1998, p. 93–96), I shall use them to designate different things. The research strategy is the overall design or logical procedure that will be followed. Given a certain research strategy, several different methods of gathering data can be used. The technique is the way in which the data will actually be analysed (see also Chapters 10–11).

The distinction made here is indicative of a certain gradation, with the researcher moving from a more global approach – the research strategy – to the practical stages of using a certain method and technique when implementing the study. In everyday practice, researchers often do not distinguish between these different phases, and the three terms mentioned are used interchangeably. One of the reasons for this is that frequently a combination of methods is used (the mixed method design), which can make it hard to define precisely what the main or dominant research strategy is.

The decision to apply a certain strategy, method and technique is guided by several considerations. First, the subject of study (the research problem) and the body of existing knowledge will be of influence. The more knowledge there is available, and the more units of study that can be included in the study, the easier it will be to apply certain statistical techniques (think of the scales of measurement discussed in Box 4.1). With more units of study, it will also be more likely that the researcher decides to follow the strategy of conducting an experiment or survey. In particular the survey is suitable for studying large numbers. The experiment is a fitting choice when the interest mainly lies in testing hypotheses derived from the theory.

Table 5.1 gives an overview of which strategies concord with certain types of research problem. In this book, four main research strategies will be discussed: namely, the experiment (Chapter 6), the survey (Chapter 7), the case study (Chapter 8), and desk research (Chapter 9). Within each chosen strategy, different methods and techniques can be applied (see Table 5.2).

Apart from the four strategies mentioned, the following methods will be discussed in this book: observation (Chapter 6), the questionnaire (Chapter 7), the interview (Chapter 8), and content analysis, meta-analysis and secondary analysis (all in Chapter 9). Most of these methods can be applied within the context of different strategies. Moreover, each method can be refined further to specific formats, such as the semi-structured interview, the written questionnaire, discourse analysis, etc. (see Table 5.2).

In the methodological literature, a distinction is often made between qualitative and quantitative methods and techniques. In actual practice, however, the words qualitative and quantitative refer to the nature of the data rather than the method or technique with which these are gathered or analysed. A

Table 5.1 Characteristics of the four main research strategies

Strategy	Research problem	Number of units	Number of variables
Experiment	Explain, test, evaluate	Small	Small
Survey	Describe, test, diagnose	Large	Large
Case study	Explore, describe, diagnose, design, evaluate	Small	Large
Desk research	All	Varies	Varies

Table 5.2 *Characteristics of diverse research methods*

Method	Approach	Variants	Strategy
Observation	Observing human behaviour, in real life or a laboratory setting	Hidden, open or participant observation	Experiment, case study
Questionnaire	Asking questions, prepared beforehand	Written, phone, online, or face-to-face questionnaire with open-ended or closed-ended questions	Survey, case study, experiment
Interview	Asking individuals questions (open-ended or closed-ended)	Open-ended interview, semi-structured or structured interview	Case study, survey
Content analysis	Interpreting the content of certain documents	Textual analysis, software supported analysis	Desk research, case study
Secondary analysis	Analysing existing numerical data anew	Statistical analysis	Desk research
Meta-analysis	Giving an overview of the results of previously conducted research	Thematic ordering and summary, statistical analysis	Desk research

questionnaire, for example, can either yield qualitative data (such as opinions or beliefs), or result in a body of numerical information (such as data on the budget of an organization, or the age or income of a respondent). In this book, methods and techniques will not be subdivided into qualitative or quantitative varieties. From here on, I shall use such labels only to refer to certain types of data (see Chapters 10–11).

Apart from the research problem and the body of existing knowledge, several other factors can be mentioned that influence the choice of research strategy, for example, a researcher's personal preferences and expertise, or practical matters like time, money or the number of staff available. The philosophy of science applied by the researcher is important as well (see Chapter 3). Whatever shape or form a study eventually takes, the reasons underlying the decision to apply a certain strategy, method or technique must be clearly specified and explained in the research design.

In principle, all strategies discussed here can be applied in research in Public Administration and Public Management, irrespective of whether a study is inductive or deductive in its set-up. It has to be added, though, that the unique features of research in Public Administration (see Chapter 1) tend to make certain strategies (such as the case study) generally more suitable, whilst other strategies will hardly ever be applied (think, for example, of the experiment). In the chapters on specific research strategies, I shall elaborate on this point.

FURTHER READING

Pierce, R. (2008). *Research Methods in Politics: A Practical Guide*. London: SAGE.
Robson, C. (2002). *Real World Research*. Malden, USA: Blackwell Publishing.

EXERCISES

1   Try to find a research proposal that you can study (ask your tutor if you have trouble finding a suitable text yourself, or check with a research council for academic funding in your country, for example, the ESRC in the UK). Judge the proposal on completeness and feasibility. Use the information given in this chapter about what a research design should contain, and defend your assessment by referring to certain sections of text. Give arguments, not personal opinions, and be constructive in your criticism: indicate what the author could do to improve the proposal. Give your comments in the first person. For example, write 'the explanation of why strategy X was chosen failed to convince me', instead of 'the explanation of why strategy X was chosen is not clear'. By making it a personal statement, and not a universal vote of censure, you allow the author to respond with counter-arguments. (Tip: follow this procedure also in other situations, for example, when acting as a discussant for a presentation, or reviewing a scientific book or article.)

2   Devise a sampling framework for, respectively, a panel, a cohort and a trend study. If you were a unit of study, which position might you occupy in such research? Use a diagram if necessary to explain your answer. For example, you can draw a large circle to represent the population as a whole, in which you insert a small circle to depict the actual sample drawn.

3   Usually, research proposals are bound to a certain word limit. To practise being concise, do the following exercise. Take a random chapter from a scientific publication (not the introduction) on a subject relevant to Public Administration; this can either be an entire book or a lengthy article from a magazine or critical journal. Summarize the publication in fewer than 300 words, and state exactly how many words you have used. Tip: write a summary first, then do a word count (Microsoft Word offers a function for this), and only afterwards start deleting what is redundant. In this way, you will prevent an excessive focus on the first part of the text.

4   Comment on the following statement: *Just as any other profession, doing scientific research requires skill and expertise, and scientists should master as many different research methods as they can.* Argue both for and against this statement, before formulating your own opinion. For self-reflection: which philosophy of science do your comments betray?

Chapter 6

The experiment

Contrary to, for example, research in psychology, Public Administration and Public Management research only rarely uses the strategy of the experiment (compare Morton & Williams, 2010; Margetts, 2011; Perry, 2012). Even so, it is important to have some basic knowledge of experiments, because researchers in Public Administration and Public Management sometimes do use certain experimental variants, such as simulations and gaming. Also, researchers in Public Administration regularly evaluate policy experiments, all of which makes it necessary to be familiar with the underlying logic of this research strategy.

Besides the experiment itself, this chapter also deals with the method of observation. This is often used in experiments, although is not exclusive to it (compare Table 5.2).

6.1 THE CLASSIC EXPERIMENT

Figure 6.1 gives a schematic outline of the classic, or pure, experiment. In the classic experiment, the units of study – called subjects – typically are people (in psychological research, experiments are sometimes also conducted with animals). Subjects are divided *at random* (R) into two groups: the experimental group and the control group. The experimental group is subjected to a certain experimental stimulus X; the control group does not undergo X. In both groups, measurements are taken at two different moments in time: O_1 (pre-test) and O_2 (post-test). By comparing both measurements, the effect of X in the experimental group can be established.

A classic experiment takes place in an environment designed and controlled by the researcher, such as a laboratory. The laboratory setting guarantees that the subjects will not be influenced by any other stimuli than those provided by the researcher. We call such a procedure manipulation: solely the researcher determines what the subjects do or experience, whilst all other influences are purposely excluded. It is easy to see why the experiment usually involves people rather than, say, organizations or countries: in the latter case, it would be impossible to create such an isolated and controlled environment.

$$R \; \frac{O_1 \; X \; O_2}{O_1 \quad O_2}$$

Figure 6.1
Schematic outline of the classic experiment

The following example can help to illustrate the logistics of the experiment. Suppose that in a study on the effects of an information campaign on the European Union (EU) subjects are asked about their opinion on the EU constitution (O_1: pre-test measurement). Subsequently, the experimental group is given an information package to read (X). The control group does not get this information, but is presented with 'neutral' reading material instead, such as a newspaper. In medical experiments, such neutral treatment is called a placebo: half of the research subjects is offered a certain experimental drug or treatment, whilst the control group is given a drug known to be medically ineffective. The subjects themselves do not know who gets the drug and who only gets the placebo. If the researcher or medical specialist does not know either, we call the experiment 'double blind' (see also the section below on validity).

To get back to our EU example: after people have acquainted themselves with the reading material they have been given, they are asked to give their opinion once more on the EU constitution (O_2: post-test measurement). During the entire experiment, both groups have remained where they are, for example, in two separate laboratories, or some other suitable set of rooms. If the researcher expects that the information package will make people more positive about the EU constitution (hypothesis), the difference between pre-test and post-test results should be bigger in the experimental group. Any difference in opinion can only have been caused by the experimental stimulus, which means that giving people an information package to read will turn out to have a proven positive effect.

As our example shows, in experiments usually just a small number of variables are considered (the experimental stimulus). Also, experimental research is predominantly of the deductive or hypothesis-testing type. Often there is no need to study a large number of subjects. Because the effect can only be ascribed to the experimental condition (and there are no sources of interference in the form of other influencing variables – see Box 6.1), a small research population suffices to test what effect the stimulus actually has.

As a rule, the subjects in an experiment are not informed in advance of the research aim underlying the study, although they are told about the procedure that will be followed. Keeping subjects 'naive' about the research aim is necessary to ensure that the change that is measured is real, and can be ascribed purely to the stimulus provided by the researcher. Of course, after the experiment has been completed, subjects have to be enlightened on what purpose the study was really meant to serve.

It goes without saying that there are situations in which it would be unethical not to inform people beforehand about what an experiment will involve or intends to demonstrate. This holds in particular for certain kinds of medical research. In such cases, the researcher has to seek permission first from an ethics committee, who decide whether or not the study may be carried out without obtaining the fully informed consent from the subjects (see also Chapter 12 on ethics).

The experiment allows for a precise measurement of the effect that the independent variable (IV: the stimulus) has on the dependent variable (DV). This research strategy is therefore ideally suited to ascertain causal relationships, as all other influences are excluded.

If one of the elements outlined in Figure 6.1 is lacking, or others are added, we do not speak of a classic experiment, but of a quasi-experimental research design. The quasi-experiment comes in various shapes and sizes. For example, a study can be done without any pre-test measurement or control group. The researcher can also decide to take several different pre-test and post-test measurements (for more variants see Cook & Campbell, 1979). Haverland (2005) argues that much of the research in Public Administration on the effects of the European integration is by definition quasi-experimental: after all, EU regulations apply to all member states, which means that a real control group is lacking. In order to measure any causal effects, he suggests following an alternative approach, such as comparing member states with non-EU members, or comparing member states that differ in terms of the pace at which EU regulations are being introduced.

BOX 6.1 EXOGENOUS VARIABLES AND INTERVENING VARIABLES

To reduce interfering influences as much as possible, the researcher will try and keep the number of variables in an experiment to a minimum. The absolute minimum set consists of the independent variable (the experimental stimulus) and the dependent variable (the effect to be measured). These variables are called 'endogenous' because they are intrinsic to the basic research design. However, a situation can also arise in which exogenous factors start to play a role. Such exogenous factors can concern variables or events that are external to the research situation itself, but whose influence can still be felt. To illustrate this in the context of the example given above, if the EU constitution is a topic of hot public debate whilst the experiment is going on, the opinion of the subjects may change independently of the stimulus. The precise moment of measurement – for example, before and after a referendum on the EU is held – can therefore be of covert influence. In theory, such an influence will be seen in all subjects, both in the experimental group and in the control group. Still, it will be hard to ascribe the effect measured entirely to the information package that the experimental group has been given to read, which means that the validity of results may be impaired.

Another possible source of interference can arise when the effect at interest is not caused directly by the independent variable. For example, people's reading skills or existing knowledge on EU regulations can influence their understanding or interpretation of the information they have been given. Such factors are called intervening variables. To reduce the interference caused by intervening variables, the researcher can decide to apply the method of matching. Instead of dividing people *at random* in an experimental group and a control group, they are first tested on their knowledge or reading skills. Low-scoring and high-scoring people are subsequently divided equally between the experimental group and the control group. This is known as matching. The source of interference is reduced in this manner, as in both groups the effect of the intervening variable will be equally large or small. The researcher has now brought the source of interference under control. Such variables are therefore sometimes also called control variables (because their influence is 'controlled' i.e. neutralized).

To summarize this section, the strategy of the experiment allows the researcher to test a presupposed causal connection. It is an efficient but also highly structured research strategy. Doing an experiment imposes stringent demands on a researcher: the research situation must be kept strictly under control, and all possible sources of interferences have to be excluded, including that of one's own behaviour as a researcher (Morton & Williams, 2010). Otherwise the so-called observer or 'Hawthorne effect' may arise: subjects are aware of the fact that they are being studied, and respond to this by modifying their behaviour (see also below).

6.2 SIMULATIONS AND GAMING

Just like the experiment, simulations and gaming involve imitating reality in a setting that is manipulated and controlled by the researcher. On the basis of theoretical knowledge, the researcher creates a situation in which the participants in the simulation game (the subjects) have to perform certain acts or do an assignment (see Box 6.2). Contrary to the classic experiment, however, subjects are not split into an experimental group and a control group. Also, more variables will be included than just one experimental stimulus. Simulations and gaming can therefore be typified as a quasi-experimental design. The research setting is the laboratory rather than daily reality, although not all conditions of the 'pure' experiment are met (compare with the field experiment below).

Typical examples of simulations and gaming research in Public Administration and Public Management are studies on decision making. In a game, the participants have to try and reach a mutual decision – for example, about how financial sources should be distributed over different policies, or the way in which a certain policy should be implemented. The participants first receive (written) information from the researcher on the problem they have to solve, the assignment they are meant to do, the different roles they can play (for example, civil servants, politicians, citizens and experts), and the conditions under which the decision must be taken (such as limited time and money, or the number of parties involved – see Box 6.2). In its simplest form, the simulation game shows which considerations or parties are important in the decision-making process, and how a decision is ultimately reached. This knowledge can be used to test, compare and improve decision-making models.

BOX 6.2 DESIGNING A SIMULATION GAME

Bots and Van Daalen (2007) have described how decision-making games can best be developed. There are three steps involved in designing the game: (1) problem selection; (2) substantive analysis of the problem; and (3) setting the scene.

1   Based on the research aim and the type of subjects, the researcher has to select a problem on which a decision has to be made. Problems can be elementary, but they can also be complex, requiring multiple sub-decisions. At this stage, time aspects such as deadlines or other constraints (money, technology) also have to be taken into account. Subjects can be stakeholders with an interest in the problem. They are either individual or corporate actors (representing, for example, an organization or society). Depending on their position and role in the simulation game, the subjects may have access to all or just part of the information on the problem at hand.

2   The structure and content of the problem have to be examined. These features form the basic ingredients for the simulation game, which has to represent and resemble reality as closely as possible. The researcher has to familiarize him- or herself thoroughly with the topic at hand, in order to be able to understand in what and how many different outcomes the decision-making process could result.

3   A setting has to be constructed, with rules and a storyline that specify in what manner subjects are allowed to behave. Games usually start with a neutral introduction, in which the simulated world and the aim of the entire exercise are explained. Next the different roles (civil servants, politicians, interest groups, experts, citizens and so on) are divided. Every participant receives the information they need, such as what exactly their role entails, their

preferences regarding the outcome, and constraints in terms of things such as time and money. People are given enough time to process all this information, after which the game begins.

Beforehand, the researcher has determined what procedure will be followed during the simulation game, and how participants will communicate with each other. To facilitate reconstructing the decision-making process afterwards, all exchanges between the participants have to be recorded, either on paper or electronically (using specialized software). The researcher keeps track of the game in other ways as well, for example by keeping a log or writing observation reports. Game simulations usually take place in a confined space: one room or a set of rooms within walking distance of each other. More than one researcher may be needed to instruct and observe the participants.

The game is over when the decision-making process has been completed, or when it is clear what the end conclusion will be (decision, no decision, or otherwise). The simulation is rounded off with an evaluation, in which the way the game developed is revised, but also what lessons can be drawn from the process.

(For more examples and guidelines, see the specialized journals or the standardized games that researchers have posted on the Internet.)

Simulations and games can also be used to improve a policy or facilitate its implementation (think of the regulative cycle discussed in Chapter 3). For example, by trying out a new implementation procedure first in a game, the later practical phase of policy execution may cause fewer problems. The aim of learning, in the sense of gaining insight into how certain processes work, is often a reason for doing simulation games, and they are regularly used for educational purposes. For example, in training programmes for crisis management, a learning tool often employed is that of enacting a crisis situation. In scientific education as well – including courses in Public Administration and Public Management – simulations and games can be a means of teaching students to apply the theoretical knowledge they have acquired to a practical, real-life situation. The evaluation of the results of the game allows participants to reflect on and explain their behaviour. This information can later serve as input for analysis, together with the observations made during the game itself (see also the section on observation, below).

Due to the increasing use of ICT applications, simulation games are now often played with the aid of computers. A concomitant advantage of this is that the acts performed by the participants in the game are all registered electronically, which information can later be used for analysis. An example is the Group Decision Room (GDR) game, which simulates decision-making processes. The participants exchange information (ideas, beliefs and opinions) via the computer, and reach a mutual decision in the end. Because all the data have been stored automatically, the researcher can easily reconstruct the various steps of the decision-making process. Moreover, measurements can be done whilst the game is still running, for example, by interviewing participants online.

Besides a term in gaming, the term simulation is also used to refer to multiple calculations with computer models for predicting the effects of certain policy measures (*ex ante* evaluations, scenarios) or those of current developments on future policy (trend analysis). Both forms of Public Administration research can provide input for the policy process (see Chapter 1). However, such variants of simulation games have little in common with the research strategy of the experiment, which is why I shall not discuss this subject any further here (but do note the section of Chapter 9 on secondary analysis).

6.3 THE FIELD EXPERIMENT

One of the main reasons why in Public Administration the strategy of the classic experiment is only seldom applied is that it can be hard to study certain research subjects in a laboratory setting, because they concern real-life, topical events (Morton & Williams, 2010; Margetts, 2011). Experiments that are conducted outside the laboratory or in the empirical world are called field experiments. In Public Administration, the field experiment is usually not carried out by a researcher but by a public or governmental organization. The researcher will merely be invited to provide guidance during the experiment, and evaluate the results afterwards. Strictly speaking, we cannot speak of a true experimental study in such a case; rather, we are dealing with a form of evaluation or action research (see Boxes 1.3 and 2.1). Numerous examples can be given of policy experiments that follow the procedure outlined here, varying from the introduction of a new law to the implementation of organizational changes (see Box 6.3).

BOX 6.3 EXAMPLES OF POLICY EXPERIMENTS

- Several national governments have experimented with vouchers for education, which are certificates that can be traded in for a specific amount of education, in time or level. For example, in a number of US cities, children from less privileged backgrounds are given the opportunity to go to a private school. In Switzerland, low-income adults are offered access to supplementary adult education. Evaluations of such experiments do not show conclusive results, though. For one thing, the number of people involved in these experiments is often very small. Second, the success of such schemes depends on the conditions under which vouchers are distributed. Third, in some cases underprivileged citizens – who are usually the main target group – appear to make less frequent use of education vouchers than more well-off people do.

- As part of the attempt to contribute to a more sustainable environment, several experiments have been implemented in the field of water management. For instance, sometimes areas of land are purposively flooded to create water basins. Examples can be found in countries such as the Netherlands, the USA (Everglades), Germany (Rhine valley), and in developing countries such as India and Bangladesh. Evaluations show that the management of such experiments is often very difficult, as there are many stakeholders involved with opposing interests. Farmers and businesses need the land, whereas interest groups will support the development of the local ecosystem. Governments, in their turn, have to keep both parties happy.
- Experiments are quite common in the healthcare sector, to test, for example, new drugs and treatment methods. However, experiments are also being applied to things like the management of care organizations or hospitals. The latter type of experiments can vary from studying innovative techniques to developing strategies for reducing waiting lists, introducing user fees to increase patients' awareness of healthcare costs, implementing performance indicators in hospital management, and allowing for new forms of cooperation between different providers of healthcare, such as hospitals and nursing homes (integrated care). Because of the large variation in these experiments, it is difficult to arrive at one single conclusion about their results. Some experiments are successful and will go on to become a 'best practice', or will even serve as a future role model for other organizations (compare with the website of the National Institute for Health and Care Excellence (NICE) in the UK).

Field experiments are, by definition, quasi-experiments, because they do not take place in a controlled environment. In other respects, as well, the basic design of the field experiment differs from that of the pure, or classic, experiment; for example, the selection of the units of study takes place in a different manner. In policy experiments, usually certain subjects are singled out for inclusion in the study, often for the reason that they have participated in similar experiments before. Sometimes, too, subjects apply of their own accord. Lastly, whereas the classic experiment always involves human subjects, in a field experiment the units of study can also consist of organizations, administrative levels, or even countries (see the examples in Box 6.3).

6.4 RELIABILITY AND VALIDITY IN EXPERIMENTS

The main advantage of choosing the research strategy of the experiment is the high level of control that it offers over the research situation. Because all other influences are excluded, the researcher can prove causality (IV creates a change in DV) and test theories. A major disadvantage is that the laboratory setting can hardly be called realistic, which makes it difficult to translate or generalize findings to other situations. Moreover, only a few variables can be considered at a time, which means that an adequate operationalization of the construct under study is crucial to success (see Chapter 4).

Experiments are sensitive to diverse sources of interference, especially with regard to validity (Morton & Williams, 2010). For one thing, the further apart in time O_1 (pre-test measurement) and O_2 (post-test measurement) take place, the greater the risk will be that the subjects are influenced by exogenous factors. Such risks apply in particular to field experiments. As to policy experiments, a change in the existing political situation can cause a certain policy measure to be adjusted, or lead to an alteration in the conditions (time schedule, money) under which the study is carried out (Margetts, 2011). Also, in-between attrition (loss of subjects because they drop out of the study) can cause results to become biased. For all such reasons, it is advisable to keep the interval between O_1 and O_2 as short as possible.

Another familiar phenomenon is the so-called observer effect. For example, if measurements are being taken frequently or regularly, subjects may grow accustomed to being tested and show increasingly higher scores, irrespective of the experimental stimulus they are given. In principle, this effect will also arise in the control group, which is exactly why it is so important to have a control group. The subjects may also adapt their behaviour to the test situation (awareness). A famous example of this is the so-called Milgram or obedience effect: subjects often wish to please the experimenter, whom they regard as an important and knowledgeable figure, and they will adjust their behaviour in a way that they think is expected of them. However, it is not just the subjects who have certain ideas or expectations regarding the experiment: the researcher can show such tendencies as well. Indeed, experimental researchers have to try and handle subjects, the experiment itself, and the data analysis in as neutral and objective a way as possible. Following fixed protocols and standardized instructions can help to achieve this. Another means of reducing researcher interference is working double blind (see above), a procedure that prevents the experimenter from knowing which subjects exactly receive the experimental stimulus.

Finally, the selection of subjects can cause a potential threat to validity, especially if only small numbers are involved. It is therefore vital to determine beforehand which requirements the potential subjects have to fulfil. In the example of the experiment with the EU information package, we saw that a subject's reading skills or knowledge might be a source of interference (see Box 6.1). Testing people first on these characteristics and matching subjects can help to increase validity in such a case. Furthermore, in policy experiments attention has to be paid to the matter of how representative the participating subjects really are. For example, if a certain change in the educational system is only implemented by larger schools, the question remains what the results of such a change would be in smaller schools (generalizability).

As mentioned in the discussion on simulation games, one of the research methods that can be applied in the experiment is observation. This forms the subject of the next section.

6.5 OBSERVATION

In this method, the researcher uses his or her own observations and interpretations (of events, persons, or acts) to arrive at certain conclusions and results. Different types of observation can be applied, depending on the degree to which the researcher actively participates in the research situation. Hidden observation means to say that the researcher remains aloof. In an open observation format, the researcher is present in the research situation but does not interact with the subjects, who may or may not have been informed about this person's role of researcher. In participant observation, there is much more interaction between researcher and subjects; also, the researcher's identity is known to those who are observed (DeWalt & DeWalt, 2002).

A second distinction that can be made is the degree of structuring applied. In a structured format, it is decided beforehand which acts or behaviours – called categories – will be observed. These categories are usually derived from the theory. For example, theories on organizational culture will describe which manifestations of organizational culture have to be included in the study (such as corporate clothing, or social norms and customs). Based on theory, a coding scheme or protocol is devised in which all possible categories are specified; during the observation phase, the researcher merely has to tick off which category has been observed most often. To give an example, in a study on leadership the researcher can examine the behaviour of politicians or civil servants by looking closely at with whom they interact, how long such meetings last, how frequently they take place and so forth. A systematic approach like this fits in well with deductive research. A disadvantage is that behaviours not included in the coding scheme will remain unnoticed. The researcher can solve such problems by following a semi-structured approach, which allows for extra categories to be added during the observation phase if this is deemed fit.

If there is little or no knowledge available on a certain research subject, less structured formats can be applied, without a coding scheme. Categories will then be derived during the observation phase, by noting events or behaviours. The researcher observes that certain characteristics and behaviours often seem to go together, creating a pattern, and combinations of categories will be added to the scheme. A full coding scheme will only be constructed after the observation phase, during the analysis of the observations that have been gathered earlier (see also Chapter 11).

Different aids are available for making observations, such as recording devices (sound, images), writing paper, a memo-recorder, or a laptop. The researcher can use these devices to make notes or recordings of everything that is said or done. These notes and recordings are subsequently transcribed and subjected to more detailed analysis.

The observation method in Public Administration research

The method of observation is employed in Public Administration (for an example, see Box 6.4), but is less popular than other methods. If researchers do make use of observation, they usually choose the method of participant observation, combining this with other methods (see also Chapter 8 on case studies).

BOX 6.4 EXAMPLE OF OBSERVATION STUDY

A classic example of observation as a main method in Public Administration and Public Management research is the study conducted by Mintzberg (1971). In his study, Mintzberg concentrated on public managers. He selected executives from five different organizations: a school, a hospital and three firms (a technological firm, a consulting firm and a consumer goods manufacturer). During one-week intervals, he observed the executives' activities in a structured manner (using an observation scheme).

Based on his findings, Mintzberg deduced ten basic roles for managers, taking into accounts aspects such as whether a manager focuses more on people, on information processing, or on decision making (including settling any disputes), or combinations thereof. He found that managerial jobs are characterized by variety, discontinuity and brevity, and often show an unrelenting work pace. Because most work activities take place in an ad hoc manner, and in interaction with other people (verbal interaction mostly, rather than written communication), Mintzberg concluded that the theoretical model of managers prevalent at the time failed to provide an accurate picture of reality. He made several recommendations on how to improve the theory on managers (compare theoretical generalization in Chapter 8).

Since 1971, Mintzberg's study has been replicated several times. It is now considered a groundbreaking study in the field of Public Management.

Participant observation

Participant observation means to say that the researcher takes part in the research situation and maintains close contact with the units of study (DeWalt & DeWalt, 2002; Kawulich, 2005). By participating in daily activities, the researcher can study people's behaviour, and gather extra information on the spot by asking them why they show a certain type of behaviour. Such contextual information can be used later, when the observation data are analysed and interpreted. As this description shows, participant observation is much more than just observing people. Everything that the researcher meets with or sees in the observation phase (documents, anecdotes, conversations, events) may be relevant. Participant observation requires the researcher to be very open minded, which makes it highly suitable to inductive forms of research (van Hulst, 2008).

Observation results in a rich body of detailed information on the research subject in its everyday context (holistic). It will come as no surprise that researchers with an interpretative philosophy of science often support or use this method. Yet there are other advantages to participating observation: for example, different aspects will come to the fore than in, say, an interview or a document analysis. An example is that of non-verbal behavioural aspects. In an interview, people can put on an act or show socially desirable behaviour, but such pretence is hard to keep up during a prolonged period of close observation. In addition, what people say does not always correspond with what they actually do.

Certain disadvantages of participant observation can be mentioned as well. For example, researchers can 'go native', because they get too much drawn into the situation or start to identify with the units of study instead of examining them objectively (compare DeWalt & DeWalt, 2002, p. 195). Indeed, it is important for the researcher to decide carefully in advance which role to assume during the observation phase. After all, he or she will be a participant in the situation as well, which means that role conflict may well arise (see van Hulst, 2008, for some practical guidance on such matters).

Reliability and validity in observation

Apart from role conflict in the researcher, the observation method may create other risks for reliability and validity. There are two main risks here: namely, selectivity and subjectivity. Whilst making his or her observations, the researcher – either consciously or unconsciously – chooses what to note down and what to ignore. In particular in situations where many things are happening at once, it will be virtually impossible to observe all events and behaviours, which means that a certain degree of selectivity is bound to result. A remedy can be found in using multiple observers, or recording behaviours first and studying them only later. Another possibility is to calculate the reliability by testing how often different observers arrive at similar conclusions (inter-observer reliability), or how often the same observer arrives at the same conclusion about similar observations (intra-observer reliability).

Selectivity can also arise from subjectivity or observer bias: the researcher's own expectations influence the observations made or the interpretation of behaviours and events. To limit such effects, it is important for observers to be well trained, and that mutual agreement is reached beforehand on the working method to follow during the observation phase and the analysis later. Such agreements can be recorded in a protocol or research code.

FURTHER READING

DeWalt, K.M., & DeWalt, B.R. (2002). *Participant Observation: A Guide for Fieldworkers*. Walnut Creek: Altamira Press.

Morton, R.B., & Williams, K.C. (2010). *Experimental Political Science and the Study of Causality: From Nature to the Lab*. Cambridge: Cambridge University Press.

EXERCISES

1 There are numerous famous – or infamous – examples of experimental research, such as the Milgram experiment in psychology and the Prisoner's Dilemma in game theory. Look up information on these two forms of experiment (for example, on the Internet), and describe in your own words what they entail (circa 1,000 words per example). Apply the terminology used in this chapter, using words and phrases such as experimental stimulus, control group and randomization. Your description should make clear whether the example in question concerns a classic experiment, a quasi-experiment, a field experiment, or a different type of research.

2 Design a small experiment of your own in an everyday situation. Your experiment can have a very simple format – for example, greeting passers-by in the street one day and confining yourself to a friendly nod on the other. Keep a log of how many people reacted spontaneously on both days by greeting you back. Is there any noticeable difference? Take care to control for any sources of interference, such as the weather, the gender of the researcher, or the units of study (how could you do this?).

3 Practise the observation method in an everyday situation. For example, whilst travelling by public transport, you can study your fellow passengers. Make a coding scheme beforehand and decide on which aspects or features to focus. A famous psychological phenomenon, for example, is that people usually sit next to someone who resembles themselves in certain respects: men sit with men, women with women, elderly people with elderly people. Can your own observations confirm this hypothesis?

Chapter 7

The survey

The survey is virtually synonymous with the written questionnaire, although there is more to it than just that. It is one of the best-known forms of research, being frequently employed by organizations and companies for purposes such as customer research and opinions polls. Almost everybody has, at one stage in their life, participated in a survey.

The strategy of the survey allows the researcher to collect a considerable body of data on a large number of subjects, which makes it a highly efficient approach to research. The information gathered is usually analysed with the aid of statistical techniques (see Chapter 10). There are also several important drawbacks to the survey and (written) questionnaire, as we shall see later in this chapter.

7.1 THE SURVEY: CHARACTERISTICS AND TYPES

A typical characteristic of the survey is its large-scale approach. Usually it comprises a sizeable number of variables and many units of study. The units of study in a survey are called respondents, whose participation in the survey results from a sampling procedure (see Chapter 4). To allow for data collection on such a large scale, the researcher will use standardized forms of measurement, such as, for example, answer scales or numerical answer categories (DeVellis, 2012; Fowler, 2002). Surveys can be employed to collect factual information, but also to gather data on people's opinions or attitudes towards a certain subject. See, for example, the European Social Survey (ESS), which studies the interaction between Europe's changing institutions, and the attitudes, beliefs and behavioural patterns of its diverse populations (www.europeansocialsurvey. org). Topics of interest are, amongst others, people's opinions on political issues, social exclusion and diverse forms of identity (religious, cultural, ethnic).

Due to the need to standardize measurements and design a scale or set of answer categories in advance, the survey is especially suitable for theory-driven or deductive forms of research. This need not always be a case of hypotheses being tested; surveys can also be conducted to explore or describe people's attitudes. Whatever the research aim, a survey is always meant for the collection of *new* data, as opposed to the research strategy of desk research (see Chapter 9). Some authors use the word survey in the sense of *review*, to describe the process of gathering and analysing a large body of *existing data* (for an example, see Babbie, 1992, p. 280). In this chapter, the term 'survey' will only refer to a research strategy for gathering fresh material.

Its large scale and high level of standardization not only make the survey an efficient way of collecting data, but the data can also easily be generalized, which means a high level of external validity. At the same time, standardization will render a certain superficiality to the information gathered. For example, if you know that someone estimates the chance of a nuclear disaster occurring to be 75%, you still have no idea why this person thinks this is so. Also, it is doubtful whether different respondents perceive such a risk in similar terms or on a similar scale; is the 75% chance of respondent A truly higher than the 50% of respondent B (compare Fowler, 2002, p. 90, and see also Box 4.1 on scales of measurement)? Indeed, usually a world of information lies hidden behind the data collected in a survey. What is more, respondents do not always reply truthfully, or they give only partial answers. Sometimes, too, respondents are unwilling to participate and do not reply at all. All these aspects can create a risk for reliability and validity (see also below).

The research strategy of the survey nearly always involves administering a questionnaire; the rest of this chapter will deal mainly with this particular method. A questionnaire can assume various shapes and forms (see also Table 5.2). Its best-known format is the written questionnaire, although questionnaires can be used in telephone surveys or in structured interviews as well (Fowler, 2002). In structured interviews, the researcher has a fixed list of questions and matching answer categories, which are read out one by one to the respondent. The interview method will be dealt with at length in the next chapter. Here, we will concentrate first on the written questionnaire.

7.2 THE WRITTEN QUESTIONNAIRE

A written questionnaire consists of a list of closed-ended questions. This means that every question is accompanied by a set of fixed answer categories. The respondents, who fill in the questionnaire by themselves, only have to tick the answers that are most applicable. Sometimes the researcher leaves room for different answers than the ones already devised (category 'other'). The advantage of the latter approach is that respondents who find none of the pre-structured answers suitable can still give a reply. An obvious disadvantage is that the level of standardization becomes lower and, concomitantly, the options for statistical analysis will be reduced (Fowler, 2002, ch.5).

Research with a written questionnaire consists of the following steps:

■ The researcher designs the questionnaire. The questionnaire includes an instruction and lists the actual questions, which are called items. The items have been derived from the theoretical framework (see also below).

■ The questionnaire is tested in a pilot, to detect whether there are any mistakes in the design, and to see how easy or difficult it will be for respondents to fill in the questionnaire (for example, whether they can do so in a specified amount of time).

■ The researcher draws a sample (see Chapter 4) and sends the questionnaire to all potential respondents. In the accompanying letter, the aim of the study is explained, and instructions are given on how the questionnaire should be filled in. These days, questionnaires are often sent and completed via the Internet (online questionnaires). In such a case, the respondent gets a letter or email with an Internet address and, if necessary, login codes for participating in the study.

■ Respondents fill in the questionnaire at a moment of their own choosing. In the accompanying letter, the researcher will have set a deadline for returning the completed forms. Respondents who have not replied after a certain period receive a reminder with a second request to participate in the study and complete the questionnaire (see also below, in the section on non-response).

■ After closing the study, the researcher enters the data (the respondents' replies) into the computer, using, for example, a statistical package, so that they can be analysed. (In case of an online questionnaire, the data has been inserted already when respondents filled in the items.) The conclusions drawn from the analysis are written down in a so-called respondent report, which is sent to all respondents who have participated in the study, or people who have shown an interest in receiving a report (see Chapter 10 for more explanation about the analytical phase, and compare Chapter 12 on reporting).

A number of the steps outlined above will be discussed in greater detail below.

The use of surveys and questionnaires is becoming more popular in research in Public Administration and Public Management, as the two examples in Box 7.1 show (compare with the ESS discussed earlier; see also Box 4.2 on the World Values Survey).

BOX 7.1 EXAMPLES OF RESEARCH WITH QUESTIONNAIRES

■ Public Service Motivation (PSM) is a term that refers to people's motivation to work in the public sector. To study this subject, a questionnaire was constructed by Perry with the aid of Likert scales (see Box 7.2). Six dimensions of PSM were distinguished: attraction to public policymaking, commitment to public interest, civic duty, social justice, self-sacrifice, and compassion. The questionnaire was filled in by 376 respondents: students, people employed in the public sector and people employed in business. The statistical analysis showed that the scales constructed do indeed provide an adequate measurement of PSM. The instrument developed by Perry is now frequently used by other researchers. For more information, see Perry's (1996) original article.

■ The COBRA network consists of a group of researchers from 30 different countries, who study the control and autonomy of semi-autonomous agencies. For this study, a special questionnaire was developed, which has now been applied in 18 countries. The items in the questionnaire aim to measure, amongst others, financial autonomy ('Can your organization act independently when taking out a loan, participating in limited ventures, or setting tariffs for customers?'), and control by the parent department ('How many performance indicators do you use to report on company performance, and who has developed these indicators?'). So far, the findings indicate that there are no clear and straightforward patterns in the type and degree of autonomy that agencies enjoy. Formal and factual autonomy are not related, and combinations of different kinds of autonomy can be observed. Moreover, there appears to be a trade-off between autonomy and control, although the exact balance between the two has yet to be determined (for more detail, see Verhoest, van Thiel, Bouckaert, & Laegreid, 2012).

Questionnaire design

Numerous handbooks are available on how to design a questionnaire (see, for example, DeVellis, 2012; Fowler, 2002). The differences between the various recommended approaches are negligible, though. The most important steps to take when designing a questionnaire are the following:

■ Choose the right variables, and operationalize these;
■ Carefully formulate the questionnaire items; and
■ Put the items in an order that makes sense (routing), with a clear layout.

As this checklist shows, designing a questionnaire starts with determining which variables will be measured. In deductive research, these variables are found in the theoretical framework. The variables must first be operationalized (see Chapter 4), after which the operationalizations have to be translated into questionnaire items. This means that the researcher has to devise questions – with options for answers – or formulate statements. The reaction of respondents to these questions or statements will show whether the variable being measured indeed had an effect on the dependent variable (DV) and, if so, what this effect exactly is. To give an example, on the basis of the theory, the variable 'bureaucratic competence' can be operationalized as 'knowing your rights and duties as a citizen'. One of the indicators for this might be whether citizens know what options they have to lodge a complaint about a governmental body. An item measuring this could read as follows:

> Which authority can citizens appeal to if they wish to lodge a complaint about the government, for example, when they think that service is inadequate? (Tick the right answer, multiple answers can be given.)

- The authority providing the service
- The ministry
- Parliament
- An ombudsman
- A court of justice

The higher the number of right answers ticked by the respondents, the greater their knowledge of their rights as a citizen, and the more bureaucratically competent they are.

A variable can also be measured by posing an open question, without pre-structured or fixed answer categories. Processing the answers will take up far more time in such a case, however, which makes this a less efficient method, in particular when large numbers of respondents are involved. What is more, it will be hard to guarantee validity, as respondents will tend to formulate their answers in different ways. Think, for example, of answers like 'the government': should this be taken to mean a minister, parliament, or something else entirely? An intermediate course can be taken by providing fixed answer categories, with one option captioned 'other'. Yet another alternative is to include answer categories such as 'I don't know', 'neutral' (for questions on opinions) or 'not applicable'. A disadvantage of the latter approach is that respondents may show a tendency to revert systematically to these vague categories (see further on in this chapter).

Often several *items* will be needed to arrive at the reliable and valid measurement of a variable. The researcher will therefore start by creating a pool of items (DeVellis, 2012), which contains several types of items for measuring the same subject. These items will all have to be judged in terms of the criteria for what constitutes a good item (see below), clarity and intelligibility, and ease of answering. Researchers can either try and judge the items themselves, or call in the aid of theoretical or methodological experts, or even ask a number of proof-respondents to take a look (in a pilot: see below). On the basis of the results of the test phase, the researcher selects the best items for inclusion in the actual questionnaire.

Criteria for formulating items

When formulating items, it is important to adhere to the following guidelines (DeVellis, 2012; Fowler, 2002):

- Devise clear-cut and unambiguous items. When reading a question or statement, the respondent has to understand right away what is being meant. If questions or statements are open to multiple interpretations, the validity of the measurement will be impaired. For this reason, it is best not to use theoretical jargon. For example, instead of the question 'What is your political preference?' the question 'Which party did you vote for during the last elections?' is far more specific, and easier to interpret. After all, someone's 'political preference' may involve many different things. Likewise, the statement 'Women are better political leaders, because they can empathize more than men', is worded too imprecisely; in effect, two different things are suggested here: 1 that women are better political leaders than men; and 2 that they empathize more. A respondent who agrees on point 2 but disagrees with 1 will find it difficult to reply to such a statement.

- The questionnaire should contain no leading questions or statements, which steer the respondent towards a particular reply. For example, few people will probably reply in the negative to a question formulated as follows: 'Don't you agree that the Western world should never cease giving developmental aid?' It is important also to avoid (double) negations, as this easily creates confusion. To illustrate, the question 'What wouldn't be a reason for you not to cast your vote during an election?' is actually a way of inquiring why people do go and vote.

- Use the same answer categories as much as possible for all items in the questionnaire. The more variation there is, the more likely it is that respondents get confused, discouraged or even annoyed, making them decide to discontinue with the questionnaire. Several formats can be used for answer categories: categories in which a certain content is specified (see the example on bureaucratic competence given earlier), dichotomous answers (yes/no), and scales (little/a lot; 1–10; seldom/never; agree/disagree). If scaled answers are used, the answer categories should describe one dimension only; avoid scales such as 'seldom/disagree' (see Box 7.2).

- Make sure that the answer categories are exhaustive, and describe as complete a range as possible (see also above). Also, answers must be mutually exclusive, and should not overlap. For a question on age, for example, a format of the type 20–29, 30–39, etc. should be used rather than categories of 20–30, 30–40 etc. The latter option makes it impossible for someone aged 30 to answer the question. By the way, answer categories that describe a certain range are often called groups (think of age groups) or classes (such as social classes or income classes).

BOX 7.2 SCALES

In scientific research, measurements are often done with the aid of scales. One of the best-known examples in the social sciences is the so-called Likert scale. A Likert scale consists of a number of items (statements or propositions) on one and the same subject; for each item, the respondent has to indicate to what extent they agree with the statement. The scores of the respondent on the diverse items are subsequently added up. A high total score usually means that the respondent also scores relatively high on the central subject of study (a construct, compare Chapter 3).

Likert scales are often used to measure personal characteristics (such as leadership or political preference), or opinions (on the monarchy, international safety issues, the privatization of governmental bodies, and such). See, for example, the Canadian Vote Compass, an online interactive tool that is run in various countries during election campaigns. In this tool, someone's responses to a series of propositions render voting advice, or give a prediction of how they will actually vote in the elections.

A typical feature of the Likert scale is that there is always an odd number of answer categories (3, 5, 7 and so forth), with a neutral option in the middle. For example, *totally disagree – disagree – neutral – agree – totally agree.*

Items are derived from the theory, and have to meet the same criteria as items in a questionnaire (unambiguity, no leading questions or statements, mutually exclusive answer categories). Several items will be formulated to measure the same variable or construct, so as to see how consistent respondents' replies are (and whether the characteristic or opinion being measured is indeed a consistent feature). To enhance reliability and validity, not all items are formulated in the same negative or positive direction; sometimes an item is formulated negatively to check whether respondents will reply differently as compared to their response to positively formulated items (see also below). Scales always have to be tested first in a pilot.

Scale measurements can be statistically analysed, even if they are only done on an ordinal level. Different techniques can be used (see Chapter 10). During the analysis, the scores of the various respondents are calculated. Also, the researcher can ascertain how closely the different items correlate, and so if they provide an adequate reflection of the research subject, or may even serve to make predictions (see Box 4.2 on the standardization of measurement instruments). On the basis of the outcome of the analysis, the researcher can decide which items do not discriminate sufficiently between respondents, and should be exchanged for others.

(For more information, see DeVellis, 2012.)

Control variables

Besides items on the variables derived from the theoretical framework, questionnaires always contain a number of items on so-called control variables as well (see Box 6.1). Usually this concerns certain personal characteristics, such as age, education, occupation, or gender. Such control variables might be of influence on people's answering patterns, which means they can interfere with the effect the researcher intends to measure (of IV on dependent variable, or DV). By studying the control variables, the researcher tries to limit such interference. In the example on bureaucratic competence, for example, a respondent's educational level might well be of influence, because higher-educated people are likely to be more bureaucratically competent. By including education as a control variable, this distorting influence can be made manifest and brought under control (see also Chapter 10).

Layout

With respect to the layout of questionnaires, several points need to be considered (DeVellis, 2012; Fowler, 2002):

- A questionnaire always starts with an introductory section (or instruction). This section gives information on the aim of the study, who will conduct the research and, if applicable, who the sponsor is. Also, it explains the way in which the questionnaire should be filled in, including whether the respondent can skip questions, and how they can correct any mistakes in their replies (see also Chapter 12 on the ethics of doing research). Lastly, something must be said about what will be done with the results of the study. Usually, the respondents remain anonymous, and results cannot be traced back to one single person. The researcher has to devise a way of making clear that anonymity is guaranteed.
- The order in which the questions are put (routing) has to be logical and plausible. This can be achieved by lumping questions on the same subject together, creating blocks or sequences. Such a sequence will be headed by a title and a short explanation of the questions that will follow; if necessary, the instructions for answering are repeated. Sometimes questions build up or refer to one another. Give a clear system of reference in such a case. Also indicate whether the respondent can tick several different answers, or provide a consistent answering system (for example, always tick the right answer, or delete the wrong answer). Do not use different answering formats alongside one another. Often the questionnaire begins with a set of simple questions, to allow respondents time to familiarize themselves with the material. Do not save the most difficult questions till last; the respondent may have grown tired by then. Sensitive questions deserve special attention, both as to how they are announced and their place in the questionnaire.
- The layout of the questionnaire has to be inviting and clear. Do not use small fonts or cram too much text onto one page, but keep things simple and easy on the eye, so as to prevent reading difficulties, or respondents being unable to see what optional answers there are. Pay special attention to headers or explanatory texts in between. Always end with a thank you

section, and offer respondents the opportunity to react to the fact that they have concluded the questionnaire (leave room for remarks, tips and comments). Such personal reactions from respondents can render new information, and prevent making the same mistakes during subsequent studies.

■ Enclose an accompanying letter in the invitation or email to participate in the study that provides the same information as in the introduction to the questionnaire.

Pilot study

Testing the questionnaire is an important stage of the research: a pilot study can contribute in several ways to the reliability and validity of the questionnaire (compare Fowler, 2002, p. 114). For example, the researcher can ask a limited number of potential respondents to try out the questionnaire and give comments. In this manner, it can be ascertained whether items are formulated clearly enough or perhaps seem vague (see the criteria outlined above), whether the questions are applicable to the everyday lives of the respondents, and how easy or difficult it will be for the target group to answer the questions. All this information (which includes the amount of time respondents actually need to complete the questionnaire) can also be used for the introductory section to the final version. For online questionnaires, in particular, it is important to gain sufficient information about technical aspects in the try-out phase, such as compatibility with operating systems.

A pilot can also be used to ask fellow researchers or experts who are familiar with the subject whether the questionnaire is complete enough as to its contents, or if certain answer categories should be added or changed. Research colleagues can also evaluate the questionnaire in terms of its research-technical quality, such as the operationalizations used, the answer categories formulated and so forth. Needless to say, the pilot is suitable, too, for detecting any linguistic mistakes that need to be corrected.

After the pilot, the questionnaire will be adapted and run in the sample that has been drawn. If many changes have been made after the first trial, a second pilot may be needed.

I have already mentioned several potential threats to the reliability and validity of survey research. There are other potential sources of interference as well.

7.3 THE RELIABILITY AND VALIDITY OF QUESTIONNAIRES

Questionnaires can be subject to three main sources of interference with reliability and validity: the operationalizations, non-response and respondents' answering tendencies.

The adequate operationalization of the variables, and a proper formulation of the items included in the questionnaire, is especially relevant for internal validity. In the previous section, several criteria were specified for well-defined items. A pilot can help to determine which items meet these criteria and which do not; also, after the survey has been completed, the statistical analysis will show if the items were sufficiently reliable and valid (see also Box 7.2 on scales).

Non-response means to say that not all people who have been asked to participate in the survey will actually do so. Such non-response can diminish the representativeness of the sample (see Chapter 4), causing problems with respect to external validity. Wright (2006) has shown that the use of online questionnaires creates additional problems with non-response. Besides the sampling problem (how representative is the online community of the entire population?), there is the larger problem of gaining access to certain closed online communities (which are based on membership only). Finally, Internet users are often bombarded with misleading and seductive information and invitations, which can make them insensitive to requests from researchers to participate in a survey.

There are two ways in which non-response can have a negative effect. First, the response rate may be so low that the sample becomes too small for certain types of (statistical) analysis. Low response rates (that is, less than 30%) are a familiar problem with questionnaires, and researchers will have to do their very best to increase response: often non-respondents are sent a reminder after a certain period, with the request to participate in the study after all. Sometimes, too, the researcher will try and increase response by phoning people before actually sending them a questionnaire, to see whether they are willing to participate. Also, a prize or some other kind of reward can be offered for participating – although this does not necessarily always boost response rates (Dillman, Smythe, & Christian, 2000).

Another way in which non-response can impair reliability and validity is when certain important characteristics of the non-respondents are not proportionally distributed in the population. For example, higher-educated people are often more willing to participate in surveys than lower-educated people. This need not be a problem; however, if education is an important variable in the study, a high non-response of the lower-educated group may cause problems for the validity of results.

These days, often a non-response study will be conducted to check on such features, in which non-respondents are asked why they failed to participate. Voogt and Van Kempen (2002), for example, have looked at the non-response in the Dutch National Voters Study (*Nationale Kiezersonderzoek*). Their findings caused some concern, as non-response does indeed seem to have an effect on the representativeness and validity of results. Also, the customary methods to correct for non-response during the phase of statistical analysis turned out to be unsatisfactory. Non-response in questionnaire research has increased in the past few years (probably because people are being asked to participate too often), and researchers will have to consider this point more closely.

However, even with those respondents who do complete the questionnaire, the researcher cannot always be certain of the reliability and validity of the findings. For example, respondents can display so-called answering tendencies – that is to say, they may adapt their answers because they are aware of being in a research situation. A well-known example is that of social desirability, with respondents giving answers that they deem politically correct, or hoping to meet the researcher's expectations. This can even occur when anonymous questionnaires are used. There are special (standardized) scales available for measuring how socially desirable respondents' answers are, and corrections can be made for this. Another option is to include a number of control items in the questionnaire: the same item is asked after in several slightly different ways, so that the consistency of a respondent's answers can be studied. If the questionnaire is filled in with the researcher or poll taker being present, it is important to be aware of the possible effect this may have on the validity of the study, and on the conclusions that can be drawn.

Research has revealed a number of answering tendencies. For example, respondents may:

- Always agree with items, or always disagree;
- Always or never choose an 'extreme' answer category;
- In case of multiple answers, always give many or always few answers;
- Use the answer to the previous question as a lead (the so-called halo effect): if someone answered positively to the last item, they will do so as well to the next; or
- Make logical mistakes by taking questions too literally.

Such answering tendencies can be countered by providing respondents with clear instructions, formulating easy-to-read and unambiguous items (see the criteria mentioned above), and testing the items beforehand (DeVellis, 2012; Dillman et al., 2000). In some cases, it can even be useful to give respondents time to practise first, before letting them fill in the actual questionnaire.

FURTHER READING

DeVellis, R.F. (2012). *Scale Development: Theory and Applications*. London: SAGE.
Dillman, D.A., Smythe, J.D., & Christian, L.M. (2000, 2nd edition). *Mail and Internet Surveys: The Tailored Design Method*. Hoboken: John Wiley and Sons.
Fowler, F. (2002, 3rd edition). *Survey Research Methods*. (Applied Social Research Methods, Volume 1.) Thousand Oaks: SAGE.

EXERCISES

1 There is free software available on the Internet that can help you to design a questionnaire for your own research purposes. Select one of these tools to create your own questionnaire for a small study on a topic of your own choice, or borrow ready-made items from the ESS or World Values Survey (but do not copy the entire questionnaire; do make your own list of questions!). Invite your family and friends or a group of fellow students to fill in

the questionnaire, making it into a sort of pilot study. Evaluate your experiences: for example, how easy or difficult was it to formulate valid items; did you notice any answering tendencies; how good or bad was your response rate, both overall and per item; how did the respondents experience their participation in the study?

2   On the website of the European Union (EU), you will find the so-called Euro-barometer surveys on a range of topics to do with the EU. In most reports, the questionnaire is given that was used to study a topic. Choose a topic that appeals to you. Evaluate the items, and the layout and routing of the questionnaire, using the information provided in this chapter. What recommendations could you give for improving the questionnaire?

Chapter 8

The case study

The case study is a research strategy in which one or several cases of the subject of study are examined in an everyday, real-life setting. A case can be almost anything: a group, an organization, a country, a city or neighbourhood, an event, a relationship, a project or process – it can even be a law or a decision. Research in Public Administration and Public Management makes prolific use of case studies (see Box 8.1 for some examples).

A typical case study takes a holistic approach, which means that a large body of – mainly qualitative – data is gathered on everything to do with the case. Usually different methods are used in combination with each other (triangulation, see Box 4.3). A method often applied is that of the interview, which will be discussed in detail in this chapter as well.

Case studies are suitable for both inductive and deductive research, although they tend to offer only limited options for the statistical testing of hypotheses (see also Chapter 10). Because of this, the reliability and validity of case study research deserves special attention.

8.1 CASE STUDY RESEARCH

The definition of the case study mentions explicitly that such research is conducted in a real-life setting ('the field'). The case study strategy is frequently applied in Public Administration and Public Management research, as it often concentrates on topical events from everyday life. Also, the subjects studied in Public Administration are usually unique or rare (see Chapter 1). This does not mean to say that case study research cannot be done on subjects that are more commonplace. When studying frequently observed phenomena, the researcher can select one or a number of cases that are thought to be representative and can serve as examples of the subject of study (see Chapter 4 on sampling). In this chapter, ample notice will be given to the selection of suitable cases.

A third reason for the popularity of case study research in Public Administration is its applied nature (compare Chapter 1). In applied research, the researcher tries to make a contribution to the solution of a concrete social issue, which means that, in principle, there is no need to study any other cases (see also Box 2.1 on action research). In sponsored studies, in particular, it will be clear from the start which case must be studied – namely, the problem or situation for which the client is seeking a solution.

Although case studies always concentrate on a limited number of situations, those situations are studied in very great detail; the researcher aims for depth instead of breadth (Timney Bailey, 1992). As a result, case study research always renders richly detailed and extensive descriptions of the phenomenon under study. Within the unique context of the case in question, the researcher can also try to arrive at an explanation of the research subject. However, usually it will be difficult, if not impossible, to generalize findings to other situations, either because the case is unique or because results only apply to the particular context that has been examined (Flyvbjerg, 2006). The external validity of case studies is therefore limited, contrary to their internal validity, which tends to be high due to the wealth of information collected.

As a last point to mention, the popularity of case study research – which is often even done in situations where others forms of research would be well suited – can also be ascribed to the predominantly interpretative approach in Public Administration and Public Management research (Ricucci, 2010), which often tends to take a rather one-sided methodological view. As stated in Chapter 1, this limits the chance of building an own, independent body of knowledge.

Even though the case study forms an independent research strategy, it is sometimes also used for the preparatory research stage (see Chapter 2), or to gather detailed empirical data in preparation for a larger-scale study, such as a survey (see Chapter 7). Because the researcher can concentrate on just one or a few cases of the research subject, a case study may seem easy to carry out. In actual practice, though, case study research usually involves extremely labour-intensive and protracted processes, which place high demands on the researcher in terms of time, commitment, expertise, and sometimes even their personality (see below).

BOX 8.1 EXAMPLES OF CASE STUDY RESEARCH IN PUBLIC ADMINISTRATION

■ One of the most classic case studies in Public Administration was carried out by Pressman and Wildavsky (see the book: *Implementation: How Great Expectations in Washington are Dashed in Oakland; or, Why it's Amazing that Federal Programs Work at All*, originally published in 1973), which laid the foundations for implementation theory. In effect, their study gave an evaluation of the implementation of a policy programme by the Economic Development Administration (EDA). The aim of the programme was to reduce the high level of unemployment in Oakland, California, by lending money or giving out grants to companies for the creation of new jobs. All conditions for success seemed to be there: a new organization, committed leaders and sufficient resources. However, results were slow to develop, and failed to meet expectations. Companies did not comply, too few jobs were created, and when the EDA changed leadership, the interest in the programme soon waned. Pressman and Wildavsky followed all these developments narrowly, conducting interviews, reading documents and collecting data from existing courses. They used their findings to formulate axioms for a new theory on policy implementation. For example, they concluded that the actual policy and its implementation are closely interlinked and therefore difficult to separate, an insight that led to the development of a new approach to the policy process. Furthermore, implementation is usually an incremental and slow process; speeding up this process to enforce change may lead to resistance rather than compliance. All in all, it is indeed amazing that some programmes do work at all.

■ Thirty years after the rise of New Public Management, it is becoming clear that public management reform has not always rendered the results that initially were expected. In fact, certain unintended and adverse effects have been witnessed. For one thing, the public sector has become more fragmented over the years: there are often numerous, single-purpose organizations involved in policy implementation, public service delivery and regulation. Bouckaert, Peters and Verhoest (2010) have studied the response of governments to this fragmentation in seven countries over a period of 25 years. Their approach is very systematic in its set-up, employing policy documents, policy evaluations and academic publications. To order the data, diagrams were used with similar symbols for similar events (as a sort of protocol), which allowed for an easy aggregation and comparison of the data. As it turns out, their findings do not corroborate with the trajectories expected on the basis of theoretical insights, which predict a trend towards a return to coordination practices. Not only did countries start at different starting positions, but new reforms have been layered on top of old policy measures rather than returning to a previous situation.

■ *International security* (Buzan, Waever & de Wilde, 1998): the theory on international security is split into two different camps. In the narrow view, security only has to do with war and peace; the broader view also takes non-military threats into account. In the international study conducted by Buzan et al. (1998), threats in several sectors or spheres of life were studied – namely, the military sector, the environment and the economy. Attention was paid to objective threats (for example, a natural disaster), but also to how these threats are perceived (think of the discussion on global warming). The threat itself was studied, as well as the behaviour of actors causing the threatening situation or – conversely – the behaviour of those responsible for finding a solution (politicians, civil servants, support groups, companies and citizens). The research team used a model in which all these elements were incorporated to study different sector threats. As they demonstrated, there are many similarities between sectors in how threats arise and how such problems are dealt with (the logic or 'mechanisms' of security). This proves that the new theoretical model forms a valid addition to existing theories.

8.2 THE SELECTION OF CASES

When selecting the cases to be studied, the researcher has to make several choices. First of all, a decision must be made as to how many cases will actually be studied. Sometimes the choice is easy, because there is just one single case. This can either be because the research subject is unique (such as a recently introduced law, or the United Nations (UN), the assassination of a famous politician, a plane crash, or a political party), or because the sponsor specifies which particular case needs to be studied. The researcher can also consciously choose to concentrate on a certain case, because it constitutes an extreme example of the phenomenon of interest, or represents the very first time that a certain phenomenon was witnessed. For example, in the wake of Hurricane Katrina several federal authorities failed to provide aid to the people of New Orleans; this particular event could form a suitable – albeit extreme – case for studying issues of political and administrative leadership.

By choosing to study just one single case, the researcher runs the risk of failing to make a clear distinction between the case itself (for example, an organizational change) and the unit of study (the organization studied). It is therefore always important to keep clearly in mind which research *domain* – compare: population – the case is thought to represent (Yin, 2008). Although there are certainly unique cases, it is nearly always possible to indicate at a higher abstraction level to what domain exactly the case belongs. For example, the Environmental Protection Agency is unique, as there is only one environmental protection agency in a country, or state in the case of a federal country. However, there are more regulatory agencies of a similar type in each country, and similar international agencies like this as well, associated with, for example, the UN and the European Union (EU). In principle, the findings of a single case study will be valid only for the case in question, yet often findings can be regarded as representative for other situations in the same research domain, even when these have not been actually studied.

In multiple case studies, several cases are included. The researcher can either decide to select a set of contrasting or heterogeneous cases (for example, large versus small municipalities), or concentrate on a homogenous set (for example, all medium-sized municipalities).

The selection of multiple cases can be compared to the process of drawing a sample: the researcher can either make a purposive selection (comparable to the non-probability sample; see Table 4.1), or apply a random procedure (probability sample). If homogenous cases are studied (*most similar systems design*; Blatter & Haverland, 2012), the researcher will expect the research findings to be homogeneous as well. This is called 'replication logic'. The accurate replication of findings is indicative of high reliability and validity (see Chapter 4), which makes it a goal worth pursuing. After all, if the same results are found in several different cases, the effects that have been measured are also likely to be valid for cases that have not been studied (generalizability).

All this does not imply that the findings will not be reliable and valid if a set of contrasting cases is chosen (*most dissimilar systems design*; Blatter & Haverland, 2012). In a heterogeneous design, the researcher can compare several cases to try to ascertain what the effect is of the variation in certain important variables. Such variation preferably concerns the independent variable, not the dependent variable (King, Keohane, & Verba, 1994, p. 141–43). For example, in a study on organizational change in municipalities, the researcher can select a case of successful implementation of organizational change, and contrast this with a case where implementation failed, but selecting cases in terms of the dependent variable makes it hard to arrive at convincing proof of causality (why does the implementation of organizational changes sometimes succeed and sometimes fail?). For one thing, success or failure is time-dependent: an initially successful change can turn out to be a failure in the long run, after the moment of measurement, and vice versa. Also, it can be difficult to trace back the outcome of certain processes (success or failure) to the original situation. By creating variation in the independent variables (such as the existing organizational model, municipal size, or project management), the causal relationship can be established more directly, and factors influencing success or failure can be identified with greater certainty. Having said all this, in research with contrasting cases, the effects that are measured will be conditioned by the context of the cases studied; internal validity will be high, and external validity will be low.

As this suggests, in order to make an adequate selection of contrasting cases, the researcher ideally has to know beforehand what the right independent variables are. In a deductive research design, the theoretical framework will provide information on this. However, when an inductive approach is followed, the independent variables will initially be an unknown quantity. Yin (2008) advises inductive researchers to study one case first as a *pilot*, before deciding upon the final selection of cases. By following such a procedure, the researcher will have at least some empirical knowledge about what might constitute important variables, which allows for a better-informed approach to the selection of cases.

It follows from the above that the selection of cases should preferably be guided by theoretical arguments. In reality, though, often a more pragmatic approach is needed. Practical issues such as having to gain access to cases or getting individuals or organizations to cooperate nearly always play a role. After all, participating in a study costs time and money; furthermore, organizations must be willing to allow outsiders to come and take a peep. Other limitations or restrictions must be thought of as well: consider, for example, the time needed to go and interview people. When planning one's study (part of the research design, see Chapter 5), all such aspects have to be taken into account.

The same goes for the number of measurements that will be taken in the course of the study. The researcher can decide on just one point of measurement, at a fixed moment in time. The alternative is to take several measurements at certain intervals during the research period (longitudinal research, see Box 5.1). The choice of which approach to go for will be influenced by various considerations: the subject studied, the research problem, but also by practical matters, such as the amount of time or the resources at one's disposal.

Besides the number of cases and the moments of measurement, the researcher has to decide which methods and research techniques to use. In case study research, triangulation is a highly suitable means of countering problems that might arise with respect to reliability and validity (see Chapter 4). This means that usually a mixed method design is chosen, in which methods such as observation (Chapter 6), content analysis of documents and other materials (Chapter 9), and the interview (see below) are combined. In section 8.3, some other ways of enhancing reliability and validity will be described.

All the choices made by the researcher are written down in a so-called case study protocol (Yin, 2008). The protocol helps the researcher to plan and structure day-to-day tasks and activities. It also enhances controllability, and allows for the replication of the study by other researchers (both important for reliability). Box 8.2 gives an overview of the various steps involved in designing a proper case study.

BOX 8.2 CHOICES INVOLVED IN DESIGNING A CASE STUDY

- Number of cases: single or multiple (contrasting or homogeneous)?
- Number of measurements: single or multiple (time frame: period, spacing)?
- Research methods: how many and which ones (triangulation)?

Case study protocol:

- Procedures: selection of (pilot) case(s), gaining access, data sources to use (people, documents), researchers involved (standardization of approach), planning the study.
- Methods: for example, designing and applying questionnaires and observation protocols, training co-researchers, exchanging and recording the data.
- Analysis: preferred techniques and way of reporting the findings (and to whom).

8.3 THE RELIABILITY AND VALIDITY OF CASE STUDIES

As indicated, the relation between case study research and theory can be an uneasy one. In the ideal situation, cases will be selected on theoretical grounds, yet in inductive research this will be problematic. In deductive studies, a small number of cases precludes the statistical testing of hypotheses. Indeed, the added value of the case study lies first and foremost in the wealth of empirical information that is collected, which can serve as a basis for developing new theories, or lead to the improvement of existing ones. Yin (2008) calls this analytical or theoretical generalization (see also Flyvbjerg, 2006). To give a more precise definition, analytical generalization means that the researcher will try to apply a certain theoretical model to one or several empirical cases (see the example of Allison in Box 3.4). The results of the case study will be used to develop the theory further or, if necessary, make certain adjustments. Theoretical generalization is especially relevant to inductive research. The results of the empirical case study are used to formulate new axioms (see Chapter 3), which can serve as building blocks for a theory or model.

The small number of units of study (n = the number of cases) in case studies can endanger the reliability and validity of case study research. Several methodological solutions can be applied to tackle this problem, the most important of which is triangulation (Timney Bailey, 1992). Box 4.3 defined triangulation as a way of collecting or processing information by using different operationalizations, data sources, researchers, or methods. By taking a diversified approach, the researcher gathers as much information as possible, so as to ensure that the data collected are valid, irrespective of the number of units studied.

Another option for countering the problem of small numbers is to distinguish sub-units within the different cases (Yin, 2008; King et al., 1994, ch.6). For example, an organization usually consists of several units; likewise, an organizational culture can often be divided into various sub-cultures. If we consider the example from Buzan and colleagues in Box 8.1, we see that the researchers have chosen not to compare the data per country (which would render too big a unit of study), but split them into units of, respectively, specific threats or sectors. Distinguishing sub-units within one larger unit of study is also known as applying a layered or nested design. An alternative is to take several different measurements, an approach that can be recommended in particular for research that traces processes, such as changes or developments (Blatter & Haverland, 2012).

Other tips for enhancing reliability are keeping a database (Yin, 2008) or a log (Miles & Huberman, 1994), in which all the steps taken in the study and the data sources used are documented, so that the whole process can be reviewed or checked afterwards. It is also useful to conduct the case study in as systematic a manner as possible, by using a case study protocol (see above) and training co-researchers as one group. Standardizing case studies allows for replication, and can ultimately even lead to meta-analysis (the analysis of several different cases: see Chapter 9 for an explanation).

Finally, researchers can present their findings and conclusions to other researchers for review, or ask independent experts for their opinion (see also Box 8.4 on the Delphi method). This extra form of control will contribute to higher (internal) validity.

Case studies are a very intensive form of research: the body of information gathered is considerable, and usually a study will extend over a prolonged period of time. Whilst the study is running, the researcher will come in close and frequent contact with the research subject, which increases the risk of subjectivity and selectivity (compare Chapter 6 on participant observation). Also, as the data are being collected, researchers will have to use all their methodological and social skills to absorb all relevant information directly and correctly. At the same time, they have to engage in a fruitful relationship with the individuals and organizations in the field (van Hulst, 2008). These long-term relationships will invariably cause the researcher to become closely involved with the subject and the individuals participating in the study, which may reduce objectivity ('going native'), or create interference with the research situation, thus lowering the validity of the study. In the analytical phase of processing large amounts of information, high demands are placed upon the researcher as well. In Chapter 11, attention will be paid to ways of analysing the qualitative data collected in case studies.

8.4 THE INTERVIEW

An interview is a conversation during which the researcher gathers information by questioning one or more people (respondents). As a method, the interview is often applied in case studies, although it is also suitable for other research strategies (see Table 5.2). An interview can be relatively structured, or have a looser, more unstructured format (see Gubrium & Holstein, 2001, for an overview of different types of interviews). In this section, two types of interview will be discussed: the unstructured or open interview, and the semi-structured interview. The fully structured interview is, in effect, an oral version of the questionnaire (see Chapter 7) and will not be treated here.

Interviews are a flexible way of collecting data. During the conversation, the researcher can ask supplementary questions to gain a better and fuller understanding of any answers that have been given (more background information, added explanation, asking someone to expand on a subject). However, its flexible format can also compromise reliability, as each interview will be slightly different from the one before (Robson, 2002, p. 273; see also below). Indeed, it is no wonder that conducting interviews – and processing the answers afterwards – requires considerable skill, and is a time-consuming process.

The open interview

In an open interview – sometimes also referred to as a qualitative interview – the only fixed item is the initial question with which the researcher opens the conversation. This question introduces the subject to be discussed, but provides no leads as to where the conversation should be heading. In other words, it is an open question, asking, for example, after the respondent's opinion on or their experiences with the research subject ('Could you tell me a bit more about that?'). The respondent's answer to the initial question forms the starting point; the researcher leaves the respondent completely free as to how to reply. By sounding out the answer given (probing, summarizing what has been said) new questions will arise (for clarification, illustration, added detail), and so on and so forth (see Weiss, 1994, for further explanation).

It will be clear that this type of interview can be rather strenuous for the researcher. After all, it does not concern a normal conversation, but constitutes a way of gathering data. The researcher has to perform several tasks at once: listen, react to the respondent's statements, gain the respondent's trust (empathise, show an interest), consider what elements of the conversation may be relevant and what is irrelevant, try and remember what is being said (if necessary, record the conversation or make notes), and formulate inviting follow-up questions to supplement the information that has been given. Also, a balance must be struck between refraining from steering the respondent in a certain direction, and providing enough guidance to ensure that the conversation will render sufficient relevant data. All this requires the interviewer to have good communication and research skills.

The open interview is especially suitable for exploratory and inductive research (see Chapters 2 and 3), or if the number of respondents is small. Open interviews have an in-depth character, which means they can take up a considerable amount of time (several hours). In Chapter 11, we will discuss some tools for processing and interpreting data gathered in open interviews.

The semi-structured interview

In the semi-structured interview, a so-called interview manual or topic list is used as a guideline. The interview manual lists a number of topics that the researcher wishes to discuss, or gives a set of questions prepared earlier (see Box 8.3). In deductive studies, the interview questions will be based on the operationalization of the variables derived from the theoretical framework. In inductive studies, the interview questions reflect the questions formulated in the research problem (see Chapter 2), which specify what kind of information the researcher aims to acquire. The variables mentioned in the research question function as so-called 'sensitizing concepts', which can guide the researcher in formulating suitable interview questions. Often it can also be useful to do some preparatory research first (reading documents, talking to experts). Information that can be accessed by other means (such as written sources) need not be included in the interview. Interviews should be conducted, in the first instance, to acquire non-factual information (on matters such as opinions, relationships, or perceptions). Of course, interviews can be a means as well of checking up on certain facts (triangulation: interviews are combined with other methods such as content analysis of documents).

When formulating interview questions, the same criteria apply as for items in a questionnaire (see Chapter 7). Be clear and understandable, and do not ask overly long or ambiguous questions. Avoid asking suggestive or leading questions by excluding certain answers or giving your own opinion ('Do you agree that the minister should have interfered?'). Make sure also to ask questions that relate to the respondents' reality and experiences; avoid jargon or difficult words and ask respondents to illustrate their answers with concrete examples. Such illustrative examples can also be of use later, during the phase of interpreting the answers.

An interview manual comprises a number of fixed elements: the introduction, the actual questions, and a concluding section (see Box 8.3). In the introduction, the researcher explains the aim of the study, and provides some information about the procedure that will be followed during the interview (compare with the questionnaire: see Chapter 7). During the introductory part of the interview, it is important to put respondents at their ease; remember that people may not be used to being interviewed (see also the ethics of doing research in Chapter 12). Taking sufficient time at the beginning also reduces the risk of respondents adapting their answers to the research situation by giving socially desirable answers, or withholding information that may be important or relevant to the study (compare the section on answering tendencies in Chapter 7).

After the introduction, the interview proper begins. Often the researcher will ask a few (neutral) initial questions to open the conversation; difficult or sensitive questions should be reserved for later. The questions listed in the interview manual can vary per respondent. After all, whether or not a certain question is applicable may depend on, for example, someone's social position. To illustrate, when inquiring after the quality of service at the municipal office, different questions may be suitable for citizens than for civil servants. Do take care, however, to use similar wording for similar questions (important for reliability and validity; see below).

In semi-structured interviews, the order in which the questions are asked can vary, depending on the way in which the conversation develops. For example, if a respondent has more or less answered question six in reply to an earlier question, the researcher may as well skip question six, instead of seeming to ask about the same thing again. It is important to let the conversation take its natural course (routing, see Chapter 7): usually this is the best way of collecting an optimal amount of information. During the conversation, the researcher can probe further if this seems necessary. In the interview manual, a number of keywords can be given for gleaning extra information (such as: 'ask for an example if the respondent is a citizen and feels dissatisfied about the service provided by the municipal office').

The conversation concludes with a thank you, and a brief explanation of what will be done with the information the respondent has given (see also below, in the section on interview reports).

BOX 8.3 THE INTERVIEW MANUAL

1   Introduction

■   What is the aim of the study? Background information on the study and the researcher.

■   Does the conversation proceed satisfactorily? Make clear that if the respondent does not understand a question they can say so. Also indicate that the respondent is not obliged to answer.

■   What will be done with the information given? The respondent will remain anonymous and will be given the opportunity to comment on the interview report. Does the respondent wish to receive a copy of the interview report?

■   If the conversation is recorded on tape: does the respondent give his or her permission to do so?

2   Questions (contents)

■   Main questions, sub-questions (in an order that seems logical to the respondent; start with neutral questions, and reserve difficult or sensitive questions for later).

■   Instructions for the researcher on how to probe for more information.

3   Conclusions and thank you; allow the respondent the chance to react to the interview

---

After the interview manual has been designed, it can be tested in a pilot interview. The researcher can check whether the questions have been formulated clearly enough, practice his or her interviewing skills, and test how long the interview will actually take. All this information will come in handy when making appointments with respondents. The interview manual must later be included in the research report as an appendix.

The selection of respondents

Once the choice has been made to conduct interviews, the researcher has to determine how many and what kind of respondents to include in the study. Deciding upon the number of respondents and the way in which these will be selected constitutes a form of sampling. As explained in Chapter 4, different sampling methods can be applied. For example, the researcher can make a stratified selection of respondents from different layers in an organization, or draw a representative sample from various social groups (citizens, companies, interest groups). It is also possible to select a certain type of respondent (Gubrium & Holstein, 2001), such as in the elite interview, where the researcher only interviews people who are highly placed in the research situation, for instance the senior management in an organization. Because of their top position, the elite are well informed, but they also often have a busy schedule and can be either unwilling or unable to make time. Another way of selecting a certain type of respondent is to use informants. Informants are people who are familiar with the research situation without actually being involved in it (any longer) – think of former employees of an organization. Often informants can provide the researcher with knowledge that current insiders would be less inclined to share (sensitive information). Another possible class of respondents are independent experts, who do not form part of the research situation but are knowledgeable about it all the same, because, for example, they do research on the subject themselves. Also, a key person ('contact') can assist in the selection of suitable respondents. A key person is someone who occupies a central position in the research situation; they will know which respondents might be suitable or available for inclusion in the study. An example of a key person is a personnel officer in an organization who knows most of the employees.

Lastly, the researcher can choose to interview several respondents simultaneously. There are special techniques for this, such as the focus group method or the Delphi method (see Box 8.4). The focus group method is actually a way of having an open discussion on a certain subject with several respondents; the discussion is led by a moderator, who will usually be the researcher him- or herself (Flick, 2002, p. 120; Robson, 2002, p. 284). Often the participants have all experienced the same event, which may or may not have been caused by the researcher (for example, an experiment; see Chapter 6). The conversation is recorded and transcribed later. Apart from the main topic, the way in which the conversation develops is also influenced by the group's dynamics. Group dynamics can have a positive effect on research results (contextualizing), or be of negative influence (interference). This particular aspect of group interviews has to be closely monitored.

BOX 8.4 THE DELPHI METHOD

The Delphi method is a technique for interviewing a group of experts on a certain subject. Different formats can be applied, such as conducting oral interviews or sending the participants a written questionnaire (per regular post or email). The answers given by the individual experts are summarized and made anonymous, and then fed back into the group. This feedback of information will lead to new responses, after which a third round can be held, if necessary. The study is concluded with a group discussion (or conference). The aim is for the experts to reach agreement on the subject in the end.

Traditionally, this technique is used for trend analysis, scenario development or making prognoses (compare Chapter 1). The Delphi method is only suitable for working with experts, which can make the selection and recruitment of respondents rather difficult. The ideal group size is 8–12. The expertise of the respondents usually renders a lot of information, but reaching consensus can be cumbersome. Summarizing the replies given, and submitting these to the group, has to be done in as transparent and objective a manner as possible. Modern techniques, such as exchanging information via email or keeping a video conference, have made the Delphi method easier to apply.

(For more information, see Linstone & Turoff, 2002.)

Rules of thumb for conducting interviews

A thorough preparation is vital to success:

- Be clear when making an appointment with the respondent about time and place, and also the duration of the interview (make sure there will be enough time to complete the entire interview). Give a first indication of the subject that will be discussed (if the respondents asks for this, a copy of the interview manual can be sent in advance), and whether or not the interview will be recorded;
- Conduct a pilot interview, and check whether the recording equipment works properly. It is also advisable to let someone else – for example, a colleague or a supervisor – take a look at the interview manual, and have them judge whether it is satisfactory; and
- Give a clear introduction and instructions at the beginning of the interview, and try to make a positive, professional impression (attitude, clothing, etc.). Physically, too, seat yourself in such a manner that you have direct eye contact with the respondent.

During the conversation, it is important for the researcher (Robson, 2002, p. 274):

- To allow the respondent plenty of opportunity to ask questions or make remarks;
- To adopt a polite and interested approach (remember that the respondent has reserved time for the interview. Exude a positive attitude: show respect and sympathy for the respondent's opinions, even if you do not share these opinions. As a researcher, try to remain as neutral as possible);
- To formulate questions in a way that is not threatening or suggestive (be clear in what you say, keep questions as short as possible, and avoid using jargon. The respondent should be able to relate to what is being asked, and feel invited to reply); and

■ To listen rather than talk (make purposive use of silences: wait a few seconds before asking the next question, and encourage the respondent to continue talking by means of non-verbal and verbal signals: nodding, 'uh-huh').

The interview report

An interview report reflects what has been discussed in the interview (questions as well as answers). A literal, verbatim account of the conversation is called a transcript; it gives the written text of the entire interview, which usually has been recorded for this particular purpose. A transcript is the most accurate and full report a researcher can give. However, this format is costly in terms of time and money (tip: there are special agencies that type up transcripts for payment). Also, the conversation has to be recorded on tape, and some respondents may object to this.

An alternative is for the researcher who has conducted the interview to draw up their own report, for example, by using the notes jotted down during the conversation. It should be kept in mind, though, that such a report will reflect the researcher's personal interpretation and summary of what has been said (see Chapter 3, on the risk of double hermeneutics, and Chapter 4 on researcher bias). To ensure that the researcher has given a valid interpretation of the conversation, the report can be submitted to the respondent. This is called a *member check*. A risk involved in doing a member check is that whilst reading the report, respondents may come to realize that actually they have revealed more than intended. Once statements are down in black and white, it will often turn out that certain shades of grey, which were there during the conversation (in the form of non-verbal signals, for example), have disappeared in the final version. For this reason, it is important to make clear agreements with the respondent about what will and what will not be done with the results of the member check. Obvious errors (such as a misrepresentation of the facts) will have to be corrected; as to the rest, the report is and does remain the researcher's interpretation of the conversation. Any adjustments will have to be considered carefully, all the more so because it will pay to remain on good terms with the respondent (Weiss, 1994). A member check will also contribute to greater acceptance of the research findings by the respondents or sponsor (I shall return to this subject in Chapter 12).

The contents of the interview report constitute the main data source to the researcher, and will be used later for analysis. In Chapter 11, I shall discuss several analytical techniques that can be applied – here, I should like to mention just one aspect of the analysis of interviews, namely, using quotes. It will be relatively easy to give literal quotes when there is a transcript. If the research report is based on notes, however, quotation becomes more difficult. The researcher will have to proceed very carefully in this case, in particular if the respondent has been guaranteed anonymity. In Chapter 12, some tips will be given for the reporting of research results.

The reliability and validity of interviews

When conducting interviews, the person of the researcher constitutes, in effect, the most important measurement instrument; he or she devises and asks the questions, after which the answers are noted down and interpreted. This imposes high demands on the researcher in terms of: 1 their knowledge on the theoretical aspects of the subject of study; 2 their interviewing skills; and 3 their communication skills. The tips and recommendations listed above provide good guidelines for conducting interviews, yet they do not guarantee a sufficient level of reliability and validity.

Generally speaking, the more structured the interview, the more reliable and valid the findings will be. In a semi-structured interview, the questions bear a clear and close relationship to the theoretical framework (operationalization); also, the interview manual ensures that the conversation follows a fixed pattern (replicability). Sometimes, though, a structured or semi-structured format cannot be applied, for example, because the knowledge needed for formulating a fixed set of questions is lacking (like in exploratory or inductive research). In such a case, the researcher should rely on his own methodological skills (or enhance them if necessary), conduct pilot interviews (to try out the interview manual), or record the interview to maximize data collection.

A final point worth mentioning here concerns the selection of respondents. There are no fixed rules for determining the ideal number and type of respondents. It will be clear, though, that the reliability and validity of a study benefits from a large research population, consisting of people from various backgrounds and social positions; such a design ensures representativeness and contributes to triangulation. Having said as much, interviews tend to be time consuming and labour intensive, which means that a large-scale approach is often not feasible. The choices eventually made, and the considerations on which these are founded, will have to be specified in the sampling framework formulated in the research design (see Chapter 5).

FURTHER READING

Blatter, J., & Haverland, M. (2012). *Designing Case Studies: Explanatory Approaches in Small-N Research*. Basingstoke: Palgrave MacMillan.
Yin, R. (2008, 4th edition). *Case Study Research: Design and Methods*. London: SAGE.

EXERCISES

1 Make a sampling plan for the selection of a case study on local problem areas such as low-income neighbourhoods. How many and which neighbourhood(s) in your own town or city would you choose, and why? What approach would you take to studying this problem? Tip: if there are

no problem areas in your own town, choose a nearby city or town you could study instead.

2   Read through one of the example studies mentioned in this chapter (see Box 8.1), or choose an example of your own (tip: pick an example that fits with your own studies). Try and reconstruct the approach taken by the researcher(s). What sort of case study design has been used? How many cases were studied, and why was this selection made? Is it an inductive or a deductive study? What role has the theory played in the study design? Which methods and techniques have been used? Have adequate measures been taken by the researcher to ensure reliability and validity? If so, which measures exactly have been taken? If not, what should have been done?

3   In internationally comparative research, every individual country forms a separate case. Develop (1) a most similar systems design and (2) a most dissimilar systems design for a research team intending to do an inter-nationally comparative study on, for example, changes in the welfare state, the meaning of citizenship, tackling crime, or another subject of your choice. Use the information provided in this chapter.

4   Practise conducting an interview on a subject of your own choice (for example, a hobby). Design a number of questions (confine yourself to a maximum of eight) and select a respondent. Do the interview, draw up a report, and present this to the respondent (member check). The crucial point in this exercise is to evaluate the interview properly. Describe how the conversation went, if the interview manual was of any use, and whether it was easy or not to conduct the interview. What should have been done differently, and why? Tip: you will profit most from this exercise if you do the interview together with a fellow student. Design an interview manual together. One of you observes the other during the interview, and writes an evaluation report afterwards. You can learn from each other's experiences and observations.

Chapter 9

Desk research

In the research strategies and methods discussed so far, researchers collect the data themselves, by means of, for example, observation or interviews. An alternative approach is that of using data that have been collected or produced by someone else. The research strategy of using existing data sources – called desk research – forms the central theme of this chapter.

Existing data sources contain information that has been produced for a different purpose than research, but can be used or re-used to this end. Examples are policy memoranda, legal documents, annual reports, or newspaper articles. Also, an increasing number of researchers put the data they have collected at the disposal of others after conclusion of their study. The World Values Survey described in Box 4.2 is an example of this. Indeed, if one knows where to look, there is a wealth of (free) information available which can serve as input for research.

Desk research is an efficient and cost-effective strategy. Moreover, the researcher need not interfere with the research situation in order to collect the data, which reduces threats to validity and reliability. This is why this form of research is sometimes also called unobtrusive research (Webb, Campbell, Schwartz, & Sechrest, 1999). It should be added, however, that desk research has certain drawbacks as well. All these aspects will be discussed in this chapter. Attention will also be paid to three different methods for gathering and analysing existing data.

9.1 USING OR RE-USING EXISTING DATA

Data sources can consist of primary or secondary material. Primary data comprise information that has been collected by the researcher him- or herself. In the strategy of using existing material, primary data refer to information that has not been produced for research purposes, or which has not been used for research before. This can concern, first of all, written or printed sources, such as annual reports, the minutes of meetings, company records, business correspondence, policy documents, legal papers, brochures, newsletters, periodicals, annual budgets, covenants, pledges, coalition agreements, results statistics, management reports, speeches and so forth. Most of these sources are freely accessible to the public, and can serve as input for research. Increasingly, archives are digitized and can be consulted on the Internet (compare Burnham, Gilland, Grant, & Layton-Henry, 2008). Consider, for example, the online archives of municipal offices, where information can be found about council decisions, council meetings and policies. With respect to research at national government level, files are frequently made available on the websites of ministries, executive agencies and parliament (see, for example, the website of the Cabinet Office in the UK). Also, there are online databases containing all kinds of legal documentation, such as the European Union (EU) website that lists EU directives and other types of legislation. Last but not least, in virtually every policy sector there are numerous organizations (such as interest groups or advisory bodies) that publish information for free. Box 9.1 gives an example of how and where a researcher can look for such sources of information.

BOX 9.1 EXAMPLE: EXISTING DATA SOURCES FOR RESEARCH ON HEALTHCARE

A researcher in Public Administration who wants to conduct a study on healthcare can consult a wide variety of existing data sources:

- The Ministry of Health will have plenty of suitable information, including policy documents, legal papers, budget documents with financial decisions, and advisory reports or trend analyses of healthcare developments.
- Hospitals keep their own records on medical results, hospital management and financial results. Often these can be accessed by independent researchers.
- The Care Quality Commission in the UK publishes numerous reports on the functioning of hospitals and other healthcare providers (such as mental healthcare or home care).
- There are also organizations that conduct independent research on healthcare; this type of research often concentrates on subjects such as hospital management, the organization of the healthcare sector, and certain medical issues. Examples in the UK are the Cambridge Institute for Medical Research, the Nuffield Trust and the CIHR (Centre for Integrated Healthcare Research).
- At the international level, organizations such as the World Health Organization (WHO) gather information on healthcare in countries all over the world. The WHO regularly publishes reports on this.
- Several medical occupational groups (general practitioners (GPs), medical specialists, nurses, physiotherapists, etc.) provide information on their websites and publish data on developments in the healthcare sector, best practices, or the results of new forms of treatment.

- Patients sometimes organize themselves into special support groups or patient associations. Often these groups provide information on waiting lists, or give hospital assessments and rankings. Diverse examples can be found on the Internet.
- Finally, there are scientific journals and periodicals in which medical specialists and researchers publish the results of their own research (check your library).

Personal documents can be a source of information in desk research as well. For example, the National Archives, which files millions of manuscripts and records, are frequently consulted by historians writing about the royal family. Personal documentation varies from private journals, diaries and letters, to the memoirs or books written by (former) politicians, biographies, interviews published in newspapers and magazines, broadcast on TV or radio, and so forth. Finally, non-written sources can be used for research, including films, photos, artistic forms of expression (including graffiti), posters, appliances and artefacts, or even clothing.

All sources listed here share two important characteristics. First, they reflect people's behaviour (compare Riffe, Lacy & Fico, 2005, p. 5), expressing opinions, chronicling events, or reporting what people decided or did. By using such sources, researchers can study behaviour without having to prompt it themselves. Second, the various types of documentation carry a communicative function, transmitting a certain message (compare Robson, 2002, ch.12). Some research methods will concentrate on analysing the contents of the message sent out (see the section on content analysis below); other methods, on the contrary, are more geared towards studying how that message is transmitted, concentrating on, for example, the purpose it is meant to serve (see Box 9.2).

As to secondary existing material, this refers to earlier research findings (data) which can be used anew in another study on the same or a related subject. Usually, secondary material consists of statistical information that has been gathered or already analysed by others, but which lends itself to more extensive study. Sometimes, too, different existing databases can be combined for studying new research questions. Frequently researchers make the data they have collected (so, the primary, unprocessed material) available to others, either for payment or for free. Finally, there are several international organizations that provide public access to internationally comparative data. For example, on the Organisation for Economic Co-operation and Development (OECD) website, statistics for the different member countries can be found on various topics of interest to researchers in Public Administration and Public Management, for example economic developments, school results, or the average income of top officials; similar databases have been set up by the EU, the United Nations (UN), the UNHCR (the UN Refugee Agency) and the WHO (on healthcare). For example, several indicators of the quality of governance in various countries are available (for an overview and discussion, see Van de Walle, 2007), such as the World Bank Government Effectiveness indicators, the European Central Bank indicators on public-sector efficiency, the World Economic Forum Growth Competitiveness Index, and the International Institute for Management Development (IMD) Competitiveness Yearbook Public Institutions Index.

Secondary sources need not always concern statistical data; the written conclusions from earlier studies can serve as input for further research as well. Scientific articles, books, or research reports can all be used for studying new research questions. The process of analysing the conclusions from previous studies is called meta-analysis. Several applications of this method will be given below.

Making a selection

Sometimes there is so much information available that it can seem harder to separate the wheat from the chaff than simply collect a new set of data. Filtering the existing information about a particular subject can be compared to drawing a sample (see Chapter 4). Suitable sources are picked from the total pool of information – just as in a sample, a selection is made from the total population of existing sources. The researcher can choose a number of existing data sources at random; however, this approach only makes sense if one has a wide range of sources at one's disposal and if it is clear from which population exactly the sample will be drawn. For example, if a researcher intends to use the minutes of council meetings of municipality X, a random selection can be made from the minutes kept in the past decade. Usually, though, the choice to use a certain dataset will result from the researcher's interest in a particular subject. In practice, it will often be more efficient to take a non-random sample and study, for example, only the council minutes with a bearing on the research subject at hand, such as, for example, housing or planning issues. Just as when designing an experiment or formulating items for a questionnaire, the use of existing data sources means that one has to consider first which material, subject and sources will be suitable for inclusion in the study. Indeed, a thorough preparation in the form of a preparatory study is vital.

In a deductive study, the researcher will know on which variables to concentrate in the research situation, which facilitates the process of looking for suitable sources and selecting what will be actually used. In an inductive study, the researcher will still be in the phase of getting acquainted with the subject, and initially it may not be that clear what sort of materials will be useful. Selection will be done more incrementally in that case.

Another crucial point to keep in mind is the context in which the existing data were collected (compare Babbie, 1992; Webb, 2000), the quality of the data (see for example Van de Walle, 2007), and who produced the database (think of the position and interests of the researchers concerned). All these aspects will have a bearing on reliability and validity, and need to be taken into account before making a final selection. If need be, reliability and validity can be enhanced by applying the method of triangulation, which means that information from several different data sources is combined (see Chapter 4). Another option is to ask a key person for assistance (see Chapter 8), or call in the aid of experts and inquire of them what they consider the most important (written) sources on the subject at hand.

From the large number of data sources collected in this manner, a second selection has to be made as to which data will actually be analysed. The documents that will not be included in the analysis can be used for background information, and to illustrate the selection process that has been applied to the research material: these sources will not have been gathered for nothing. Indeed, it is important not to settle for the first source you can lay your hands on, but to keep looking until you can make a well-considered, informed choice. All the steps taken during the search process, and the choices that are ultimately made, have to be reported in the sampling framework (part of the research design; see Chapter 5).

The principal drawback of using existing data sources is the operationalization problem. As the information to be used was originally produced for a different purpose, the data will often not entirely match with the central variables or research question. To solve this problem, the researcher has to be pliable and creative enough to: 1 find information that meets the research needs as adequately as possible; and 2 use the existing information in such a manner that its contents will come to concur with the research subject.

An example from my own experience can illustrate this procedure. In a study on agencification in the Netherlands (Van Thiel, 2001), my principal interest lay in the effects of corporatism in policy sectors on the number of decisions to establish a semi-autonomous agency. My main hypothesis was that corporatism has a positive effect on agencification. The number of decisions to create an agency (per policy sector, per year for the period 1900–93) was derived from a study conducted by the Netherlands Court of Audit in 1994. This particular study did not contain any data on corporatism, however, which meant that another source was needed. In the end, I decided to use the number of recognized advisory bodies in each policy sector as a yardstick, using the listing given in the State Directory of 1994 for a source (note that I used one fixed measuring point). Interest groups often participate in advisory bodies, or are consulted by them, which made me decide to use interest groups as a proxy for corporatism. The operationalization I chose constituted a sub-optimal solution, but other (numerical) sources for measuring corporatism were simply not available. By the way, the hypothesis formulated could not be corroborated.

Desk research in Public Administration and Public Management

When exactly will a researcher decide to use desk research? For obvious reasons, this strategy is ultimately suitable for research of an historical nature (describing developments over time), or when exploring the background or context of a certain research problem – for example, in the preparatory research stage (see Chapter 2) or during pilot case studies (see Chapter 9).

Existing sources are suitable, too, for studying subjects that can be approached only indirectly, either because they are taboo or because the phenomenon of interest cannot be observed directly in people's behaviour. Primary data reflect or reveal behaviour in real-life situations, which makes such sources less susceptible to negative influences such as social desirability or other answering tendencies (compare Chapter 7). But, be aware that secondary data have been collected by other researchers and check how well they have countered the risks for validity and reliability. Other situations in which existing data can provide a solution are, for example, when a unique case is studied, without there being any control case available for comparison. To illustrate, there is one only voting system in the UK; someone interested in studying what the effect of a different system would be can use information on the voting procedures in other countries. Also, it may be unethical and therefore not legitimate to conduct a certain study. For example, in research on subjects such as Detention at Her Majesty's Pleasure or residence permits, the researcher cannot ask for certain psychiatric treatments to be given at random, or for permits to be withheld, just to see what the effect would be (see also Chapter 6 on ethics committees). In such cases, the best solution often lies in using existing longitudinal or internationally comparative data.

The main advantage of using existing data is that usually there is a lot of information available, which makes this research strategy relatively efficient and cost-effective. Internationally comparative research, for example, can be carried out without any travelling being needed (Babbie, 1992, p. 336–38). Moreover, the researcher can act independently, without the help of others, although assistance may be needed to gain access to non-digital records and archives. The major disadvantage is the operationalization problem mentioned earlier. Also, gathering and analysing the data can be labour intensive and time consuming, which means that a very systematic approach is required (see Chapter 11). Often the research will seem easier at first than it actually turns out to be.

Existing information can either be of a qualitative nature (such as written texts or images), or be quantitative (numbers). For each category of data, there are suitable methods and analytical techniques (see, for example, Riffe et al., 2005; Fischer, 2003; Roberts, 1997). In Public Administration and Public Management research, both qualitative and quantitative data are used, although still slightly more qualitative data (compare Pollitt, 2006, and Perry, 2012). See Box 9.4 for examples. Existing data can be employed in both deductive and inductive studies.

9.2 THREE METHODS FOR GATHERING AND ANALYSING EXISTING DATA

In this section, three methods for gathering and analysing existing data will be discussed: content analysis, secondary analysis and meta-analysis. As these labels suggest, we are not just dealing with different ways of collecting data here, but also with techniques for processing data. The analysis of quantitative and qualitative data will be treated in, respectively, Chapter 10 and Chapter 11. In this section, I shall give only a brief explanation of how existing data sources can be analysed.

Content analysis

Content analysis means to say that the researcher studies the content of the existing data source, which will usually consist of written material or documents. The main interest lies in the message that the author of the text tries to convey to the audience. The researcher first selects material that is relevant to the subject of study. The data may have been produced in the research situation itself (for example, texts published by an organization), or stem from an external source (for example, reports on the organization produced by a review committee). To give an example, in a study of the influence of executive agencies on the development of new policies, texts can be studied about how the new policy was developed (policy documents, parliamentary reports, advisory memos, reports on the consultation procedure between the parties involved, policy drafts), and the role that a certain executives agency played in the policy process. Such a reconstruction will involve both the facts and the opinions expressed by the relevant parties (that is, in as far as the written sources express the latter). Different forms of ordering can then be applied: making a chronological reconstruction, studying the process from the perspective of different actors, or looking at the different phases of policy development. Another possibility is doing a textual analysis (see Box 9.2) to see whether certain phrases or words in the policy text can be traced back to the contributions originally made by the implementation agency. For example, some executive agencies carry out *ex ante* cost-benefit analyses (CBA) to ascertain the feasibility and efficiency (cost, results) of a certain new policy. Such a cost-benefit analysis can constitute an important input for policy. If the text of the new policy refers to the CBA-report, or sections thereof have been copied into the policy text, the conclusion might be that the executive agency has had a significant influence on the policy process.

BOX 9.2 TYPES OF TEXTUAL ANALYSIS

A lot of information that can be used for research is expressed in language, for example, the text of a written document or what has been said in an interview. Language is more than just a means of conveying information, however; it is also used to assign meaning to subjects, persons, or events. For example, the way in which respondents formulate their answer often says a lot about how they feel about the subject being discussed, or what it means to them or their community. Also, whilst formulating an answer, respondents use language to give shape to their view of reality: language contributes to perception. As this

---

implies, language plays a role at various levels, which has special implications for doing research.

Different methods or techniques have been developed for the analysis of language, three of which will be described here (for more information, see Fischer, 2003):

- Narrative analysis focuses on identifying and analysing the stories that people tell. The answer given by a respondent in an interview illustrates this: whilst talking, the respondent makes the reply into a story. Stories can assume different shapes (genres) and structures (plot, characters, climax). The researcher uses these elements to deconstruct the respondent's answer, and try and construct the respondent's 'story' – as well as the function of that story. Is it, for example, more of a myth, a drama or fairy tale; also, what is the role of the narrator (hero, supporting role, onlooker)? By comparing the stories told by different respondents, the researcher can then construct a new, composite story, which will be the researcher's own story (that is, his or her conclusions).

- Discourse analysis focuses on discovering linguistics patterns. The term discourse refers to a common or shared way of talking or thinking about something. The participants in a particular discourse speak the same 'language', for example, because they have the same educational background (such as law), similar jobs (civil servants), or belong to the same generation. As a rule, every form of discourse strives to dominate other forms of discourse, and different discourses compete in society. To give an example of the influence of discourse, the increasing popularity of New Public Management (NPM) can be seen as a rise in economic discourse in the public domain, claiming as it does that the government ought to function like a private company or market economy. This also shows that a certain discourse can influence reality to a substantial degree: due to the influence of NPM, quite a number of governmental changes have been implemented in various countries. Yet forms of discourse themselves tend to change as well. Discourse analysis aims to identify certain types of discourse, and how they evolve over time. This information is subsequently used to explain certain changes in society. Attention is paid, amongst other things, to how (and by whom) change is effected by certain forms of discourse.

- Rhetorical analysis focuses on the techniques used by the producer of a text or speech to convey a certain message to the audience (compare Perelman & Olbrechts-Tyteca, 2003). For example, the producer of the text can use certain metaphors, or give examples to make the audience identify with what is being said. Other techniques include rousing positive or negative emotions, such as pride

('Britannia rules the waves') or fear ('Terrorism lurks in every corner'). The speaker can also substantiate an argument with facts and figures, or relate an apt anecdote. Researchers who use the method of rhetorical analysis will usually read a text several times to try and detect such techniques. The analysis results in an overview of the rhetorical qualities of the text; the aim is to expose the (implied) message that the speaker has been trying to convey to the audience.

To sum up the above, content analysis can be used to: 1 establish facts and opinions; and 2 reconstruct the arguments used in a text. Box 9.3 gives some examples to illustrate these two functions. The reconstruction of a programme theory (as described in Box 1.2) is another typical example of content analysis. Also, in virtually all case studies discussed in Chapter 8, content analysis of documented material took place.

After gathering and selecting the data, the phase of analysis begins. The basic principle here is for the researcher to read a text or look at an image, and assign a value to parts of the text or image. The value assigned can either be quantitative ('score': compare Roberts, 1997; Riffe et al, 2005) or qualitative ('code': see also Chapter 11).

A score may refer to, for example, how frequently a certain concept occurs in a text ('How often are citizens mentioned in the party's political programme?'). It can also describe the frequency of an event ('How often are executive agencies asked to contribute to the development of new policies?'), or be used to assign a value to particular aspects of the text ('In this speech, cut-backs are mentioned more often than the improvement of service to citizens'). See also the example on the negotiation positions of EU member states in Box 9.3.

A code is a summary of the contents of a certain concept, and can be compared to an operationalization (see Chapter 4). For example, politicians can be interviewed about their motives for standing as a candidate in the elections. Each motive mentioned can be given its own label (the code): 'the public cause', 'gaining fame', 'it is a family tradition', etc.

In Chapters 10 and 11, I shall explain how such scores and codes can subsequently be used to draw conclusions. At this point, it is mainly important to realize that content analysis concentrates on the literal contents of the source of information (for example, the researcher counts how often a certain word appears in the text), whereas qualitative forms of analysis require the researcher to give an interpretation of the text: the empirically observed material is translated, as it were, into theoretical concepts. Such an interpretation can be derived by means of deduction (the theory indicates which concepts are important) or induction (generating axioms; see Chapter 3). To ensure a systematic approach to such qualitative forms of analysis, often specialized software is used.

BOX 9.3 EXAMPLES OF THE APPLICATION OF CONTENT ANALYSIS IN PUBLIC ADMINISTRATION

- During the first round of negotiations about the EU constitution, the national governments involved produced thousands of texts in which they stated their viewpoints. Benoit, Laver, Arnold, Pennings, and Hosli (2005) analysed these texts with the aid of a computer program; the program counted how often certain words occurred in the various texts. On the basis of the frequencies found, it could be established what positions certain national governments took on certain aspects of the EU constitution ('dimensions'). In the next stage, the data were compared with the results of a survey amongst experts in the field. The calculations from the computerized content analysis turned out to be reliable; they could adequately predict the negotiation positions of the diverse national governments.

- An analysis of the rhetorical techniques used by three different governments (the Netherlands, Sweden and Australia) to introduce the agency model in their home country has shown that agencification is indeed an international trend: the same arguments were used by all three governments. However, in each country studied certain adaptations were made, both with respect to the legal and organizational configuration of agencies, and in the stated motives for introducing this form of privatization. Such adaptations are probably needed to make the international trend fit in with the national political-administrative context and culture, and create sufficient support for the agency model (Smullen, 2010).

(For more information on qualitative or interpretative content analysis of policies, see Yanow, 1996.)

Secondary analysis

The analysis of data that have been collected by other researchers is called secondary analysis. In this approach, (parts of) existing datasets are combined with each other, after which the resulting new dataset is analysed. Above, several examples of sources that can be used for this form of research have been given. Generally speaking, secondary analysis involves using *statistical* data; this method is especially suitable for deductive or hypothesis-testing forms of research. Secondary analysis can also be part of trend analysis, using information over a longer period of time. Sometimes trend studies result in prospective scenarios or prognoses (simulations; see Chapter 6), which can subsequently be used by policymakers for designing new policies (see Chapter 1 on the relationship between policy and research).

The main problem when doing a secondary analysis is the operationalization problem mentioned earlier. If different datasets are combined, the researcher has to decide whether the data allow for adequate measurement of the research subject (and whether they pertain to the right level of measurement; see Box 4.1). If necessary, adaptations have to be made, or the data must be recalculated. For example, the total amount of employees in an organization may be expressed in one database as the number of persons employed, and as full-time equivalents (fte) in the other. These different measures do not always correspond with each other, which means that a way must be found to make them directly comparable. All such adjustments and recalculations have to be described and motivated in the research design or research report (with a view to validity and reliability).

As our discussion shows, the researcher needs to know how exactly the existing material came into being, and which choices were made by his or her predecessors whilst collecting the data. Box 9.4 gives some examples of research with secondary sources. In the example on corporatism and agencification given in the previous section (Van Thiel, 2001), secondary analysis was used as well. In Chapter 10, I shall elaborate further on the opportunities that secondary analysis offers for processing quantitative research data.

BOX 9.4 EXAMPLES OF SECONDARY ANALYSIS IN PUBLIC ADMINISTRATION

- As more and more public-sector organizations start using performance indicators and publish their performance indicators (often online), researchers have increasing access to data for studying changes in the performance of public organizations. They can link these changes to other trends, such as new policies, changes in the internal organizational structure (e.g. the appointment of a new manager) or changes in the wider environment (demographic changes, market changes), or changes over time. Provided that comparable data are available, cross-country comparisons are also a possible subject of study. See, for example, the comparative studies on the independence of regulatory authorities conducted by Maggetti (2009; work carried out by Majone and Gilardi also deals with this topic).

- Do party programmes and election promises really address the issues voters find important (the so-called gap between citizen and government)? Politicians ask for a mandate from voters for governing the country; however, sometimes it is unclear whether they will indeed try and tackle certain issues. To study this matter, Pennings (2005) used several existing databases. During his research, it turned out that the way in which certain matters were operationalized in one type of documents (the contents of government agreements) did not match the operationalizations applied in other texts (which described voters' preferences). To solve this problem, the data had to be recoded before they could be analysed (see also Chapter 10). Political parties proved to be hardly responsive to voters' needs, by the way; the wishes expressed by voters were seldom mentioned in the various election programmes. An explanation for this might lie in the fact that political parties have to serve the public interest (and not merely respond to the private interests of individual voters). Especially in countries where coalition governments are the custom, political parties must be prepared to compromise.

■ European countries differ significantly in how frequently or easily asylum seekers are granted a residence permit. It is unclear, though, whether such differences result from the number of asylum seekers a country receives per year, or inter-country difference in immigration policy. To study this subject, Vink and Meijerink (2003) conducted a statistical analysis on the annual number of asylum seekers, the number of residence permits granted (source: UNHCR), immigration or asylum policies (source: legislation), and the demographic and economic circumstances in 15 different EU countries (source: EU and national bureaux of statistics). Their conclusion was that contrary to what is generally believed, a strong relationship exists between the immigration policy of a country and the number of asylum seekers it receives each year. The EU could use this knowledge to synchronize their immigration policies better.

Meta-analysis

As the label meta-analysis indicates, this method transcends the level of just one piece of research, and makes use of several previously conducted studies. In a meta-analytical study, the results of all kinds of existing research – inductive or deductive, different strategies and methods, collecting qualitative or quantitative data – are brought together, with the aim of arriving at new conclusions. As these conclusions will be based on a wide array of research situations and units of study, they tend to have greater external validity and reliability (representativeness; see Chapter 4). For example, a case study on the leadership qualities of a certain mayor does not allow for statements on the average mayor. However, if 20 such case studies are analysed, conclusions at the higher level can be drawn.

Meta-analysis can be applied both deductively and inductively. In a deductive design, the data gathered are used to test certain hypotheses. In case studies, hypotheses usually cannot be tested (see Chapter 8), but meta-analysis of several case studies makes this a feasible option. In a so-called review study – which is a way of reporting the results of a meta-analysis – the researcher can provide an overview of the conclusions so far obtained on a certain research subject and thus test hypotheses.

If an inductive approach is followed, the findings of a large number of studies can be used to generate axioms or discover certain patterns (see Chapter 3). Finally, meta-analysis can also result in the identification of a new knowledge problem: the analysis will show on which subjects or aspects knowledge is still incomplete, and whether perhaps conclusions from previously conducted studies are contradictory (see the examples in Box 9.5). Such observations can result in a new research problem being formulated (see Chapter 2).

BOX 9.5 EXAMPLES OF META-ANALYSIS IN PUBLIC ADMINISTRATION AND PUBLIC MANAGEMENT RESEARCH

- Pollitt and Dan (2011) have collected over 500 evaluation studies and reports on the results of NPM reforms in 27 different countries. The majority of these reports deal with core executive bodies, healthcare organizations and local governments; usually they are written by academics who offer an overview of the effects or results of NPM reforms (most often the focus lies on the introduction of performance measurement). Pollitt and Dan (2011) have used the same coding scheme for all reports. Results showed that most reports offer only a description of changes that have taken place over the years; less than one quarter of all reports actually specifies the results of NPM reform (mostly in terms of output). In about half of the reports listing results, a positive result was noted. In about 20% of all cases, performance was said to have worsened; 30% of the reports listed no change at all. (Compare the meta-analysis by Hodge and Greve (2007) on the performance of public-private partnerships.)

- Seppänen, Blomqvist, & Sundqvist (2007) reviewed 15 studies on inter-organizational trust. Trust is expected to be an important variable in policy networks and other forms of collaboration, such as partnerships. The review conducted by Seppänen et al. (2007) shows, however, that most studies remain unclear about what exactly trust is, or how it can be used to manage networks and partnerships. The concept of trust has many different dimensions, varying from benevolence to things such as reliability and keeping agreements. As a result of this complexity, a truly reliable and valid instrument for measuring trust still has not been developed. (The reader should also note that most studies on trust focus on the private sector, which raises the question whether trust could take on another, still unexplored meaning in the public domain.)

- Policy convergence refers to the imitation and copying of policy programmes between different sectors and countries. Because governments often face similar problems, it is generally assumed that they will prefer similar solutions to those problems. Bennett's (1991) review of a number of studies on different policy sectors led him to discern four different patterns of convergence: emulation, harmonization, elite networking and penetration. Due to the influence of globalization and Europeanization, more policy convergence can be expected in future.

- Yildiz (2007) carried out a meta-analysis of secondary material by reviewing a large number of existing studies on the concept and practice of e-government. The review shows that the concept of e-government is often not clearly defined. It has not been properly studied either: several methodological shortcomings still do exist. For one, the development of e-government processes is often oversimplified, without taking the influence of complex political and institutional environments into account. Yildiz draws several lessons from this, and gives a number of recommendations for future research. Amongst others, he suggests that the subject of e-government should be connected more closely with the mainstream research in Public Administration and Public Management.

Different methods compared

Desk research can be applied for different purposes: description, explanation, testing, diagnosis and so forth. Likewise, the three methods distinguished above can be used for various types of research, although they differ in their emphasis. For example, secondary analysis requires an existent body of (statistical) data, which means that it is suitable for testing, but less so for exploration. Content analysis, on the other hand, can be used well in exploratory research. To illustrate the differences in emphasis between the three different methods, I shall describe three fictive examples of subjects in Public Administration and Public Management that can be studied by using existing material:

Example 1. The subject is the application of the management technique of performance indicators in hospitals. A content analysis could be carried out to reconstruct why the decision was made to introduce this technique, and how exactly it was implemented. A secondary analysis would sooner consist of comparing information on the number and types of performance indicators used, and which results have been measured (or obtained) by these. A meta-analytical approach could focus on comparing experiences in different medical sectors (hospitals, home care), and trying to establish the conditions under which performance indicators can be applied successfully.

Example 2. The subject is finding a solution to the problem of school segregation along social or racial lines. By doing a content analysis, the researcher could try to ascertain what legal options are available to the government for tackling this problem. A secondary analysis could be done of the data collected by the Ministry of Education on schools and pupils, focusing on questions such as: In what respects do highly segregated schools and more mixed schools differ? In a meta-analysis, an overview could be given of case studies of successful schools with a high number of pupils from minority groups.

Example 3. The subject is why so few women reach top positions in certain organizations or companies. A content analysis of personal documents of successful women could throw light on the constraints and conditions for rising through the ranks. A secondary analysis could provide an overview of the number of female top managers and CEOs in different economic sectors or in different periods (coupled to data on economic growth, employment levels and such). In a meta-analysis, an international comparison could be made between countries with a relatively high or a relatively low number of women in top positions, and test for the influence of relevant legislation or other variables.

These examples could be easily supplemented with other variants of research questions and approaches, but they serve to indicate the differences between the three methods.

To conclude

As a final point, I would like to stress that designing a theoretical framework is not a form of content analysis or meta-analysis as described here. In this chapter, I have discussed the application of content analysis and meta-analysis as a form of *empirical* research. Gathering the necessary literature to develop one's theoretical framework does resemble the collection of existing empirical material in certain respects; however, it serves a different purpose, and belongs to a different stage of research.

Review studies can be of great informative use, however, when developing a theoretical framework. The confusion on this point will arise in particular if theoretical insights and the scientific literature are the object of analysis, for example, in philosophical debates or comparative research aimed at testing the validity of certain theories. In such cases, it is important to distinguish clearly between theory as a guideline for research and theory as a subject of study.

FURTHER READING

Fischer, F. (2003). *Reframing Public Policy: Discursive Politics and Deliberative Practices*. Oxford: Oxford University Press.

Riffe, D., Lacy, S., & Fico, F.G. (2005, 2nd edition). *Analyzing Media Messages: Using Quantitative Content Analysis in Research*. Mahwah: Lawrence Erlbaum Ass.

Roberts, C. (1997). *Text Analysis for the Social Sciences: Methods for Drawing Statistical Inferences from Texts and Transcripts*. Mahwah: Lawrence Erlbaum Ass.

Yanow, D. (1996). *How Does a Policy Mean? Interpreting Policy and Organizational Actions*. Washington: Georgetown University Press.

EXERCISES

1   Write an essay (circa 3,000 words) on a key figure in Public Administration (for example, Max Weber, Alexis de Tocqueville, Woodrow Wilson, Christopher Hood, or B. Guy Peters). Use several sources, such as texts written on or by this person. Motivate your choice of sources (see also Box 3.5 on literature skills).

2   Try to get hold of the transcript of a speech made by a (local or national) politician. Tip: sometimes such speeches are printed in the newspaper, or posted on a website or blog. Make a rhetorical analysis of the speech. For example, who is the intended audience? What is the main message? Which rhetorical techniques have been used? Apply the information given in Box 9.2 (see also the reference given in this box).

3   Look up the latest version of the 'Government at a glance' report on the OECD website. Select a chapter that contains data on a topic of your preference. Formulate a research question and aim (see Chapter 2) that could be studied with these data (other than what is already discussed in the chapter). Next, develop a research design (see Chapter 5) to study this particular research problem, using a secondary analysis of the OECD data. If possible, conduct the analysis and report your findings.

4   Find a so-called review article from an international refereed journal in Public Administration or Public Management on a subject of your preference. (Tip: use the keyword review or meta-analysis during your search.) In what way has the author conducted the meta-analysis? Give your opinion on the approach followed. Could the author have done things better or differently?

Chapter 10

Analysing quantitative data

The aim of this chapter is to offer an introductory guide to researchers who are new to using quantitative data. It is not my purpose to provide an exhaustive review of all possible statistical techniques and formulae. A single chapter would not suffice – besides, there are plenty of other, specialized textbooks on statistics and analytical techniques (see, for example, McClave, Benson & Sincich, 2007). The focus here will rather be on the different phases that researchers have to complete when analysing quantitative data. I shall also give an overview of a select number of statistical techniques, and discuss their suitability for answering certain research questions.

When applying statistical techniques, it is always a good idea to seek some external advice first: from other researchers, from specialists in research methods and techniques, by consulting textbooks, or using the help function of the computer program employed for analysis. Do not be intimidated by statistics! Researchers have to be able to think logically, but need not be mathematicians in order to be able to conduct a quantitative study.

Broadly speaking, a study with quantitative data consists of three phases: data collection, data ordering and data analysis. Below, all these three phases will be discussed. The chapter concludes by listing a few points worthy of consideration with respect to the reliability and validity of quantitative data.

10.1 QUANTITATIVE DATA

Quantitative data are always numerical in kind. They can either be numbers that have a certain intrinsic meaning (such as money in pounds sterling, a date, or a number of units of something), or consist of numerical scores (for example, an evaluation of a respondent's answer on a scale from 1 to 10). Researchers can assign scores to all kinds of variables. For example, the replies given by a group of respondents to the question 'Which political party did you vote for during the last elections?' can be quantified by assigning a separate score to every possible answer (for example, 1 = Conservative; 2 = Liberal Democrat; 3 = Labour). The score number constitutes a shorthand way of expressing a respondent's answer.

There are several advantages to working with numbers. First of all, numbers are far more clear-cut than words. Using numbers forces the researcher to think logically and be precise, and prevents reverting to ambiguous language. Numbers are also shorter than words, enabling the researcher to have an easy overview of the data. Finally, numbers can be used in statistical calculations: logical procedures that obey certain rules (see the regulative ideas discussed in Chapter 3). Having said all this, the researcher must always keep closely in mind that a number or score has a certain meaning. In the end, it is not the numbers themselves that count, but the conclusions that can be drawn from them (see also below on interpretation).

Not everybody is equally convinced of the advantages that quantitative data can offer. Some researchers are even opposed to using numbers, alleging that quantification leads to simplification and a reduction of information, and therefore does not do justice to the complexity of reality. A more principled but related argument is that people – who are the central subject of social science research – cannot be captured in numbers. The latter view is closely associated with the predominantly interpretative philosophy of science of the anti-quantitative faction in Public Administration (see Chapter 3).

Lastly, opponents of numerical analysis often contend that quantitative research is not as transparent and truthful as its adherents tend to allege. A title frequently cited in this respect is *How to Lie with Statistics* by Huff (1993). In his book, Huff describes how researchers can use – or rather misuse – statistical analysis to give inflated, overly positive results. It is indeed true that there are ways and means of manipulating numbers to enforce certain conclusions ('data massage', or fraud); still, such practices are more indicative of the lack of integrity of the researchers involved than the accuracy or inaccuracy of statistical analysis as a method.

The analysis of quantitative data can be either theory driven or data driven (compare Robson, 2002, p. 399). Theory-driven analysis is geared at the statistical testing of hypotheses that have been formulated beforehand (deduction). In a data-driven analysis, on the contrary, the dataset is exploited or 'cannibalized', in the sense that numerous analyses are carried out to mine the available information for all kinds of patterns and relations between variables, so as to arrive at new theoretical insights. This approach is more or less comparable to induction. In practice, however, a deductive researcher will want to cannibalize the data as well, after having tested the original hypotheses. Such a procedure can be used to generate new or supplementary hypotheses (compare Babbie, 1992, p. 425; Kuhn, 1996 [1962]).

In itself, there is nothing wrong with cannibalizing the data, yet the researcher must take care not to create a *post hoc, ergo propter hoc* argument (literally: after this, therefore, because of this, or: seeing causation in correlation). By the way, the analysis of quantitative data is always a continuous process. The results of one step in the analytical process will generate new questions, which will need analysing in their turn.

10.2 COLLECTING AND ORDERING THE DATA

When designing a study, a researcher decides which variables will be measured (by means of, for example, items in a questionnaire), and what numerical values these can assume (see Chapter 4 on operationalization). The more clearly all such aspects of the data collection are specified in the initial research design, the easier it will be to process the data later. Consider, for example, the difference between asking respondents to confine themselves to ticking just one answer per item, or allowing for several different answers to be given. In the latter case, each separate answer category must be assigned its own score, which will make the dataset much bigger. As this example shows, the quantification of the research data already begins in the operationalization phase. For all such reasons, inductive research is less suitable for quantitative analysis, although sometimes quantitative methods can be successfully applied in an inductive study (see also below).

If quantification takes place only at a later stage, the situation may arise that certain analytical techniques will turn out to be unfit for the data that have been collected. In Chapter 4, it was explained that variables which have been measured at a certain level (nominal, ordinal, etc.) will be only of limited use for statistical analysis (see Box 4.1). Remember also Chapter 9, in which we discussed that when a secondary analysis is conducted, the operationalization problem can arise; the way in which the data have been operationalized in the different sources may not concur with each other, which means that the researcher has to find some kind of solution before being able to proceed with the analysis.

If meaningful numbers are to be used (that is, numbers with ecological validity; compare Chapter 4), the choice for a certain numerical value will be a matter of course. For example, an organization's budget will be expressed in pounds sterling, euros, or some other currency. Yet even in such seemingly simple cases, several subsequent choices have to be made: what kind of budget exactly is of interest (personnel costs, materials, consolidated budget, or income and expenses), and whether prices will have to be indexed to correct for inflation. Another example is the number of civil servants employed by the government: are we dealing with the total number of people or full-time equivalents (fte)? Also, do people employed by semi-autonomous agencies and privatized companies count as well? The researcher has to be absolutely clear which aspects will be included in the study, and what exactly will be measured.

When assigning scores to non-numerical variables, the advice is always to choose values that seem logical (compare Robson, 2002, p. 257). There are no hard and fast rules for this, but often scores will describe a rising scale, ranging, for example, from (1): totally disagree with a certain statement, via (2): disagree, (3): neutral, and (4): agree, to (5): totally agree. Positive answers usually score higher than negative ones (0 = no; 1 = yes). In case of dichotomous variables, it is best for statistically analytical purposes to choose the values 0 and 1 (for example, 0 = male; 1 = female).

Furthermore, it is important to pay close attention to answer categories such as 'not applicable', 'don't know', 'neutral', or any missing answers. Each of these answer categories has their own particular meaning; someone failing to respond to a certain statement or someone choosing a neutral reply can lead to different research results. The best way to prevent confusion on this point is by assigning all such answer categories their own score. This is particularly important for missing answers ('missing values'), as a lack of information can have serious consequences for the statistical analysis later. Always take care to choose a value that is easily distinguishable from the other answer categories. For example, if a respondent has not filled in his or her age, a value of 0 for the missing score does not discriminate sufficiently – after all, the value of 0 can indicate a certain age as well (although it seems doubtful that an infant would fill in a questionnaire). Rather, choose a score such as, say, -1 for the missing value.

Code book

All possible scores are noted down in the so-called code book. The code book provides an overview of all the variables that are included in the study, plus their accompanying values. Table 10.1 presents a simple example of a code book for a fictive study with questionnaires. Respondents will be asked after their gender, income, age, which political party they voted for in the last elections, which newspaper they read, and how much confidence they have in politics. The variables gender, newspaper and vote are all assigned a certain value by the researcher; the other variables are numerical of their own accord.

Data matrix

Using the code book as a guideline, the researcher enters the data that are being collected into a so-called data matrix. A data matrix looks like a spreadsheet; it is a matrix in which the quantitative data are arranged by units (the rows) and variables (the columns). In Table 10.2, an example is given of a data matrix for five fictive respondents; the code book from Table 10.1 has been used to fill in the data matrix (reading guide: the first respondent is a female

Table 10.1 Example of a code book

Variable	Description	Values
Respondent	Respondent number	0 etc.
Gender	Respondent's sex	0=male; 1=female; 9=missing answer
Income	Net monthly income in pounds sterling	0 etc.; –1=missing answer
Age	Age in years	0 etc.; –1=missing answer
Vote	Which party voted for in last elections	0=abstained; 1=Conservative; 2=LibDem; 3=Labour; 4=Green Party; etc.
Newspaper	National newspaper	0=no paper; 1=Guardian; 2=Times; 3=Daily Mail; 4=Daily Telegraph; 5=Sun; 6=other
Confidence	Confidence in politics, on a scale from 1 to 10	1–10; –1=missing answer

Table 10.2 *Example of a data matrix*

Respondent	Gender	Age	Income	Vote	Paper	Confidence
001	1	21	500	3	5	7
002	0	22	1,275	1	3	6
003	1	43	2,150	2	1	8
004	1	16	220	0	4	4
005	0	23	780	0	4	4

aged 21, who reads the *Sun,* and has a net monthly income of £500. She has voted Labour and her level of confidence in politics is reasonably high (7 on a scale of 1–10)).

Researchers can enter the data themselves, but there are also specialized data entry agencies, which enter data for payment (compare Babbie, 1992, p. 383–84). If online questionnaires are used, respondents' answers can be entered directly into the data matrix, and there is no need for the researcher to type out the answer sheets (the latter which invariably leads to mistakes being made). The computer transmits all this information to the accompanying data matrix.

There are several computer programs for analysing quantitative data, such as SPSS, Excel, Stata, R and SAS. All these programs are based on data matrices like the one described here. In Public Administration and Public Management research, SPSS is most frequently used. It is a menu-driven program, which is compatible with Windows (see Field, 2009, for a useful guide to statistics and SPSS). The data matrix is found on the opening page, the second tab page shows the code book.

Computer programs provide several advantages to the researcher: they offer an array of statistical techniques, can handle sizeable datasets with large numbers of respondents, and give ample assistance to the user (help function, handbooks, internal coach). Most programs also provide room for adding non-numerical information, such as names and labels (of an organization or a profession), or text containing the answers given to open questions (category 'other'; see Chapter 7). Such non-numerical or text variables are called string variables. It goes without saying that string variables are unsuitable for numerical calculations; other techniques are needed for analysing these data (see below).

Data inspection

During the process of data entry, mistakes can be made, both by the respondents and the researcher. Therefore, the first thing the researcher has to do when the data matrix has been completed is to check the dataset for errors. We call this the phase of data inspection. For the data inspection, the researcher creates a frequency distribution for each variable, which is an overview of how often certain values occur. The frequency distribution makes it easy to spot any irregularities in the data. For example, in Table 10.2, the frequency distribution of the variables 'gender' and 'newspaper' ought to look as follows:

Gender: Male 2, Female 3, Missing answer 0;
Paper: No paper 0, *Guardian* 1, *Times* 0, *Daily Mail* 1, *Daily Telegraph* 2, *Sun* 1.

If mistakes have been made during the data entry (for example, the value 22 is found for a respondent's gender, which would probably be a typo), these errors have to be corrected. *In order to be able to do this, it is imperative that the original data have been saved in a separate file, so that the source of the mistake can be traced.* Always keep a file of the original data therefore, and make several copies of the data file. In our fictive example, the researcher will have to trace for which respondent exactly a faulty entry was made, and which original questionnaire corresponds with this respondent (this information can be found by looking up the respondent number). If it turns out that the necessary detail cannot be tracked down, the researcher can remove the faulty answer, or try and make an informed guess about what the right value should have been (in case of a typo, this will not be too difficult). Either which way, the error case must be noted down in the log, as it may have consequences for the reliability and validity of the study.

Data inspection can be a very time-consuming process, especially when the dataset is large. Still, it is an absolutely vital step in the analysis, which will prevent potential problems at a later stage. An alternative to checking the entire dataset is taking a sample of a few units (respondents), and using this group for verification.

Besides tracing mistakes, the data inspection serves a second purpose: namely, to check the dataset on certain statistical features, such as the population mean and standard deviation. To calculate the mean and standard deviation, different measures and formulae can be applied. The two measures used most often are given below.

- The arithmetic mean (also simply called the mean or average) is the total sum of all scores, divided by the number of units. In the example given in Table 10.2, the average age is 25. The age distribution turns out to be less than optimal, by the way: there are four relatively young respondents, and one respondent who is older. Extremely deviant scores are called *outliers*. With some forms of statistical analysis, it is best to remove such outliers from the dataset (and make a note about this removal in your log).
- The standard deviation (SD) is a measure that indicates how big the distance is between a certain score and the mean. This measure is standardized, which means to say that one SD from the average or mean (over or under) will cover two thirds of the entire population. Some 95% of the population will lie within the boundaries of two SDs; this range is called the reliability interval. To illustrate mean and SD, in Table 10.2, monthly income is listed: the lowest value is £220; the highest value is £2,150; the mean is £985; and the standard deviation is £758.9. In general, the higher

the standard deviation, the more spread there will be (the data are more heterogeneous): there are relatively big differences between scores, which means the differences between individual respondents are relatively big as well. Statistical analyses aim to identify the causes of such differences or spread (also referred to as variation or dispersion).

As a no doubt redundant remark, it is of little use to calculate the mean and standard deviation for nominal variables. For example, the mean of the variable 'vote' in Table 10.2 carries no meaning; likewise, a vote for Liberal Democrat (2) is not twice as much as a vote for Conservative (1).

By way of the mean and the standard deviation, the researcher can gain an idea as to whether the data have a so-called normal distribution. The normal distribution forms the basis for most statistical techniques. Figure 10.1 depicts what a normal distribution looks like. Right in the middle we find the mean; 68% of all scores lie within one SD; 95% lie within the range of two SDs. Besides calculating these measures (and establishing, for example, that the population distribution is skewed rather than normal), computer programs can also give a graphical presentation of the research results, so that the researcher can see at a glance whether the data are normally distributed or not.

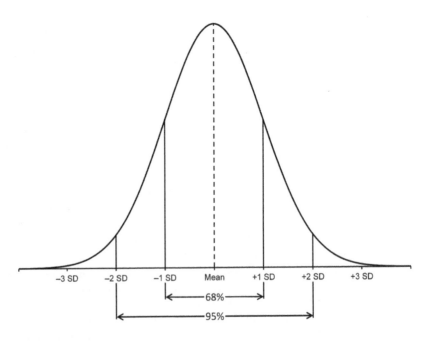

Figure 10.1
Normal distribution

By inspecting the data, the researcher gets a real feel for the dataset, which can help to make a better-informed choice as to which statistical techniques to use for analysis (see below). A separate goal of the data inspection is to check on the representativeness of the sample (if applicable). In order to do so, the sample and the population as a whole must be compared on a number of relevant characteristics. For example, in a questionnaire study, it is the custom to compare the sample's age, gender and educational distribution with national averages. In this way, the researcher can see in which respects the sample deviates from the entire population. During the later stage of analysis, such additional information can be taken into account, by giving certain groups a lower or higher weight in the calculations, for example (see what has been said on non-response in Chapter 7).

Recoding, categorizing and processing

In principle, the data that have been entered into the data matrix form the starting point for the statistical analysis. Sometimes, though, the data have to be recoded or processed first, because the distribution of the scores on a certain variable is less than optimal. A correction can be made for this by redefining the values that the variable can assume, for example, by creating categories. To refer back to Table 10.2 once more, instead of the values initially specified, a number of classes or categories can be created for the variable income, such as: 1 minimum wage; 2 minimum wage to median family income; 3 average to twice the median income; and 4 more than twice the median income. An alternative is to make a classification on the basis of the scores that have been measured: if three categories (low, medium, high) are used, every category will contain circa 33% of all respondents.

The advantage of such recoding procedures is that the distribution of the new scores will resemble the normal distribution more closely, which will facilitate the analysis later, as most statistical techniques require variables to be normally distributed. Also, the data become readily comparable; they are standardized, as it were. This can be helpful when datasets with different operationalizations are joined together (see Chapter 9 on secondary analysis). Finally, recoding also leads to a reduction (simplification) of the data, which may be particularly useful if big datasets are used (to avoid overestimation, see below). On the down side, recoding invariably entails a loss of information, which could have been used to draw firm conclusions. Also, every form of recoding creates an extra risk for reliability and validity. For example, a researcher's bias can influence the decision to recode the data (see Chapter 4). For these and related reasons, every choice made during the recoding process has to be well motivated and carefully documented.

The original data will also need recoding if they consist of non-numerical, string variables. Statistical analyses can only be done with data of a numerical format, and after the information on non-numerical variables has been gathered, scores must be assigned manually. For example, if in a questionnaire certain respondents have given a 'different' reply rather than using any of the pre-structured answer categories, the researcher can make an overview of such replies by means of a frequency distribution. Worded replies that are similar or identical get the same score. In this manner, a new variable is created with accompanying values, which can be included in the data matrix and the code book. In the example given in Table 10.1, for example, people are asked which newspaper they read. Besides the five papers listed, there is the option to give the name of a different, unlisted newspaper, 6: 'other ... '. The answers in the 'other' category are studied, gathered together, and assigned new scores (which means the code book has to be adjusted as well).

10.3 ANALYSIS

There are numerous statistical techniques for analysing quantitative data. These techniques can be divided into two groups: 1 descriptive statistical techniques; and 2 inferential statistical techniques. The first category of statistics concentrates on a number of characteristics of the variables in the dataset, and the relations that exist between these variables. Descriptive statistics are particularly suitable for nominal and ordinal data, or when making a first exploration of the data, which is why they are sometimes also referred to as exploratory statistics.

Inferential statistics focus on whether the relations as described are systematic ('real'). In deductive research, inferential statistics can also be used to ascertain whether the hypothesized relations are indeed present (confirmatory analysis). In order to do so, the data must have been measured at minimally the ordinal level (but preferably a higher level). Also, for every particular inferential technique additional requirements will have to be met, besides that the variables are distributed normally. Before using a certain statistical technique, always check whether the data meet such assumptions. If they fail to do so, an alternative method of analysis must be sought.

Inferential techniques are sometimes also referred to as 'explanatory statistics'; however, to call this form of analysis 'explanatory' seems somewhat premature. Statistical analysis can indeed demonstrate that two or more variables are related, yet this does not necessarily mean that the relation is of the cause-and-effect type (causality). To illustrate, in the data matrix of Table 10.2, we can see that there are two respondents who did not vote during the last elections; both respondents have also indicated they have little confidence in politics. These data seem to suggest some kind of relation, but which one exactly? Are these people disappointed by politics, and is that the reason why they failed to vote? Or did they decide to abstain from voting and only afterwards lost their confidence in politics? As this example shows, a researcher must first interpret the results of the statistical analysis and give them meaning, before being able to draw any conclusions that make sense (hold true). In practice, there are only very few techniques that can establish causality in an effective manner (see below on structural-equation modelling).

10.4 DESCRIPTIVE STATISTICS

Besides the techniques mentioned in the section on data inspection (see above), we can mention two other relevant descriptive techniques: namely, cross-tabulation and correlation.

Cross-tabulation

In a cross-tabulation, the results of two or more variables are tabulated against each other, creating a multivariate frequency distribution. By inspecting the table, the researcher can easily establish whether certain combinations of values occur more frequently than others, which can be indicative of a theoretically relevant relation. Cross-tabulations are also suitable for nominal data, as the example in Table 10.3 shows. In this cross-table, the relation between gender (columns) and voting behaviour (rows) is shown for 162 respondents.

The cross-tabulation makes clear that – looking at the rows rather than columns – the Liberal Democrats and the Green Party are more popular with female voters, whereas the Conservatives draw a relatively high number of male voters. It is important, by the way, not to regard cross-tables from a purely absolute point of view, but also to consider the relative numbers or percentages. After all, the numbers of male and female voters in this sample are not equal (and most votes have been cast for the Liberal Democrats in this example).

Correlation

Correlation is a measure of how strongly two variables are interrelated. The correlation (or correlation coefficient) ranges between 0 and 1; the higher the correlation, the stronger the variables are statistically related. A negative correlation indicates a negative relation; a positive correction coefficient indicates a positive relation. Do take note that the correlation only expresses whether a relation exists, and how strong this relation is: it does not specify if the two variables are causally related. A statistical correlation might even be wholly devoid of meaning. For example, a researcher may observe a correlation between the colour of respondents' eyes and their voting behaviour, but this would in all likelihood just be a coincidence (the composition of the sample might be of influence here).

Table 10.3 *Example of a cross-tabulation*

	Male	Female	Total
Conservative	22 (32.8%)	17 (17.9%)	39 (24.1%)
Liberal Democrats	23 (34.3%)	41 (43.2%)	64 (39.5%)
Labour	18 (26.9%)	22 (23.2%)	40 (24.7%)
Green Party	4 (6%)	15 (15.8%)	19 (11.7%)
Total	67	95	162

Correlations can be calculated in different ways, either as a simple correlation between two variables – so without taking the possible influence of other variables into account (bivariate correlation) – or with a correction being made for such influences (partial correlation). With respect to the last option, again different measures can be used, such as Pearson's r and Spearman's rho. Which measure exactly will be most suitable depends on the level of measurement (ordinal level or higher), and the different values that a variable can assume.

To illustrate the meaning and use of correlation, consider once more the example given in Table 10.2. In this sample, there is a correlation of 0.928 between income and age (Pearson's r, bivariate). This means that the older someone grows, the higher their income will be (the correlation is positive). A strongly simplified way of interpreting the same result is that for every additional 10% of years of age, income rises with 9.3% (or vice versa). For a more detailed interpretation of correlation, and more information on how correlation coefficients are calculated, I refer to the statistical literature.

10.5 INFERENTIAL STATISTICS

Inferential statistical analysis aims to establish whether a certain (theoretically presupposed) relation between two variables is systematic. This type of analysis is based on the principles of probability theory. The simplest but most often used test statistic is the t-test, which can only be applied to variables of ordinal or higher level. For nominal data, the so-called chi-square test can be used, which would be suitable, for example, for the data in the cross-table given earlier (see the statistical literature for further explanation and more examples).

In this section, the t-test, regression analysis, variance analysis, factor analysis and the construction of scales will be briefly discussed. Regression analysis and factor analysis, in particular, are frequently applied in Public Administration and Public Management research with quantitative data. For example applications, see Box 7.1, where a number of survey studies using statistical analyses are discussed (see also Box 10.2).

T-test

A t-test measures whether the difference found between two scores (for example, between a pre-test and post-test measurement, between the sample and the population, or between two groups of respondents), is systematic, and unlikely to be caused by random factors such as coincidental circumstances, interference by other variables, or a wrongly constructed sample. To illustrate the use of the t-test, consider once more Table 10.2. In the sample, there were two male respondents whose confidence in politics was less than the average level of confidence of the sampled females (male mean of 5, female mean of 6.3, on a scale of 1–10). The question presents itself whether this is a *true* difference, or should perhaps be attributed to coincidence. A t-test can measure this: it shows whether the difference observed is real or random. If there is a real and systematic difference between the two groups (men have less confidence in politics than women), we call the effect of the variable gender statistically significant. Only if an effect is shown to be statistically significant can the hypothesis on the supposed relation between two variables be confirmed or rejected. The conclusion here would be that there is indeed a true relation between a respondent's gender and their level of confidence in politics. If, however, the results of the t-test had not been statistically significant (n.s.), it would remain uncertain whether the two variables are truly related (the hypothesis cannot be rejected).

How does a t-test work? In a t-test, the mean scores of two groups on a certain variable are compared (for example, male versus female respondents, with confidence in politics as the variable of which the mean scores are considered). The t-test estimates the chance that the difference found is purely random. The researcher states beforehand how large this chance of a random result may be; the standard maximum value (p) is 5%. If $p < 0.05$, the difference observed between the two groups is not random, but systematic (with 95% reliability). This difference is statistically significant, which means that the variables (gender and confidence in politics) are systematically related. Sometimes other p-values are used, such as 0.10, 0.01, or 0.001. In scientific research, certain conventions apply on how to report on the significance of results (see Box 10.1).

BOX 10.1 REPORTING ON RESULTS

The results of statistical analyses are reported both in tables or figures (graphs, diagrams) as well as in words. These two respective formats have different functions, and always have to be used in combination with each other (which will contribute also to the readability of a research report). Tables and figures give the numerical results of the analyses, specifying things such as sample size (n), the p-value used for tests, and the scores and differences in scores found in the analysis. The interpretation of what all these numbers mean is given in words. For example, a certain table may show that the variables gender is statistically related to voting behaviour, which means (in words) that, as compared to men, women vote Labour more often: about once more every four times that a vote is cast by women. *Only by translating the numerical results (= interpreting) into words do analytical results gain meaning.*

Depending on the system used for literature references (see Box 3.5), the layout of tables and figures is subject to certain rules. Whichever system is applied, it is always important to number your tables and figures, and give them a full, complete title. In the APA system used in this book, a table title takes the shape of a header; for figures, the title is displayed as a caption below the figure. Take care also to specify sample size (n) and whether results are significant. For statistical significance, asterisks are used: * means to say a p-value of 0.05; ** indicates a p of 0.01, etc.

> To get a feel for layout and the different ways of reporting on results, you can study some tables and figures in scientific articles or research reports. It is also advisable to try and master the appropriate function keys in your word-processing program.

As explained, t-tests give information on whether the relation between two variables is systematic. The results of the analysis also give an indication of the direction of the relation (for example, a negative t-value shows a negative relation), and of its strength (effect size: the size of the t-value). However, the t-test cannot be used to draw conclusions on causality (which variable caused which effect?). The researcher has to interpret the estimated t-value by looking at the hypotheses formulated earlier (in deductive studies), or by comparing the results with the other data that have been collected (inductive). Also, the mathematical properties of the data have to be taken into account: relations between variables will sooner be statistically significant in larger samples, if a smaller p-value is used, or if the difference between mean scores is sizeable (compare Robson, 2002, p. 401). All such aspects have to be kept closely in mind (indeed, it is a well-known fact that researchers with little integrity sometimes manipulate results, for example, by consciously setting the p-value higher; compare Simmons, Nelson, & Simonsohn, 2011).

A drawback of the t-test is that it can only be used to study the difference between the group scores on one single variable; it performs a so-called uni-variate analysis. Furthermore, if several t-tests are done, an accumulation of the probability error arises. After all, for every t-test, there is a probability of 5% that the effect found is just random (the researcher accepts this probability – sometimes referred to as a type I error). Every subsequent t-test will add another 5%, which means that ultimately there is a substantial risk that the effect which has been found is spurious after all. Fortunately, there are techniques to correct for this, such as variance analysis (see below).

Regression analysis

Regression analysis tests whether the relation between two variables (the dependent variable and the independent variable) is linear; the analysis results in a mathematical expression of that relation. A positive linear relation means to say that an increase in the independent variable (for example, political knowledge) leads to an increase in the dependent variable (for example, political involvement). Such a relation can be expressed in a so-called regression function (equation):

$$Y = a + bX + e$$

In the regression function given above, Y is the dependent variable (political involvement), whereas X is the independent variable (political knowledge). The explanatory effect of X on Y is expressed by b (which can be either positive or negative); a is a so-called constant; and e is the estimation error. The constant is the base score of all respondents (everyone has at least some political involvement, for example, through being a voter); the estimation error expresses the fact that the independent variable alone cannot explain all variation that is observed in the dependent variable.

The actual regression analysis consists of calculating the values of a, b, and e. An indication will also be given (by the computer program used) of whether b is statistically significant (see above). With the values that have been computed, the researcher can formulate the regression function, which can be used to draw a line in a scattergram (see Figure 10.2). In the scattergram, the regression coefficient b is, in essence, a numerical expression of the slope of the regression line. The line shown in the scattergram depicts the relation between the independent variable (x axis) and the dependent variable (y axis).

A scattergram is a graphical representation of the scores of the units of study (people, organizations, countries, etc.) on the research variables. Figure 10.2 gives a simple example of a scattergram of political knowledge (x axis) and political involvement (y axis). The sum of all the differences between the scores measured is also called the variance. Statistical techniques aim to explain the variance (so, the differences between the units of study); they calculate the influence of the independent variables (the characteristics of the units of study). The regression analysis not only shows which variables have a significant effect, it also gives an indication of the magnitude or strength of their explanatory value: it specifies the percentage of explained variance (R^2).

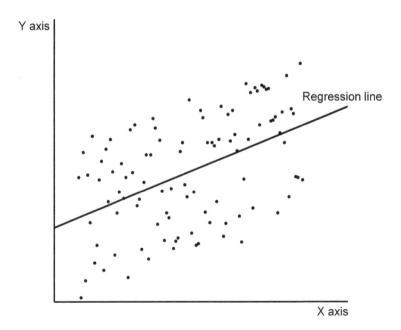

Figure 10.2
Example of a scattergram

If there is more than one independent variable, the regression function can be extended to a multiple regression function. A regression function with two independent variables may look as follows:

$$Y = a + b_1X_1 + b_2X_2 + b_1b_2X_1X_2 + e$$

Apart from X_1 (political knowledge) and X_2 (age), the combination of X_1 and X_2 can also have an effect on Y (political involvement). For example, the older people grow, the more political knowledge they will have gained. Such a combined influence of two independent variables is called an interaction effect.

A note of warning: variables can be added to the regression function in only limited numbers, depending on the so-called degrees of freedom (df). The degrees of freedom rule states that the number of variables that can be added may not exceed the total number of respondents in the sample minus 1 (df = n-1). Also, the greater the number of variables in the regression function, the more complicated any interaction effects will be (interaction effects of a higher order).

Researchers doing a regression analysis can study different combinations of variables and regression functions, based on the theoretical expectations formulated earlier (see Box 2.3 on hypotheses). As an alternative, the dataset can be cannibalized by trying out all possible combinations. Different combinations of variables are called different (statistical) estimation models. Usually the analytical process starts with a simple model of one or a few variables, after which other variables can be gradually added. The influence of possible sources of interference (see Box 6.1) and control variables has to be considered as well. The best model will be the one that renders the highest percentage of explained variance with the smallest combination of variables (compare Chapter 3 on the criterion of parsimony).

The results of the regression analysis are presented in a table, which specifies the parameters (a, b, e, etc.) found for each estimation model. An indication is also given of the respective R^2 values (see also Box 10.1).

Variance analysis

Variance analysis tests whether there are differences in the mean scores of two groups on one variable (analysis of variance: ANOVA), or more than one variable (multivariate ANOVA or MANOVA). The underlying assumption is that a significant difference in mean scores indicates that the variable used to create the groups (for example, men versus women) offers an explanation for the differences found in the dependent variable (for example, confidence in politics). As an alternative to testing the differences between two groups (between subjects design), the researcher can also consider just one unit of study (within subjects design) at two different moments in time, comparing, for example, pre-test and post-test scores. The latter option makes variance analysis a popular choice in experiments; it also explains why, in Public Administration and Public Management research, variance analysis is used less often than other techniques such as regression analysis or factor analysis (see Chapter 6).

The biggest advantage of variance analysis over the t-test is that in case of multivariate testing, there is only a small risk of error accumulation. If more than two groups are analysed (think of age groups, for example), or several variables are included in the analysis, variance analysis is to be preferred over the t-test.

Variance analysis is based on the principle of falsification; if the difference in the (mean) scores between the two groups or two measuring moments is statistically significant, the null hypothesis is rejected, and the alternative hypothesis becomes valid (see Box 3.1). The underlying assumption is that the independent variable explains the change in the dependent variable. The test value F (with accompanying p-value) expresses whether the difference (variance) between two groups or moments is significant.

Factor analysis

Factor analysis aims to find the underlying or latent relation between a set of variables. Taken together, these variables constitute one 'factor'. The factor itself cannot be observed or measured; it is merely a theoretical construct (see Chapter 3). For example, political leadership is a construct based on a combination of personal characteristics, such as charisma, background (educational background, family background), and management style (all of which are constructs in their turn). To measure the construct of leadership as a whole, the researcher will have to perform a factor analysis, combining the measurements of all these separate dimensions (see also the example on Public Service Motivation in Box 7.1).

A factor analysis estimates for each individual variable the extent to which it co-varies with other variables, and so whether the variable in question forms part of the factor. We speak of a variable 'loading' onto a factor (this can be seen in the correlations). The Eigenvalue or degree to which the factor forms a unified whole is also calculated: this shows if the factor found does indeed explain all variance. It should be as high as possible (at least > 1).

In a deductive study, a researcher will have formed certain expectations about which (independent) variables are closely related and contribute to the dependent variable (the factor). Such expectations can be put to the test in a factor analysis (confirmatory analysis). The results will indicate whether the expected relations do indeed exist, and how strong or statistically significant they are. On the basis of the results, the hypotheses formulated can either be rejected or confirmed, after which the theoretical model can be refined or adjusted. If the researcher has no clear-cut expectations, an open factor analysis (or 'principal component analysis') can be performed. In the latter case, the computer calculates the statistically strongest factor. What this factor means from a conceptual point of view will have to be explained (interpreted) by the researcher.

The advantage of doing a factor analysis is that one factor can say more about the unit of study than a whole group of measured variables taken together (reduction). Ultimately, the factor itself can become a new variable in a subsequent study (see Box 4.2 on the validating measurement instruments).

Constructing scales

In Box 7.2, the concept of scales was explained. By means of a statistical analysis of respondents' replies to questions or statements, the researcher can try and establish how closely certain items (such as questions and statements on political knowledge) are related, and whether or not they can predict the value of a certain construct (such as political involvement). Items that are closely related are called a 'scale' (see also Box 4.2; compare DeVellis, 2012).

The procedure to follow when constructing a scale can be compared to doing a factor analysis. For each item, the researcher calculates the degree to which this item interrelates with other items (see the section on correlations), and also, to what extent it relates to the scale to be constructed (load). The reliability of the scale as a whole is expressed by means of the test value Cronbach's Alpha. This test value ranges from 0 to 1, and must be as high as possible (ideally higher than 0.7). Different combinations of items can be tested; the scale that is ultimately constructed will consist of the minimal number of items with the highest combined reliability (the Alpha value).

BOX 10.2 EXAMPLES OF STUDIES IN PUBLIC ADMINISTRATION AND PUBLIC MANAGEMENT USING QUANTITATIVE DATA

- Meier and O'Toole (2001) have collected data from several Texas school districts in order to study the management of public organizations, in particular public organizations in a network environment. They have published several articles based on these data, using different variables and different linear regression techniques. One of their findings is that the performance of schools is influenced to a great extent by the involvement of superintendents in network contacts, and is not just determined by good public management (Meier & O'Toole, 2001). The data collection is replicated frequently and new analyses are still being carried out.

- To study patterns of democracy in 36 countries, Lijphart (1999) used a number of existing, secondary data sources. Data were collected on political party system, electoral volatility, judicial review, economic indicators and so on. Subsequently, Lijphart tested a number of hypothesized differences between countries with a majoritarian political system and countries with a consensus-based system. He applied and combined several techniques, such as regression analysis and scaling (to create indexes on which the countries in the database could be ranked and compared). His main finding was that consensus-based systems are qualitatively more democratic, because they are more open to diversity and societal participation.

■ The World Values Survey (see Box 4.2) was founded on Hofstede's 2001 study on culture, a piece of research that has been replicated in over 40 countries. Hofstede's study comprised questions (often with answering scales) on values and norms, attitudes and the behaviour of citizens. One of its most famous central concepts was the so-called power distance measure, which expresses the degree of hierarchy in society, both between groups in society, and between individuals. The large scale of the study allowed for a standardized index to be calculated, which made a comparison of different countries possible, and could help to explain why a certain democracy model will be successful in one country but will fail in another. Indexes like these can be created by means of scale construction or factor analysis.

Other forms of analysis with quantitative data

The statistical methods discussed above are the most popular forms of analytical testing in Public Administration research (see, for example, Box 10.2). However, there are numerous other options for analysing quantitative data. Some of these alternative techniques are based on different assumptions (for example, structural equation modelling, which proceeds from the principle of the covariance of variables instead of correlation), or are more suitable for variables at a lower level of measurement (for example, Q-sorting, which sorts respondents' opinions). For the analysis of variables over time, there are various specialized analytical techniques (such as time series, event history analysis and survival analysis). Yet other methods are more suitable for a so-called nested design, in which variables at different levels of measurement are analysed. An example is multi-level analysis, which can be used to link individual-level variables (for example, school performance) to institutional characteristics (of schools), or even certain features of a system (the educational system as a whole). Finally, there are diverse forms of regression analysis which allow for the analysis of dichotomous dependent variables or variables at a lower level of measurement (such as logit, probit, or log-linear analysis). Indeed, for nearly every possible research situation, a suitable technique can be found. Often it is useful to seek some expert advice first before actually deciding which statistical technique to use for analysing the research data.

10.6 RELIABILITY AND VALIDITY WHEN ANALYSING QUANTITATIVE DATA

In previous chapters, the subject of reliability and validity regularly cropped up. When it comes to statistical analysis, a few points have to be added to what has already been said.

First, the representativeness of the sample deserves some extra attention. According to the laws of probability, a random sample is representative, which is why randomization is usually the recommended approach. In practice, though, certain problems may arise – for example, non-response may lead to distorted results (see also Chapter 7). Always check the composition of your sample before doing a statistical analysis (see also the section on data inspection). If the sample turns out to be less than representative, there are several options to counter the negative effects this might have. For example, parts of the over-represented groups can be excluded from the analysis (selection), or the scores of certain units can be weighed proportionately to their representativeness (compare with recoding and processing). Of course, such manipulations should be carefully considered and reported.

Second, statistical analysis can suffer from so-called statistical artefacts, which are by-products of the calculations that are being carried out. I shall not go into the technical details here, but it will be clear that such features are undesirable. It is always important to check beforehand whether the data meet the assumptions of the analytical technique to be used, such as the normal distribution requirement. It can also help to exclude any outliers from the analysis, as such deviant scores can interfere with results (remember that statistics and probability operate on the basis of averages and means).

Third, statistical analyses are merely an aid for arriving at a theoretical explanation of a certain phenomenon: they are a means to an end, not an end in itself. Give thorough consideration to which analytical technique would be most suitable for the research aim you have selected, and also weigh up the possible advantages or disadvantages of the chosen technique (after all, no technique is perfect). Cannibalizing the data is not unethical, but care must be taken that statistics does not become the main purpose of the exercise.

Fourth, no analysis is ever complete, and a certain amount of unexplained variance will always remain (this is called the estimation error). Ideally, there would be no variance left at all after the analysis. On the upside, unexplained variance does provide some food for further thought.

FURTHER READING

Field, A. (2009, 3rd edition). *Discovering Statistics Using SPSS*. London: SAGE.

EXERCISES

1   Devise a questionnaire or (pre-structured) observation scheme on a subject of your own choice. Construct the accompanying code book, and conduct a small-scale study with the questionnaire or observation scheme. The main point here is to practise these matters; the intention is not to construct a large body of data. Enter the information you have

gathered into a data matrix, using, for example, SPSS. Go through all the necessary steps in the program, including the t-test described above. Write a short report on your findings, using illustrations in the form of tables and figures in which you present the results.

2 Read an article or report of your own choice in which the results of a statistical analysis are reported. Select one or more tables, and explain what exactly the researcher has done, and how this shows in the table. Use your own words to make clear that you understand what is depicted in the table. Do not make things too easy: choose a table that seems somewhat less clear-cut.

Chapter 11

Analysing qualitative data

It is a frequent misconception amongst researchers (and students) that analysing qualitative data is easier than doing statistics. In practice, conducting a systematic and scientifically sound qualitative analysis can be quite difficult. Perhaps the analysis of qualitative data makes even higher demands on the researcher, as it requires a great capacity for logical reasoning and the ability to oversee a large body of data.

Just as within research with quantitative data, a study with qualitative data basically consists of three phases: data collection, data ordering and the actual analysis. However, in inductive research – which often makes use of qualitative data – these phases seldom occur in sequence; rather, the process tends to be iterative or cyclical in character.

This chapter is based on two premises: namely, that although the analysis and interpretation of qualitative data will usually be an iterative process, it is still important to take a systematic approach. Only then can results be repeated (reliability) and do they gain credibility (validity). Below, I shall give some tips on how to achieve the right standards. I shall also refer frequently to the literature for more information on how to use certain analytical techniques.

11.1 QUALITATIVE DATA

Qualitative data are non-numerical units of information, for example statements, text or interview fragments, and images (photos, posters). Usually, qualitative data are unstructured and cannot be arranged hierarchically – contrary to quantitative data, for which we can distinguish different levels of measurement. Moreover, qualitative data are often hard to circumscribe. For example, it is not always clear where exactly a text fragment begins or ends: are we dealing with sentences, paragraphs, or entire pages?

To create the right configuration, the researcher will first have to structure the data and delineate the boundaries between the different units of information. Such structuring is done by means of coding: the researcher interprets the qualitative data, and subsequently assigns codes or labels to the different pieces of information. In this way, the data are categorized and subdivided, so that they can be compared at a later stage. The process of coding will be discussed at length below. First I shall outline some other characteristic features of qualitative data analysis.

The literature on qualitative research – as research with qualitative data is usually called – often goes far beyond a simple listing of methods for data collection and analysis. To most qualitative researchers, doing qualitative research is closely associated with their philosophy of science, which will usually be of the interpretative variety (see Denzin & Lincoln, 1998a, 1998b). Adherents of qualitative research prefer to focus on describing and understanding reality in the context in which actors operate or in which certain phenomena occur. Because they think that such aspects cannot be summarized in numbers, qualitative data are said to be needed, which would provide better insight into and do more justice to the complexity of reality (see, for example, Yanow, 1996). As this description suggests, sometimes qualitative research can seem more of a perspective on doing research than a true strategy, method, or technique. It should be added, though, that within the mainstream, different views are held on the exact nature of the qualitative research process (see Denzin & Lincoln, 1998a, 1998b, for an overview). Box 11.1 gives some examples of the many shapes that qualitative research can assume.

BOX 11.1 FORMS OF QUALITATIVE RESEARCH

■ Grounded theory is a research tradition that is geared at formulating specific theories which explain a certain case that is being studied. As this form of research tends to concentrate on one case only, it does not strive for generalization (compare Chapter 9). Sometimes the inductively developed theory is not merely bound up with the research subject, but also place- and time-specific, which means that the theory only applies to the particular situation studied. The researcher conducts the study in the research situation itself, using methods such as participant observation or open interviews. Cases, data sources and respondents are chosen for their theoretical value (or the contribution they might make to the theory that the researcher hopes to construct). In the course of research, several measurements are taken: the phases of data collection and analysis constantly alternate. Once the moment has been reached when the addition of more data would not contribute anything new to the theory, the study is ended.

- Ethnography refers to in-depth, descriptive studies of small groups of people, or some other restricted research situation. Ethnographic research often concentrates on groups in society who diverge from the norm, but are homogeneous in other respects (think of social minorities). It can also tackle subjects that are difficult to grasp, such as culture. The researcher tries to gain insight into what is happening in the group or situation, and translate these insights into an explanatory hypothesis. The approach is one of analytical induction; the researcher follows a predominantly inductive path, whilst using existing theoretical notions as well. Analytical induction also strives for falsification; if an existing theory is proved wrong, this can provide an impetus to further research. The process continues until the theory cannot be refuted any longer.

- Thick description aims to arrive at a detailed description (or understanding) of the phenomenon that is studied. Information is analysed whilst being gathered, and preferably regarded from several different angles. Language and subjects often constitute important sources of information; the context and history of the case under study will be taken into account as well (compare Chapter 3 on holistic approaches). The vital instrument in this type of research is the reflexivity of the researcher, who is both a participant and an outsider, and who can therefore regard the information that is collected from several different perspectives (see also action research in Box 2.1). In addition to the empirical data collected (such as interviews or documents), the notes and memos that the researcher makes on the procedure that is being followed, the decisions that are taken in the course of the study, and the actual observations made constitute a rich source of information. By testing the total body of information on its logical consistency, or contrasting it with other data, the events under study acquire meaning.

In this chapter, we will not concentrate on one particular analytical technique, but will mainly consider the different phases through which a researcher nearly always has to go when conducting a qualitative study. Indeed, the methodological pluralism of qualitative research makes it difficult to give firm and generally valid guidelines (compare Chapter 3 on regulative ideas). For more information on how to use certain techniques, I shall refer to the appropriate literature.

Qualitative research is typically geared towards the exploration and description of the research subject, which means that it is predominantly inductive in nature. This does not mean to say, however, that qualitative data would be unsuitable as an input for deductive research, as the examples given in Box 11.2 show.

BOX 11.2 EXAMPLES OF QUALITATIVE RESEARCH IN PUBLIC ADMINISTRATION AND PUBLIC MANAGEMENT

■ The work done by street-level bureaucrats (Lipsky, 1980) is often studied by means of case studies, in which observation methods are combined with interviews. Occasionally, questionnaires are used as well, or even experimental designs. Examples of such studies are easy to find in research on, for example, policemen, nurses and doctors, social workers, or teachers. These studies usually pay attention to different aspects of the daily work of the people concerned, including the impact of changes in their task load or work environment (e.g. new ICT systems, the introduction of performance measurement indicators), the interaction with clients, job satisfaction, and whether someone can influence new policy-making processes (and, if so, how they can exert an influence). As will be clear, the data collected in such studies are mostly qualitative. There are numerous publications (too many to list here) describing case studies of this type.

■ Rhodes, 't Hart, & Noordegraaf (2007) have used an ethnographic approach in their study of government elites, observing seven such elites in Sweden, the UK, the Netherlands, and the European Union (EU). Their study has resulted in a thick description, which is rendered in the form of a narrative. Besides giving an account of their observations and findings, the authors also pay attention to their own experiences during research, relating, for example, to the culture shock they underwent when joining the daily lives of government elites.

■ Knill and Lenschow (1998) have studied the implementation of EU environmental policies in Germany and the UK. Based on the literature on regulatory styles, they expected to find differences between these two countries as regards their level of compliance with EU legislation. To be more specific, they thought that Germany (which they characterized as 'an interventionist regulator') would strive after full compliance with all parties involved, whereas the UK was thought to favour flexibility and discretionary authority (adopting a mediating style). In practice, however, Germany's federalist structure turned out to be more conducive to decentralized implementation, contrary to the more centralist approach taken by the British executive. The implementation processes of two cases in each country were reconstructed by means of content analysis of official documents. The authors concluded that the more pressure there is exerted at the national level to implement a certain policy, the better the fit will be with national traditions and institutions, leaving a smaller so-called implementation gap.

11.2 COLLECTING AND ORDERING THE DATA

The first step after qualitative data have been collected is to start ordering them (compare Flick, 2002). In order to be able to do so, it is important that the data have been stored in a systematic manner. Miles and Huberman (1994, p. 45) advise using a clear index or filing system, so that every piece of information can be easily found when needed. There are numerous computer programs that can be used for setting up such a filing system, such as NVivo and ATLAS.ti. Such programs operate in a similar fashion: data are stored digitally in a database structure, which sorts the interview transcripts, the scanned documents, or the images collected. The program usually also provides room for adding research notes or memos with supplementary information about the study, which can come in handy during the analysis that will be conducted later. Besides storing all the information gathered, the computer program can analyse the data as well (hence the name: qualitative data analysis, QDA). More about this will be said below.

Using computer programs has several advantages (compare Robson, 2002, p. 462; Flick, 2002, p. 252–54). First, it allows the researcher to store a large body of data in a systematic manner. Also, usually diverse special functions are available for retrieving and analysing the research material, with far greater capacity than the average word processor or the human brain could offer. Besides, exchanging information and results with other researchers will be easier, with the annotation that these colleagues will have to know how to use the program as well. Regrettably, not all QDA programs are equally user-friendly.

The systematic storage of qualitative data will be vital to the success of the analysis to be conducted later. Moreover, if a computer program is used, it will be easier to add new or additional information that is being gathered in the course of the study. As stated earlier, incremental data collection is an important characteristic of most qualitative studies.

A few practical tips:

- Do not wait too long before actually storing the information you have collected. It is best to start this process straight away, right at the beginning of your research. For example, immediately after completing an interview, you can write a report or make a transcript, which you then store electronically in the computer.
- Use filenames that make sense. For example, store the file under the respondent's name, and add a label with the date of the interview. This will make it easier to find the right information later.
- Create a list of contents of all the information that has been gathered, subdivided by type. Relevant sub-categories could be: interview reports, documents, observations, or research notes (memos).
- Add new information directly, and continue to update the list of contents. By doing so, you will keep the overview.

Once the qualitative data have been stored, the information can be ordered conceptually. The aim is now to gain insight into which data or sub-categories will be relevant to the study, and what can be disregarded. In effect, the phase of data reduction – as this process is called – constitutes the first part of the analysis (compare Miles & Huberman, 1994, p. 10–12). The researcher does a so-called quick scan per data unit (which can be an interview transcript, a text or an image), and selects the data or parts thereof that will be included in the analysis. Needless to say, the data to be analysed are not selected at random. In a deductive study, the researcher will follow the guideline of the oper-ationalizations and the hypotheses developed earlier: these will help to decide what is relevant to the study, and what is not. In an inductive study, selecting the right data will be trickier, although the questions and concepts specified in the research problem will help to show the way (so-called sensitizing concepts). The researcher has to take care, by the way, to document all the choices that are made, and write these down in a log or memo. The log or memos will have to be stored as well, preferably in the same database as the one that was used for the qualitative data.

After the data selection, the main part of the analysis begins (see below). Yet even at this stage, the qualitative researcher will continue to gather new mate-rial, to supplement the information gathered before, or to add clarification to the interim analytical results. The additional material must be stored in the same systematic manner, and be judged on its relevance before it can actually be analysed.

11.3 ANALYSING THE DATA

In a nutshell, the analysis of qualitative data consists of dividing the data units into even smaller units, labelling these units with a code, and comparing the different codes with each other. This process is often one of trial and error, which places great demands on the researcher in terms of creativity and logical thinking (compare Miles & Huberman, 1994, p. 9; Robson, 2002, p. 456; Flick, 2002, ch.15; Silverman, 2011). Hard and fast rules cannot be given here. Below, I shall describe what the coding process usually involves. However, individual researchers can take a different path from the majority travels, depending on which methodological principles they prefer to follow (see also Box 11.4 on fuzzy set qualitative comparative analysis, QCA).

A code is a shorthand way of indicating what a certain qualitative data unit (such as a text fragment or interview report) actually means. It is, as it were, a brief summary of the main attributes or features of the unit. By assigning the same code to data units that pertain to the same or a similar subject, the researcher creates the possibility to compare the different data units. If a com-puter program is used – as will normally be the case – the code is stored as a key word, which can be used later to retrieve certain fragments, and compare and combine them with each other.

Codes can be assigned to all kinds of things: opinions, behaviours, motives, activities, meanings, relations, situations, events, or perceptions (Miles &

Huberman, 1994, p. 61). Besides the contents of a data unit, codes can also be used to classify or describe the situation in which the information was gathered. An example can illustrate this. Box 11.3 gives the transcript of an interview with an alderman in a fictive study on politicians' motives for going into politics. The interview report is divided into fragments of a single question plus answer. Every fragment is assigned one or several codes. Sometimes these will be situational codes (of the type of respondent, or the interview situation); sometimes the code is substantive (indicating the motive mentioned). In this particular interview, there was one fragment that did not render any relevant codes, but the interviewer persisted by probing for more information.

BOX 11.3   CODING AN INTERVIEW: EXAMPLE

Fragment 1

A is a 45-year-old male, who has been an alderman in municipality Z since 2004. He is responsible for the portfolio of Public Works and City Maintenance, and has joined the city council on behalf of Interest Z, a local party. He was interviewed in his office on a weekday afternoon.

Codes: Respondent alderman; Respondent male; Respondent member political party; Interview on weekday; Interview in work situation.

Fragment 2

Question: Can you tell me how you became an alderman?

Answer: Yes, of course. I'd been a party member for quite some time, but was never really active. With my full-time job [A is a solicitor, ed.], there was simply no time. But I was acquainted with several members of the council's parliamentary group, and of course my brother works with the council.

Codes: Motive membership party; Motive familiar with council; Motive family connections.

Fragment 3

Question: What does your brother do, if I may ask [extra question inserted, ed.]?

Answer: He runs the Department of Social Welfare. Because he works in the sector of social services, I couldn't become an alderman there, of course. That's why I was given the portfolio of Public Works.

(No codes.)

Fragment 4

Question: I see – maybe we can return to that point later. First I'd like to get back to my question of how you became an alderman.

Answer: Oh yes. Well, actually, it all went rather quickly. During the elections, we hadn't really gained or lost any seats, but as it turned out, Labour didn't have enough seats to obtain the majority. In the past, they always used to form the executive council – I think they had been in office in Z for some 12 years running. During the formation, they approached our group to form a coalition, and we did rather well. We could supply one alderman, and the party group thought that I might be suitable. I was a bit surprised, because I thought our leader might want to take on the job, but he said he'd rather stay in the parliamentary group – or it would have to do without his expertise and experience. Between you and me, if I'm honest, I think he didn't find the alderman salary that appealing. He's an estate agent, you see, and makes quite a lot of money.

Code: Motive forwarded by parliamentary group.

Fragment 5

Question: But wasn't the low pay a reason for you to refuse? After all, a solicitor usually has a good income.

Answer: Oh, my business can continue without me. And in this way, I could do something in return for the people of Z, which rather appealed to me. I used to be a member of the chamber of commerce, you know. And to be able to have a say in decisions, help to shape the region and what happens there; that was an attractive idea. As an alderman I can do even more; we have big plans.

Codes: Motive not financial; Motive previous experience in public domain; Motive serve the public good; Motive exerting influence; Motive help to shape the living environment.

Generating codes

Codes can be generated in several different ways. In a deductive study, the codes will correspond with the operationalizations, and are decided upon in advance. In an inductive study, on the contrary, the codes are only gradually developed, and refined during the process of analysis (open coding; Flick, 2002, p. 177). The inductive researcher usually starts by studying a number of data units, paying special attention to similarities (literally, or looking for synonymous materials) and differences (variations and contrasts) between the fragments that have been selected. To illustrate, in the interview in Box 11.3, alderman A mentions several motives for becoming active in politics. The researcher registers these motives by adding notes in the margin of the interview report, or marking parts of the text and labelling these with the aid of a computer program.

The researcher will use the codes initially constructed as a starting point for analysing the subsequent interview. Should any new motives be mentioned, the coding scheme has to be supplemented. If necessary, the analysis of the first interview is replicated to see whether the newly found codes were not missed out on earlier. This process is repeated until no new codes are found, which means that the researcher has arrived at a so-called exhaustive coding scheme. Some computer programs will even offer the option to let the computer generate codes, making the program count how frequently certain words or concepts appear. Of course, such a list is just a machine product, which has to be interpreted by the researcher afterwards. For example, the computer may have imputed several synonyms with separate codes, whereas in fact one single code would suffice. The list that ultimately results is a gross list, which will be ordered later (see below).

Different types of code

Codes can be simple numbers (see Chapter 10). Usually, though, they are concepts with a certain meaning or content, such as theoretical constructs, characteristics of the units of study, relations or mechanisms, conditions, or causes and consequences (Miles & Huberman, 1994, p. 70). Indeed, the process of coding can often be compared to that of developing axioms, constituting a form of 'backward operationalization' (see Chapters 3 and 4). A great deal of logical thinking is required at this stage; also, effective coding demands a certain degree of theoretical sensitivity (compare Flick, 2002). The researcher constantly has to look for patterns and themes in the data, and compare these with each other, so as to decide which different codes there actually are, and how relevant these will be for the ultimate aim of describing, understanding and explaining the research subject. The questions and concepts specified in the research problem will form a guideline here (see above). In addition, the researcher's expectations and theoretical knowledge will play a role (Flick, 2002, ch.15). This last factor can also create the risk of personal bias: the researcher may put a one-sided emphasis on certain themes or – conversely – fail to spot other features which could have been of interest. During the discussion on reliability and validity, I shall return to this point.

We can distinguish several types of code (Flick, 2002). Interpretative codes reflect a certain interpretation of a data fragment, such as the different motives specified in Box 11.3. Thematic codes are more interrelated constructs. To illustrate the use of thematic codes, 'motive' can be seen as one thematic code, which may be subdivided into different sorts of motive (family connections, political party, financial motives), each of which has either a positive or a negative relation with the research subject. As this shows, codes tend to interrelate, and show a certain order (see also below). Both interpretative and thematic codes are to do with content. Descriptive codes, on the other hand, are used to denote certain characteristics of a respondent or data source. They can also reflect the researcher's observations, or the physical aspects of the research situation (compare with situational codes, see Box 11.3).

It is important to keep well in mind that codes must be singular in meaning, mutually distinctive, and closely related to the theory. However, the intention should not be to create a separate code for each and every text fragment or data unit, which would make comparison between the various units impossible. A good code can be assigned to different fragments that all reflect comparable (or even synonymous) information. Conversely, one fragment that touches upon various subjects of interest can receive several different codes (see Box 11.3).

Irrespective of what codes exactly are developed and used by the researcher, all the choices made during this process must be well-founded and carefully documented. During the phase of generating codes, the researcher can keep a log or write memos (addressed to him- or herself) on what decisions were taken, and why.

Axial coding

Once an exhaustive set of codes has been generated, the next phase of the analysis begins: namely, that of axial coding (compare, for example, Flick, 2002, p. 181). The aim is now to concentrate on the patterns that can be found in the codes that have been assigned to the data. An example is the categorization of the different motives mentioned in Box 11.3. The researcher can decide to order such codes hierarchically, but the original codes can also be grouped (because they turn out to be related) or be subdivided (because, on second thoughts, they seem to relate to different things). Earlier, the procedure of following the content of codes was called thematic coding. When the researcher concentrates the analysis on a limited number of codes, we call this selective coding.

Generally speaking, the ordering of codes is needed to ensure that the analysis remains succinct (reduction), and also that the codes used in the analysis are comparable and theoretically interesting relations are identified. Ordering codes is an important step in the formulation and development of new theories (inductive research) or the decision making about the tenability of certain hypotheses (deductive research).

The results of the axial coding phase can be given in different formats, such as a taxonomic scheme or an arrow diagram. Figure 11.1 presents an example of a taxonomic scheme based on the interview in Box 11.3.

Interpretation and theory development

In the final phase of the qualitative data analysis, the researcher will try and generate new theories, to find answers to the research questions formulated in

1 Motives

    1.1 Political

    1.2 Personal

        1.2.1 Family connections

           1.2.1.1 Positive influence

           1.2.1.2 Negative influence

        1.2.2 Serving the public good

        1.2.3 Exerting influence (power)

    1.3 Financial

Figure 11.1
Example of a taxonomic scheme of codes

the beginning. In this phase, the data that have been collected and coded are integrated; the different codes are compared and contrasted with each other to search for patterns, cause and effect relations, and other forms of interconnection. Several techniques can be used for this. The handbook by Miles and Huberman (1994) provides the most comprehensive overview:

- Clustering persons, events and characteristics (for example, are aldermen with the same political allegiance inspired by similar motives?);
- Developing metaphors and analogies (sketching, for example, a prototypical course of events in the research situation);
- Counting the number of data units that go with a certain code, on the reasoning that the more frequently a certain feature is observed, the more important it will be for the description or explanation of the research problem (compare Box 11.4);
- Devising a theoretical construct by grouping codes that seem interrelated (compare with axial coding);
- Identifying intervening variables or sources of interference (see Box 6.1).

Yin (2008) mentions a few additional techniques, such as pattern matching. In deductive research, the technique of pattern matching tries to answer the question of whether the effects predicted (by the hypotheses) are indeed observed in reality. If they are not, the question arises whether an alternative explanation can be found for the empirical data that have been gathered. In inductive research, on the contrary, the focus will rather lie on the gradual development of an explanation for the phenomenon being studied. The researcher tries to trace the causes of what is observed in the research situation by putting the codes for causes and effects together. In this manner, building blocks for a new theory are created (see Chapter 3 on axioms); step by step, new variables (codes) are added to the model to develop the theory further. If necessary, a schematic overview can be made of the model, so as to show how exactly the theory works. Such an overview can take the shape of a checklist, a table, a matrix, an event flow chart, a network diagram of actors and relations, or a time bar (see Miles & Huberman, 1994, ch.5–6).

Finally, a number of other techniques can be used. For example, the researcher can do a chronological reconstruction (retrospectively, or prospectively to predict future events) by coupling codes to dates or years. Another option is to create a chain of events by linking cause-effect relations over time.

The computer program that is used for analysis will offer several algorithms for the techniques described here. For example, usually the researcher can do a search for combinations of two or more codes in a single data fragment (cause and effect), or try and distil different combinations in a certain fragment (for example, different codes found in one single interview, within a span of ten sentences of a document, or in interview reports of respondents who share a certain characteristic). For each combination of codes, the computer program will give a full overview of the data fragments in which a particular combination was encountered. The researcher can use this information to establish if the combination is relevant (for example, by counting the number of fragments in which the combination occurs), and what it means as to content (theoretical interpretation). Data fragments can also be used to illustrate the conclusions that have been drawn from the study; in the research report, the researcher can quote from interviews, or insert a passage from one of the documents that has been analysed.

BOX 11.4   FUZZY SET QUALITATIVE COMPARATIVE ANALYSIS (QCA)

New methods and techniques for the analysis of qualitative data are being developed all the time. Fuzzy set QCA is one of those new techniques (see Ragin, 2000). In essence, QCA enables researchers to analyse large sets of qualitative data – or ordinal data – in a systematic and comparative way. An example can illustrate best how it works: Vis (2007) used QCA to test for 16 countries whether they moved from a welfare state regime to a workfare regime – as some theorists would predict. Based on that theory, three central variables were identified and operationalized: the obligation to work (activation), the objective of maximal labour participation (generosity), and labour protection. Each country is assigned a score for each variable, based on a set of explicit decision rules. Such scores can be continuous or dichotomous, depending on the data and the preferences of the researcher. For example, in Vis's study protection was measured by an index based on a sum score on 14 relevant legal rules. This was a continuous score between 0 and 1.

Assigning scores can be done by the researcher him- or herself, or by independent experts. In the example, countries could be characterized as belonging to a certain type of welfare or workfare state (Vis distinguished five types), based on the total scores of all three variables, in different combinations and at different points in time. The hypothesized trend was not found for most countries, except in the case of Ireland.

11.4 THE RELIABILITY AND VALIDITY OF QUALITATIVE DATA ANALYSIS

The controllability and repeatability of qualitative data analysis is a far less clear-cut matter than it is in quantitative data analysis – after all, the greater part of the analysis takes place in the researcher's mind. This is why with qualitative data we usually do not speak of validity and reliability in a strict sense, but apply terms such as the comprehensibility of the analysis, its transferability, and the plausibility of the conclusions drawn. If the analysis is comprehensible, it can be repeated (reliability); transferability means that the results can be generalized (external validity); and plausibility corresponds with the notion of internal validity.

Opponents of qualitative research often contend that this form of research is too subjective: in essence, the research findings consist mainly of the researcher's own interpretations and are therefore, by definition, bound to just one person. Most qualitative data analysis is indeed subjective; however, certain measures can be taken to ensure reliability and validity. Several of these measures, such as triangulation, were already discussed in previous chapters (see Chapters 4 and 8). As regards coding, it has been stressed repeatedly that all the choices made during the analysis must be noted down in a log or memo. Another piece of advice is to have the coding scheme checked by other researchers, experts, or a group of respondents (in a member check). By inviting other people to comment, the researcher can ascertain and ensure a certain degree of inter-subjectivity and inter-researcher reliability (compare King, Keohane, & Verba, 1994, p. 157). If the analysis is carried out by a team of researchers, the recommended approach is to devise a protocol beforehand, in which the rules for gathering, storing and interpreting the data are specified (compare Chapter 8 on case studies).

A second objection typically raised by adversaries of qualitative research is that it is virtually impossible to prove causality with qualitative data. In principle, the same was said of quantitative data (see Chapter 10). It is true, though, that a qualitative data analysis will not give any indication of the (statistical) significance of results, which makes it far more difficult to arrive at firm conclusions. Moreover, qualitative research is often based on small numbers (think of case studies), which means there will not be enough power for the testing of hypotheses. It is for this reason that in some approaches such as grounded theory (see Box 11.1) the theory that is developed will only be considered applicable to the particular case that has been studied (situation, time and place).

In general, qualitative researchers are recommended to adhere to the following guidelines (Miles & Huberman, 1994; King et al., 1994):

- Make a good, representative selection of cases, units of study (respondents), and data sources. Because qualitative datasets are always sizeable, you need to be efficient in your approach. Do not be afraid to be selective, but keep a close tag on which data exactly are being gathered.
- Use a computer program during the phase of data collection, as well as for the analysis. By using a computer program, you will force yourself to take a systematic approach. Also, make memos and plenty of notes. Keep the empirical observations well separated from your research notes.
- Keep in mind that the researcher can be a source of interference with the research situation (compare Chapters 4 and 6). All researchers involved in the study will have to be well informed, and must be trained in the methods and techniques to be used.
- When analysing the data, keep an eye on unexpected or deviant results (outliers). If necessary, such information can be used to develop an alternative explanation (see Box 11.1 on analytical induction). Only ignore certain pieces of information if it is absolutely clear that they are redundant.
- Do not just aim for confirmation of your hypotheses or codes, but also look for counter-evidence (so, strive after falsification; Flyvbjerg, 2006). Counter-arguments force you to pay extra attention to building solid foundations for your theory.
- Try to replicate results by taking several different measurements in sub-units (see Chapter 8), or ask respondents for feedback in a member check.

FURTHER READING

Flick, U. (2002, 2nd edition). *An Introduction to Qualitative Research*. London: SAGE.

Miles, M.B., & Huberman, A.M. (1994, 2nd edition). *Qualitative Data Analysis: An Expanded Sourcebook*. Thousand Oaks: Sage Publishing Inc.

Silverman, D. (Ed.). (2011, 3rd edition). *Qualitative Research*. London: SAGE.

EXERCISES

1   There are several computer programs available for qualitative data analysis (QDA). You can download a demonstration version of NVivo or ATLAS.ti from the Internet. Use one of these programs to analyse a text or interview report (or use one of the examples in the demo). Follow the guidelines in the program (help function).

2   Conduct a few short interviews, and apply codes to the interview tran-
    scripts in the manner explained earlier. First create a gross code list, and
    proceed with axial coding to get a set of thematic codes and sub-codes.
    Describe the procedure you have followed, and how you have created
    your axial codes. Give a scheme as well.
3   An alternative for exercise 2: Use a limited set of documents (for example,
    policy memos) as input for a qualitative content analysis. First make a
    gross code list, and then proceed with axial coding. Explain what you have
    done and why. Give a graphical presentation of your findings as well.

Chapter 12

Reporting results

Every piece of research ends with a report of the results. After all, both in the scientific community and in society, research findings will only matter if they are published.

A report can be written in various ways, depending on which audience the researcher wishes to address. Also, as I shall explain in this chapter, different formats can be applied. I shall say a few words as well about what happens – or sometimes does not happen – with the results of research in Public Administration and Public Management.

12.1 FORUMS

Research findings may be of interest to diverse forums or groups, and often they will be considered relevant by more groups than one. It is customary for results to be reported in multiple publications, targeted at different audiences. We can distinguish four main forums.

The first is the scientific community, which consists of researchers, lecturers and students. Increasingly, scientific publications are intended to reach an international audience, and usually they are written in English, even if the research has taken place in a non-English-speaking country by non-English researchers (about which more will be said below).

A second important forum, which is especially relevant to practical research, is the sponsor, i.e. the person or organization that commissioned the study. As a rule, the sponsor will be mainly interested in the practical use of the study, and the research report will have to reflect this. Later in this chapter some tips will be given on how to write a report that meets the needs of sponsors and practitioners.

A closely related target group is that of society in general. Research in Public Administration and Public Management often serves an important public function; it leads to the accumulation of knowledge and – in many cases – contributes to the solution of practical issues. Disseminating knowledge does not necessarily mean, however, that a researcher has to be actively involved him- or herself in the public or political debate. The knowledge acquired can reach a wider audience via other channels as well (compare Pawson & Tilley,

2004). For example, if a study has been commissioned by a professional interest group, company or public organization, the researcher can simply report to the sponsor, who may later decide to share the information received with other parties.

Depending on their philosophy of science, researchers differ in opinion about whether and how far they should participate in the public debate. Empirical-analytical researchers are usually hesitant about this, fearing it might conflict with their goal of staying objective. Other researchers, on the contrary, consider it their duty to make a contribution to society. As a discipline, Public Administration and Public Management are characterized by applied research, which owes (the greater part of) its existence to active participation in the public debate (see Chapter 1).

Last, but by no means least, there is the forum of the units of study or respondents. Respondents have actively contributed to the study, usually on a voluntary basis and at the expense of their own time and cost, and reporting to this group is a way of thanking them for their trouble. Indeed, it is of vital importance to stay on good terms with the respondents, so that they remain willing to participate in any follow-up studies (compare Chapter 7). Respondents reports, which give the survey results, can help to prevent respondent attrition.

Respondent attrition can also be countered by other means, which brings us to the subject of the codes of conduct for researchers, or their professional ethics. For several scientific disciplines, such a professional code of conduct has been specified, usually by the professional association (see, for example, codes for psychological researchers or for researchers who work with human subjects) or by universities for its academic staff members. There is no specific international code for research in Public Administration and Public Management yet, but there are some general codes, like the one developed by the European Union (EU), which all recipients of research grants have to abide by (ESF, 2011).

Generally speaking, researchers have to abide by five ethical rules (compare Burnham, Gilland, Grant, & Layton-Henry, 2008, p. 286). These rules apply to all phases of research, including that of reporting. The five ethical rules for research are:

- Beneficence. A study should be positive in its aim, which means that it has to constitute an attempt to contribute to the acquisition of knowledge or the solution of a problem. Research may not be intended to do harm – to people or otherwise. The case may arise, however, that the knowledge to be acquired might lead to, for example, someone being prosecuted (think of research on integrity), or the abolition of a certain policy or subsidy. The researcher has to consider such likely consequences beforehand, and decide whether this aspect of the study is acceptable or not.
- Veracity. Research should never be misleading. A study may require that the units of study are not fully informed about the main research aim. For example, in certain experiments it is important that the test population remain naive (see Chapter 6). In such cases, the researcher will have to explain to people afterwards what the study meant to achieve. Also, before

the research is actually carried out, the ethical commission has to give permission for the units of study to be temporarily misled.

■ Privacy. The units of study have the right to refuse to participate in the study, or to withhold information. The researcher has to respect such decisions, and needs to stress (for example, in the instructions to the questionnaire) that the respondent is free to refrain from replying to certain questions. Sometimes, however, the researcher will want to prevent non-response (think of questions on taboo subjects), and will try to force an answer. In an online questionnaire this can be easily achieved as it can be designed in such a manner that the respondent can only proceed to the next question if the previous one has been answered. Such constructions should not be decided upon lightly, though, and require serious forethought (and sometimes permission from the ethics committee).

■ Confidentiality. The researcher has to reach a clear agreement with the units of study and the sponsor on how exactly the information will be used, both by the researcher and by the sponsor. Sometimes it can turn out to be quite difficult to guarantee anonymity: an obvious example is that of a unique case being studied, a situation that frequently arises in Public Administration and Public Management (see Chapter 1). The matter of how the research data will be used needs to be negotiated well in advance.

■ Informed consent. The researcher has to gain permission from the units of study to carry out the study and publish the results later. These days, it is customary to draw up a special contract for subjects or respondents, sometimes with a clause of confidentiality. As regards the publication of results, researchers frequently do not own the full copyright of their own research findings. Sometimes the sponsor decides if and when the study results may be published in a format that is accessible to other forums. If the results are published in a journal or a book, it is usually the publisher that gains the copyright.

12.2 REPORTING FORMATS

A number of formats can be applied when reporting to the forums mentioned. Although often a particular format will be most suitable for a particular forum, in principle various formats can be used for various forums. Research results can also be reported in multiple publications, for different forums and in different formats. To give an example, in a multiple case study (see Chapter 8), results can be reported in an overall report reflecting the entire study, or be given per case studied. It is not unusual either to write a partial report, in which a particular sub-question is addressed (see Chapter 2). Due to the influence of the modern-day 'publish or perish' culture (one of the most important performance indicators in the scientific community is a researcher's publication rate), there are ever more researchers who go for the option of publishing several articles on the same study (cannibalizing one's research).

A study can be reported in a written format or in non-written form. For written forms, there is a choice between:

- An article in a scientific, international, refereed journal. The number of journals is virtually endless, offering researchers from all kinds of disciplines (such as economics, political science, or sociology) the possibility to publish on a certain subject (such as the EU, Public Management, or political theories), a specialized policy field (education, healthcare, planning or financial management), or a certain methodology (for example, action research). Box 12.1 presents some examples of journals that have published Public Administration and/or Public Management articles in the past years. Do note that ever more journals are only published online.

- Scientific book publications come in various shapes and forms, such as monographs (written by one or several scientists), edited volumes (with chapters authored by different people and one or more editors being responsible for the book's composition and end result), or theses (also called dissertations: books written to acquire a PhD degree).

- A research report or policy advice. This format is typically used to report to the sponsor; it is also the most suitable format for policy research (see Chapter 1). The report will consist of an introduction, a motivation, the study's main conclusions and some recommendations. See also the section on writing for practice below.

- A respondents report. A respondents report is meant for those who have participated in a study, in particular when the study has used questionnaires. It gives the first results of the data analysis, often in the form of a number of descriptive statistics (see Chapter 10). Reports like these usually follow the order of the questions used, and provide an overview of the main findings per question.

- A case study report. In case studies, the researcher usually writes a separate report for each case study. Such reports are characterized by a high density of information (see Chapter 9 on thick description), listing in detail all the information that has been gathered. A scientific article on a case study will usually give only a short summary of the individual case study reports. Case study reports can be organized in different ways: for example, information can be presented in a chronological order (for more options, see below).

- A professional publication for practitioners. A professional publication is an article in a specialist journal for practitioners. It can also be a self-published book, which is produced without the intermediary of a publisher, or a handbook. Publications like these are often more popular in tone, and give practical tips and guidelines for how to solve certain problems, for example using a more efficient working method, or ways of developing a new management instrument or organizational structure.

- A popular science publication. Scientists frequently contribute to the public debate by writing critical articles or op-eds for national papers, or by giving interviews to weeklies or monthlies. Sometimes, too, they contribute to a radio or TV programme, such as the news, a series on science (think of the Open University, for example), or a talk show.

BOX 12.1   SELECTION OF INTERNATIONAL, REFEREED JOURNALS IN PUBLIC ADMINISTRATION AND PUBLIC MANAGEMENT (IN ALPHABETICAL ORDER)

Administration & Society, American Review of Public Administration, Governance, International Journal of Public Administration, International Public Management Journal, International Review of Administrative Sciences, Journal of Comparative Policy Analysis, Journal of European Public Policy, Journal of Public Administration Research & Theory, Journal of Public Policy, Local Government Studies, Policy & Politics, Public Administration, Public Administration & Development, Public Administration Review, Public Management Review, Public Performance & Management Review, Public Personnel Management.
    (For a full list of journals, see your library catalogue.)

The format of popular science publications brings us to the subject of non-written formats. Besides cooperating in radio or TV programmes, or publishing on the Internet, researchers can also show their work directly to the sponsor, or attend national or international conferences. They can also participate in workshops or seminars organized for scientists or practitioners, where they present their findings and discuss them with others (see, for example, the increasing number of TEDx online seminars).

To generate interest in noteworthy research results, it is customary to publish a press release after having concluded a study (see Box 12.2).

BOX 12.2   GUIDELINES FOR WRITING A PRESS RELEASE

1   Only write a press release if you genuinely have anything new or noteworthy to report. Send your text preferably via email to press agencies and newspaper editors, and do so early in the morning.
2   Choose a grabbing title, which adequately expresses what the study is about, but is concise all the same. Confine yourself to just one subject per press statement.
3   In the first paragraph (the *lead*), you outline the main research findings, and indicate their scientific or societal interest. Try to explain in two or three sentences who has discovered what, when and where, and why this should be important (the five w's).

---

4 In subsequent paragraphs, separated from each other by a line space, you can describe certain elements or sub-items. Think like a journalist: what would interest people? If the editor or journalist wants to know more, they will contact you.

5 Pay close attention to layout. Indicate at the top of the page that the text concerns a press release, and list your personal details (name, phone number, email address) at the bottom, so that the person reading the press statement knows where to contact you. The text should not exceed one sheet of A4. Do not add appendices, and clearly state the date on which the statement was written.

6 Use the spell check and grammar check functions. Avoid using abbreviations or difficult jargon.

7 Never give in to the temptation to lard your statement with super-latives. Another no-no is phoning the editor to ask if your press statement will be published.

A final note of warning: do bear in mind that journalists will want to write a popular article, which will be less nuanced than a scientific publication would be. Ask the journalist if you can review the article before it is actually published, and reserve the right to correct any mistakes (in particular regarding quotations).

12.3 THE PURPOSE OF REPORTING RESEARCH RESULTS

In a commissioned study, writing the research report usually signals the moment when 'the goods' are delivered that have been promised to the sponsor. The report concludes the researcher's job, and the sponsor gets the wished-for advice or policy design (see Chapter 2 on research aims). Reporting the research findings to others can serve other purposes as well. In Chapter 3, I explained about the accumulation of knowledge; nearly every scientific study contributes to our knowledge of society and reality. Needless to say, such a contribution can only be made if research results are disseminated in the scientific community. Newton's famous phrase 'standing on the shoulders of giants' makes this quite clear: a true body of knowledge (see Chapter 1) can only be built if researchers share and exchange their theoretical and empirical insights. (By the way, when referencing other people's work, it is important to adhere to the right conventions (see Box 3.5), and fully acknowledge the shoulders on which you are standing.)

A third goal or function of reporting research findings has to do with the aim of contributing to society (compare Pawson & Tilley, 2004). This aim can be achieved by making knowledge public and letting it be used by others, or by trying to contribute to political or social agenda setting. For example, a researcher can strive to get a certain policy annulled by showing what disadvantages its implementation would bring. Such an approach closely relates to action research (see Box 2.1). It has to be said, though, that in practice research findings are not always taken seriously, or sometimes fail to meet with a positive reaction (see Box 12.4 below).

A final, less idealistic, reason for publishing research results is the desire of most scientists to showcase their work or reach certain publication targets. Academic sponsors often take a researcher's number of publications as a measure of quality, which will influence their decision whether or not to subsidize a study. Research institutes such as universities, too, increasingly operate on a 'publish or perish' basis (Harzing, 2011), using publication rates as a performance indicator in their human resources policy.

To measure a researcher's publications output, several systems can be applied. In most systems, scientific and international publications are given a greater weight than articles in professional journals or articles written in someone's native language (if this is not English, that is). As a consequence, people increasingly strive after publishing in internationally renowned scientific journals. Another weighing factor is which particular journal or publisher prints the article or research report. Scientific journals are ordered or ranked by impact; the more often the articles from a certain journal are cited, the more prestigious it is, and the higher the rank it is assigned. For researchers themselves, such rankings are created as well. A good example is the so-called citation or h-index, which expresses how frequently a certain author is quoted, and how highly the author's scientific output is rated in the international scientific community.

Some people think it could be useful to create a similar index for the societal value of researchers and their research. It may come as no surprise that the adherents of different philosophies of science are divided on this subject.

12.4 WRITING DOWN THE RESULTS

Writing a report is an essential part of research. The way in which the results will actually be reported has to be specified in the research design (see Chapter 5). It is important to keep in mind that writing a research report is a sizeable task – irrespective of the format chosen or which forum will be addressed – and enough time must be planned for this. The actual writing of the report usually takes place in stages; interim drafts can be given to read to colleagues or the sponsor (or the supervisory board: see below). By asking people to read along and comment, you can improve the quality of your texts. It can also create a platform, and be a means of gaining the sponsor's acceptance of the conclusions of the study.

A few general guidelines

Numerous handbooks can be found that give instructions on how to write a research report (see, for example, Dunleavy, 2003, on how to write a dissertation). Of course, a good command of language is a must. Also, you should always check on typos and linguistic mistakes in the grammar and spelling. A few other guidelines can be given:

- Be precise and accurate, and avoid ambiguous language. For example, instead of saying 'research has shown that', you should refer to the authors whose research you mean.
- Motivate all the choices you have made in the course of the study (think of reliability and validity: see Chapter 4), and build a sound set of well-founded conclusions. It is important that the conclusions can be traced back directly to the research that has been done, or that you indicate that something concerns uncertain or untested interpretations.
- If the units of study have been guaranteed anonymity, this should be respected in the entire report. Striking details, which could betray the identity of a certain organization or person, must be handled with care. In case studies, you can solve part of the problem by using fictive names for the cases.
- Clearly specify what sort of contribution has been made by third parties such as respondents, key informants, fellow researchers, or experts. If the report is authored by several people, the authors' names must be listed alphabetically, or in an order that expresses their relative contributions (the person who has put in most work is mentioned first, etc.). In some accreditation systems for scientific research, the number of publications someone has to their name may depend on whether they were mentioned as the first or second author of an article.
- Adhere to the appropriate conventions for citations and literature references. Avoid all semblance of plagiarism: never copy texts without giving your source, and use quotations sparingly. Write your own text, but give references to sustain your argument.
- Choose a clear, concise title that reflects the contents of the study. Literary-sounding titles may seem appealing, but are not always suitable. For example, if someone is searching for literature references during the preparatory research stage (see Chapter 1) or when developing a theoretical framework (see Chapter 3), usually the title of a publication will be seen first. If this title does not clearly express the subject of the book or article, it will be disregarded and not be cited.
- Write a summary, which you preferably place at the beginning of the report. A summary of a scientific publication (called an abstract) has a different format from an executive summary in a professional journal. An abstract is a succinct summary stating the research questions and the main conclusions of the study; it is a mini version of an article or chapter, usually comprising fewer than 200 words. Contrary to a normal summary, the abstract does not give any information about how the research developed whilst being carried out. An executive summary provides an overview of the research question, the conclusions of the study and all recommendations (see also below).
- Choose a clear, logical order for your argumentation. Explain the set-up chosen to the reader: take your readers by the hand, as it were, and guide

them through the text by regularly indicating which step will be taken next, and why. Some authors prefer to give their conclusions first and only then explain what has brought them to these conclusions; others prefer the format of building up to a climax (the conclusion). Styles and tastes differ, but do take care to adhere to the same style throughout, to guarantee readability and avoid confusion on behalf of the reader.

■ Before actually starting to write the report, make a plan or design. A list of contents provides a first systematic ordering, which will facilitate the writing process later.

Scientific writing

In deductive research, the scientific reporting usually follows the logic of the research itself (compare Robson, 2002, p. 505–6). The article or book starts with an introduction, in which the research problem, the literature review, and the scientific and societal relevance of the study are set out. This is followed by an introductory outline of the rest of the text. After the introduction, the theoretical framework is delineated, resulting in a number of hypotheses. After the operationalizations, the research design is explained and motivated (think of reliability and validity), after which the results of the analysis are presented. The report ends with a set of conclusions, which constitute the answers to the original main research question and sub-questions. In practice, the conclusions do not just concern the contents of the research, such as which hypotheses have been rejected or confirmed, but they also specify what the findings mean with respect to the validity of the theoretical framework. The latter is sometimes also labelled separately as 'discussion'.

With regard to inductive research, there is no fixed format; the way in which the argument is built depends on which particular methods have been employed. For example, narrative research and grounded theory (see Box 11.1) each have their own specific format. A potential rule of thumb is to use the different phases of the inductive study as a structure for the research report: the introduction (research problem, literature) is followed by a discussion of the method and the research design chosen, a description of the data that have been collected, the results of the analysis, the discussion (as a building block for theory development), and finally the conclusions (the answers to the research questions). Actually, the main difference with the deductive format is the point at which the theoretical framework is discussed (see Box 12.3).

BOX 12.3 MODEL FOR REPORTING RESEARCH RESULTS

■ Introduction: research problem, relevance, reading guide
■ Theoretical framework (in deductive research)
■ Research design: strategy, methods, techniques, sampling frame, etc.
■ Results of empirical study and analysis (choose a clear order)

- Building blocks for theory development (in inductive research)
- Conclusion: answers to research questions, reflections on the study, recommendations
- Bibliography
- Appendices: measurement instruments, lists of respondents and data sources, coding schemes

The deductive format is especially useful for experiments and surveys. In case of desk research or a case study, the model chosen for an article or book can vary, depending on the particular research design that has been followed. In case studies, results are often published per case in separate case study reports, which can vary structurally as well (compare Yin, 2008; Miles & Huberman, 1994, p. 301–4; Robson, 2002, p. 512–13). One option is to describe for each case what the research problem was (introduction plus literature), which method was chosen and how the case was selected, followed by a description of the find-ings, the analysis and the conclusions. In effect, this creates a deductive format. A drawback of such a model is that the text can become repetitive, because each separate case is first described (findings) and only then analysed. Such repetition or reiteration can be prevented by integrating description and analysis. A more narrative format can be chosen as well: for example, an historical or chronological overview of the case can be given. This model often works well when reporting a qualitative content analysis.

For multiple case studies, the researcher can choose to describe the cases studied as a series, or to order them in terms of certain theoretical variables (constructs). This can only be done, however, if a deductive research design has been followed, with an accompanying theoretical framework and a set of operationalizations. In an inductive multiple case study design, the patterns observed (see Chapter 11 on axial coding) can function as a guideline for writing the report. The conclusions will then consist of a set of axioms (see Chapter 3).

Academic writing style

The academic writing style is characterized by a businesslike, neutral tone. Dull as this may sound, scientific publications are not meant to be journalistic pro-ducts or literary prose. Theoretical and methodological jargon has to be used consistently and appropriately, so that the scientific reader will know on which theories the researcher builds. This will generate additional interest, and raises the possibility that the research results will be used by others. What is more, definitions are often contested ground, and by using terminology in a consistent manner, a lot of criticism can be prevented.

Opinion differs greatly on the use of personal pronouns ('I'). It is generally agreed upon, however, that frequent use of passive constructions makes a text less reader-friendly. It is important to find the right balance between a readable, fluent text and meeting scientific quality criteria (see Boxes 3.5 and 10.1). One way of creating a livelier text is by inserting quotes from interviews or documents that have been analysed, although such means should be used sparingly. A quote should not be taken as evidence or support of a conclusion, but only be meant to illustrate the main argument. Also pay close attention to layout, and use tables and figures to create more variation. Another way of keeping your account lively is to put certain chunks of information in an appendix instead of including them in the main text. Think, for example, of questionnaires, interview manuals, respondent lists, data sources, coding schemes, and all such detailed background information. Do bear in mind that the bibliography is not an appendix, but forms part of the text.

Finally, it is important to create a clear distinction between findings (facts), the interpretation of the findings by the researcher, assessments (in terms of scores, scales, or evaluations), and conclusions or recommendations (see also below).

Review procedure for scientific publications

Before being published, scientific articles and books are usually reviewed by so-called referees. Referees are fellow researchers and academics who are active in the same field, who read the draft article or book to judge it on its merit (peer review). Often the peer review will be double-blind, with the referee and the author remaining unaware of each other's identity. In this manner, personal details and relations (such as admiration for the other's work, or someone's good or bad reputation) cannot play a role, and objectivity is guaranteed. The editorial board of the journal or publishing house uses the referees' comments to decide whether the article or book meets the required standards. Sometimes several drafts are needed to reach the right level of quality, or the author has to try more than one journal before succeeding in placing an article. Because of the refereeing process, it often takes quite a while before a book or article is actually published, especially if revisions are needed. Indeed, researchers who want to publish in a scientific journal or with an academic publisher must be able to handle (sometimes severe) criticism. (For some practical guidelines, see also Germano, 2001.)

Writing for practical purposes

Most tips given so far also apply to reports intended for practical usage, by sponsors or other agents in society. For example, it is always worthwhile to strive after a lively and readable text. Usually, when writing an advisory report, a scientific format will be suitable, although sometimes a sponsor may request a different type of text. The main interest of most sponsors tends to lie in the conclusions and recommendations of the study, which means that the theoretical framework need not receive that much attention. For similar reasons, information of a more technical nature, such as the research material and the methodology followed, are often best put in an appendix instead of the main text. This will keep the report accessible to the layperson.

Generally speaking, writing for practical purposes diverges from scientific writing in two major respects. First, an executive summary has to be given for practitioners, such as managers or policymakers, who wish to apply the research findings to everyday practice. Second, sometimes a so-called supervisory board is installed, which can consist of representatives of the sponsor or the organizations studied, people active in the field, independent experts, or representatives of certain other interested parties (stakeholders). The supervisory board discusses with the researcher how the study is progressing and what knowledge it will render. The board also comments on any interim reports, hereby guarding the quality and practical use of the study. The obligation to report to the board means that the researcher has to answer for any decisions that have been made; also, results must be presented at regular intervals. Such interim reporting has to be incorporated in the planning (see Chapter 5).

12.5 PRESCRIPTION

Most research in Public Administration is geared at everyday practice. Prescription, in the form of making recommendations and giving advice, usually forms a principal ingredient of the reporting phase (see the regulative cycle discussed in Chapter 3 and the research aim in Chapter 2). Prescription is not something to be done casually, or just on an informal basis (Pawson & Tilley, 2004, p. 210–11); it is a value-driven and normative activity. Do take care to avoid voicing just your own opinion (bias); readers should be able to trace the recommendations made back to the study. Be aware, too, that implementation of your recommendations may have important social consequences, for example the discontinuation of a certain policy, or the reallocation of financial sources (see Chapter 1 on the relation between research in Public Administration and policymaking).

Functions of prescription

A researcher can make recommendations to other researchers or to practitioners. Recommendations for future research indicate what sort of research is needed to gather new, relevant knowledge on a certain subject. They can specify or state something about content (what needs to be studied), or consist of advice as to which theories, research situations or methods need further attention or might be suitable for future studies (the how).

The nature of recommendations for practitioners depends on the aim and subject of the research. For example, if a study has concentrated on a practical problem, recommendations will take the shape of suggested solutions. The researcher provides insight into what caused the problem, reporting on, for example, the reconstruction (description) or bottleneck analysis (diagnosis) that has been carried out. This information can serve as a basis for suggested instruments for solving the problem, which may vary from a new policy design to a suitable organizational format. Usually several alternatives will be sketched, so that the sponsor can make their own choice. For each alternative, an indication must be given of the costs of implementing the measure, in terms of time, money and human resources. (For some practical tips, see below.)

If a study were mainly meant to acquire substantive knowledge, such as in research for policy purposes (see Chapter 1), the recommendations that the researcher gives will bear a different character. In such cases, the purpose will be to give policymakers insight into which factors should be taken into account when new policies are developed, and which criteria can be applied for deciding between the different alternatives. For example, if the researcher foresees that implementing policy scenario A would be far less costly than scenario B, the first alternative can be recommended. Of course, other factors need to be considered as well, such as the legitimacy of a certain policy, and what would be fair to different social groups. In this manner, the researcher can sketch the consequences of different policy alternatives, which insights policy-makers can subsequently use for motivating their policy choices (Pawson & Tilley, 2004).

A third possible function of prescription is closely related to evaluation research. Evaluations are used to judge certain events or behaviours, and can constitute a basis for formulating recommendations on how such events or behaviours can be prevented in future, or what an alternative way of handling a particular situation could be. A code of conduct can even be developed, or existing policies can be adapted (compare with parliamentary inquiries, which have a similar function).

Practical tips for formulating recommendations

It is important to formulate recommendations in practical terms, specifying, for example, *who* should do *what* under which *conditions* (time, money), in order to achieve a certain *effect*. Instead of just giving the advice to 'do something about the organizational culture', it is better to state that 'a more open organizational culture might be attained by the board by sending a weekly update on the reorganization to all personnel, who can then respond via email to the board'. Also, recommendations should clearly follow from the research findings (no 'afterthoughts'). Often it is best to provide several options to the reader. These can consist of several recommendations on the same subject, or be variations of one and the same recommended change to be implemented.

Recommendations are usually formulated whilst the study is still in progress, instead of only after the analytical phase. As an outsider, the researcher can provide a fresh perspective, and will be sooner inclined to question certain aspects of an existing situation. Suggestions for improvement or solving a problem may also present themselves during interviews with people. You can make a note of such thoughts or ideas in the log or a memo (see Chapter 11) to store them for later use. Finally, certain suggestions may arise during discussions with colleagues. By involving as many people as you can, you will increase the chance of your recommendations being accepted and followed (compare Pawson & Tilley, 2004, and Robson, 2002, p. 517). This is an extremely important point because, as the examples in Box 12.4 show, research results do not always receive an equally warm welcome.

BOX 12.4   UNWELCOME TIDINGS*

Research results do not always find favour with others, whether this concerns sponsors, such as social organizations or companies, or fellow scientists (whose work may have been used or discussed in the study). Disgruntled parties can respond in different ways, from trying to ignore a study (by mothballing the results), to refuting findings and conclusions by claiming that they are incorrect, or blame the methodology followed ('the study has been carried out in a sloppy manner, which means its conclusions must be disregarded'). For example, the sample can be labelled as non-representative. Sometimes people say that measurement errors have not been corrected or invalid questions have been posed to the respondents. The most extreme reaction is for the researcher him- or herself to be discredited, with damage to their reputation as a result. Several infamous examples can be mentioned of such smear campaigns, which have seriously harmed people's careers.

As to what inspires such attacks, big financial interests can be at stake in research; after all, studies in Public Administration and Public Management often instigate an evaluation of existing policies or the development of new ones. The conclusion that a certain policy proves ineffective, or that certain plans are bound to fail, will be unpleasant news to proponents of that policy, but will also find a sympathetic ear with opponents. If a study refutes the results of fellow researchers, concerns may arise that further research grants will be withdrawn. Doing research costs money, and the competition between researchers, research agencies and consultants can be quite fierce.

Criticism of one's research can be parried in different ways, varying from admitting that mistakes have been made (and adjusting the research report accordingly), negotiation (trying to reach a compromise, or demanding compensation), to retaliation (leaking information or finding counterarguments).

* 'Unwelcome tidings' refers to the title of a Dutch book on this topic, authored by Köbben and Tromp in 1999. It describes a number of examples of mothballing and other negative reactions to research. In many cases, these examples concern studies in Public Administration and Public Management.

The impact of Public Administration and Public Management research

As Box 12.4 shows, recommendations are not always followed, and advice is not always taken. This can be caused by something as simple as a political reshuffle, which leads to a shift in priorities or policy preferences (compare Pawson & Tilley, 2004). Other circumstances that can render a running study obsolete, or even redundant, are changing economic circumstances (think of the recent financial crisis), the introduction of a new law, or a natural disaster or some other big crisis (for example, the effects 9/11 on national and international security policies). Closely tied as it is to policymaking and policymakers, in Public Administration the actual impact of a study is never a matter of course.

Having said all this, researchers can take certain measures to ensure that their research findings do make a difference (compare Pawson & Tilley, 2004). First, it is vital to match the research problem as closely as possible with the questions posed by policymakers and practitioners: the better the two correspond, the more likely it is that the study will make a difference (Verschuren & Doorewaard, 2010). Also, when reporting results, it is important to try and choose a format that meets the sponsor's wishes. Remember to include an executive summary, and give carefully formulated and qualitatively sound recommendations. Finally, it might be useful to inquire beforehand (*ex ante*) if a certain piece of advice is likely to meet with a positive response. This remark should not be taken as an invitation to manipulate research results; rather, the idea is to arrive at recommendations that can and will be listened to by the sponsor (Pawson & Tilley, 2004). Indeed, doing research that leaves an impact is one of the things that makes Public Administration and Public Management such a useful subject of study – as well as great fun!

FURTHER READING

Dunleavy, P. (2003). *Authoring a PhD: How to Plan, Draft, Write and Finish a Doctoral Thesis or Dissertation*. Basingstoke: Palgrave Macmillan.

Pawson, R., & Tilley, N. (2004). *Realistic Evaluation*. London: SAGE.

EXERCISES

1   Reports by the National Audit Office (NAO) do not just give research results but also recommendations. Select an NAO report (you can find reports on their website), and read the recommendations. Then search the Internet for a response from, for example, parliament or a ministry (tip: media attention can direct you to who has responded to a certain report, but make sure to look up the official response document). What can you conclude from what you have read? Was the report well received? What will happen with the recommendations?

2   Find two scientific articles on a subject of your own choice; use the digital databases in the university library, Google Scholar or some other search engine. Study these articles on their format, paying attention to things such as the quality of the abstract, the way the argument is built, the use of jargon, tables and figures, and the conventions for literature references followed. What target group does the publication have? What does it try to achieve, and is this explained to the reader?

3   Read two articles from a professional journal of your choice, and do a similar analysis as in exercise 2. Do these articles strike you as different compared to the articles you studied for exercise 2? What differences can you see?

4   Use one of the texts from the previous exercises to formulate a number of concrete recommendations. Be as practical as possible: indicate who should do what, what effects are to be achieved, and which conditions (time, money and instruments) might be of influence on the results.

5   Numerous organizations publish their own press statements. Look up a few examples of such press statements on the website of a university, ministry or research institution. Try and ascertain how much media attention the press statements received: can you find newspaper articles about them? (If so, check to see whether certain passages were copied literally or a selective form of quotation was applied.)

6   Use the guidelines given in Box 12.1 to write a press statement on an event that has taken place in your own life. What matters here is the exercise; you need not present some earth-shattering study result (for example, 'student discovers that his college room is infested with mice').

Bibliography

Allison, G.T. (1980). *Public and Private Management: Are they Fundamentally Alike in all Unimportant Respects*. Proceedings for the Public Management Research Conference, 1980 – US Office of Personnel Management.

Allison, G.T., & Zelikow, P. (1999, 2nd edition). *Essence of Decision: Explaining the Cuban Missile Crisis*. New York: Longman.

Babbie, E. (1992, 6th edition). *The Practice of Social Research*. Belmont, CA: Wadsworth Publishing Company.

Bass, B.M. (1990). From Transactional to Transformational Leadership: Learning to Share the Vision. *Organizational Dynamics* (winter), 19–31.

Bennett, C. (1991). What is Policy Convergence and What Causes It? *British Journal of Political Science, 21*(2), 215–33.

Benoit, K., Laver, M., Arnold, C., Pennings, P., & Hosli, M.O. (2005). Measuring National Delegate Positions at the Convention on the Future of Europe Using Computerized Word Scoring. *European Union Politics, 6*(3), 291–313.

Black, T.R. (1999). *Doing Quantitative Research in the Social Sciences*. London: SAGE.

Blatter, J., & Haverland, M. (2012). *Designing Case Studies: Explanatory Approaches in Small-N Research*. Basingstoke: Palgrave Macmillan.

Bots, P.W.G., & van Daalen, E. (2007). A Design Method and Support Tool for Decision-making Programs. In I. Mayer & H. Mastik (Eds.), *Organizing and Learning through Gaming and Simulation: Proceedings of ISAGA 2007*(pp. 67–77). Delft: Eburon.

Bouckaert, G., Peters, B.G., & Verhoest, K. (2010). *The Coordination of Public Sector Organizations: Shifting Patterns of Public Management*. Basingstoke: Palgrave Macmillan.

Bozeman, B., & Bretschneider, S. (1994). The 'Publicness Puzzle' in Organization Theory: A Test of Alternative Explanations of Differences between Public and Private Organizations. *Journal of Public Administration Research and Theory, 4*(2), 197–224.

Burnham, P., Gilland, K., Grant, W., & Layton-Henry, Z. (2008). *Research Methods in Politics*. Basingstoke: Palgrave Macmillan.

Buzan, B., Waever, O., & de Wilde, J. (1998). *Security: A New Framework for Analysis*. Boulder: Lynne Rienner Publishers.

Christensen, T., & Laegreid, P. (2008). Post New Public Management Reforms – Exploring the 'Whole of Government' Approach to Public Reform. In A.M. Bissessar (Ed.), *Rethinking the Reform Question*. Cambridge Scholars Publishing.

Cook, T.D., & Campbell, D.T. (1979). *Quasi-experimentation: Design and Analysis Issues for Field Settings*. Boston: Houghton Mifflin Company.

Daniel, J. (2012). *Sampling Essentials: Practical Guidelines for Making Sampling Choices*. London: SAGE.

De Groot, A.D. (1969). *Methodology: Foundations of Inference and Research in the Behavioral Sciences*. Berlin: Walter de Gruyter Inc.

Denzin, N.K., & Lincoln, Y.S. (Eds.). (1998a). *The Landscape of Qualitative Research*. Thousand Oaks: Sage Publications Inc.

——(1998b). *Collecting and Interpreting Qualitative Materials*. Thousand Oaks: Sage Publications Inc.

DeVellis, R.F. (2012). *Scale Development: Theory and Applications*. London: SAGE.

DeWalt, K.M., & DeWalt, B.R. (2002). *Participant Observation: A Guide for Fieldworkers*. Walnut Creek: Altamira Press.

Dillman, D.A., Smythe, J.D., & Christian, L.M. (2000, 2nd edition). *Mail and Internet Surveys: The Tailored Design Method*. Hoboken: John Wiley and Sons.

Dryzek, J.S., Honig, B., & Phillips, A. (Eds.). (2006). *The Oxford Handbook of Political Theory*. Oxford: Oxford University Press.

Dunleavy, P. (2003). *Authoring a PhD: How to Plan, Draft, Write and Finish a Doctoral Thesis or Dissertation*. Basingstoke: Palgrave Macmillan.

ESF. (2011). *The European Code of Conduct of Research Integrity*. Retrieved from: www.esf.org/fileadmin/Public_documents/Publications/Code_Conduct_ResearchIntegrity.pdf (19 May 2013).

Ferlie, E., Lynn, L.E. Jr., & Pollitt, C. (Eds.). (2007). *The Oxford Handbook of Public Management*. Oxford: Oxford University Press.

Field, A. (2009, 3rd edition). *Discovering Statistics Using SPSS*. London: SAGE.

Fischer, F. (2003). *Reframing Public Policy: Discursive Politics and Deliberative Practices*. Oxford: Oxford University Press.

Flick, U. (2002, 2nd edition). *An Introduction to Qualitative Research*. Thousand Oaks: Sage Publications Inc.

Flyvbjerg, B. (2006). Five Misunderstandings About Case-Study Research. *Qualitative Inquiry, 12*(2), 219–45.

Fowler, F. (2002, 3rd edition). *Survey Research Methods*. (Applied Social Research Methods, Volume 1.) Thousand Oaks: Sage Publications Inc.

Germano, W. (2001). *Getting it Published: A Guide for Scholars and Anyone else Serious about Serious Books*. Chicago: Chicago University Press.

Gubrium, J.F., & Holstein, J.A. (Eds.). (2001). *The Handbook of Interview Research*. London: SAGE.

Hart, H. 't, van Dijk, J., de Goede, M., Jansen, W., & Teunissen, J. (1998). *Onderzoeksmethoden*. Amsterdam: Boom.

Harzing, A.-W. (2011). *The Publish or Perish Book*. Melbourne: Tarma Software Research Pty Ltd.

Haverland, M. (2005). Does the EU Cause Domestic Developments? The Problem of Case Selection in Europeanization Research. *European Integration Online Papers, 9*(2).

Hodge, G., & Greve, C. (2007). Public-private Partnerships: An International Performance Review. *Public Administration Review* (May–June), 545–58.

Hofstede, G. (2001). *Culture's Consequences: Comparing Values, Behaviors, Institutions, and Organizations across Nations*. Thousand Oaks: Sage Publications Inc.

Hood, C. (1991). A Public Management for all Seasons. *Public Administration*, *19*(1), 3–19.

——(1994). *Explaining Economic Policy Reversals*. Buckingham: Open University Press.

Huff, D. (1993). *How to Lie with Statistics*. New York: Norton & Company Inc.

Kawulich, B. (2005) Participant Observation as a Data Collection Method. *Qualitative Social Research* (online journal), *6*(2), art. 43. Retrieved from www.qualitative-research.net/fqs-texte/2-05/05-2-43-e.htm (3 July 2007).

Kickert, W.J.M., Klijn, E.H., & Koppenjan, J.F.M. (Eds.). (1997). *Managing Complex Networks*. London: SAGE.

King, G., Keohane, R.O., & Verba, S. (1994). *Designing Social Inquiry: Scientific Inference in Qualitative Research*. Princeton University Press.

Knill, C., & Lenschow, A. (1998). Coping with Europe: The Impact of British and German Administrations on the Implementation of EU Environmental Policy. *Journal of European Public Policy*, *5*(4), 595–614.

Köbben, A.J.F., & Tromp, H. (1999). *De onwelkome boodschap of hoe de vrijheid van wetenschap bedreigd wordt*. Amsterdam: Jan Mets.

Koppenjan, J.F.M., & Klijn, E.H. (2004). *Managing Uncertainty in Networks*. London: Routledge.

Kuhn, T.S. (1996 [1962]). *The Structure of Scientific Revolutions*. Chicago: University of Chicago Press.

Lapsley, I. (2008). The NPM Agenda: Back to the Future. *Financial Accountability & Management*, *24*(1), 77–96.

Leeuw, F.L. (2003). Reconstructing Program Theories: Methods Available and Problems to be Solved. *American Journal of Evaluation*, *24*(1), 5–20.

Lijphart, A. (1999) *Patterns of Democracy: Government Forms and Performance in Thirty-six Countries*. New Haven, CT: Yale University Press.

Linstone, H.A., & Turoff, M. (2002). *The Delphi Method: Techniques and Applications*. Retrieved from www.is.njit.edu/pubs/delphibook/delphibook.pdf (19 May 2013).

Lipsky, M. (1980). *Street-level Bureaucracy: Dilemmas of the Individual in Public Services*. New York: Russell Sage Foundation.

Maggetti, M. (2009). The Role of Independent Regulatory Agencies in Policy-Making: A Comparative Analysis. *Journal of European Public Policy*, *16*(3), 445–65.

Margetts, H. (2011). Experiments for Public Management Research. *Public Management Review*, *13*(2), 189–208.

Marsh, D., & Furlong, P. (2002, 2nd edition). A Skin, Not a Sweater: Ontology and Epistemology in Political Science. In D. Marsh & G. Stoker (Eds.), *Theory and Methods in Political Science* (pp. 17–41). Basingstoke: Palgrave MacMillan.

McClave, J.T., Benson, P.G., & Sincich, T. (2005, 9th edition). *Statistics for Business and Economics*. Upper Saddle River: Pearson/Prentice Hall.

McMenamin, I. (2006). Process and Text: Teaching Students to Review the Literature. *Political Science & Politics*, *39*(1), 133–35.

Meier, K.J., & O'Toole, L.J. Jr. (2001). Managerial Strategies and Behavior in Networks: A Model with Evidence from U.S. Public Education. *Journal of Public Administration Research and Theory*, *11*(3), 271–94.

Miles, M.B., & Huberman, A.M. (1994, 2nd edition). *Qualitative Data Analysis: An Expanded Sourcebook*. Thousand Oaks: Sage Publishing Inc.

Mintzberg, H. (1971). Managerial Work: Analysis from Observation. *Management Science*, *18*(2), 97–110.

Moran, M., Rein, M., & Goodin, R.E. (Eds.). (2006). *The Oxford Handbook of Public Policy*. Oxford: Oxford University Press.

Morton, R.B., & Williams, K.C. (2010). *Experimental Political Science and the Study of Causality: From Nature to the Lab*. Cambridge: Cambridge University Press.

OECD. (2002). *Distributed Public Governance. Agencies, Authorities and other Autonomous Bodies*. Paris: OECD Press.

Osborne, S. (Ed.). (2009). *The New Public Governance?* London: Routledge.

Parsons, W. (1995). *Public Policy*. Cheltenham: Edward Elgar Publishing Ltd.

Pawson, R., & Tilley, N. (2004). *Realistic Evaluation*. London: SAGE.

Pennings, P. (2005). Parties, Voters and Policy Priorities in the Netherlands, 1971–2002. *Party Politics, 11*(1), 29–45.

Perelman, C., & Olbrechts-Tyteca, L. (2003). *The New Rhetoric*. London: University of Notre Dame Press.

Perry, J.L. (1996). Public Service Motivation: An Assessment of Construct Reliability and Validity. *Journal of Public Administration Research and Theory, 6*(1), 5–22.

——(2012). How Can We Improve Our Science to Generate More Usable Knowledge for Public Professionals? *Public Administration Review, 72*(4), 479–82.

Perry, J.L., & Wise, L.R. (1990). The Motivational Bases of Public Service. *Public Administration Review, 50*(3), 367–73.

Pierce, R. (2008). *Research Methods in Politics: A Practical Guide*. London: SAGE.

Pollitt, C. (2006). Academic Advice to Practitioners – What is its Nature, Place and Value within Academia? *Public Money & Management, 26*(4), 257–64.

Pollitt, C., & Dan, S. (2011). *The Impacts of the New Public Management in Europe: A Meta-analysis*. Retrieved from www.cocops.eu (19 May 2013).

Pollitt, C., & Talbot, C. (Eds.). (2004). *Unbundled Government: A Critical Analysis of the Global Trend to Agencies, Quangos and Contractualisation*. London: Routledge.

Popper, K.R. (2002 [1953]). *Conjectures and Refutations* (pp. 43–78). London: Routledge.

Power, M. (1994). *The Audit Explosion*. London: Demos.

Putnam, R.D. (1993). *Making Democracy Work: Civic Traditions in Modern Italy*. Princeton: Princeton University Press.

Raadschelders, J.C.N. (2011). *Public Administration: the interdisciplinary study of government*. UK: Oxford University Press.

Ragin, C. (2000). *Fuzzy-set Social Science*. Chicago: University of Chicago Press.

Rainey, H.G. (2009, 4th edition). *Understanding and Managing Public Corporations*. San Francisco: Jossey-Bass.

Rhodes, R.A.W., Hart, P. 't, & Noordegraaf, M. (Eds.). (2007). *Observing Government Elites: Up Close and Personal*. Basingstoke: Palgrave Macmillan.

Ricucci, N.M. (2010). *Public Administration: Traditions of Inquiry and Philosophies of Knowledge*. Washington, DC: Georgetown University Press.

Riffe, D., Lacy, S., & Fico, F.G. (2005, 2nd edition). *Analyzing Media Messages: Using Quantitative Content Analysis in Research*. Mahwah: Lawrence Erlbaum Ass.

Roberts, C. (1997). *Text Analysis for the Social Sciences: Methods for Drawing Statistical Inferences from Texts and Transcripts*. Mahwah: Lawrence Erlbaum Ass.

Robson, C. (2002, 2nd edition). *Real World Research. A Resource for Social Scientists and Practitioner-Researchers*. Malden, USA: Blackwell Publishing.

Rossi, P.H., Lipsey, M.W., & Freeman, H.E. (2004, 7th edition). *Evaluation: A Systematic Approach*. Thousand Oaks: Sage Publications Inc.

Seppänen, R., Blomqvist, K., & Sundqvist, S. (2007). Measuring Inter-organizational Trust – A Critical Review of the Empirical Research in 1990–2003. *Industrial Marketing Management*, *36*(2), 249–65.

Silverman, D. (Ed.). (2011, 3rd edition). *Qualitative Research*. London: SAGE.

Simmons, J.P., Nelson, L.D., & Simonsohn, U. (2011). False-Positive Psychology: Undisclosed Flexibility in Data Collection and Analysis Allows Presenting Anything as Significant. *Psychological Science*. Retrieved from www.socio.mta.hu/dynamic/simmons_et_al_2011.pdf (19 May 2013).

Smullen, A.J. (2010). *Translating Agency Reform: Rhetoric and Culture in Comparative Perspective*. Basingstoke: Palgrave Macmillan.

Stringer, E.T. (1996). *Action Research: A Handbook for Practitioners*. Thousand Oaks: Sage Publications Inc.

Swanborn, P.G. (1996). A Common Base for Quality Control Criteria in Quantitative and Qualitative Research. *Quality and Quantity*, *30*(1), 19–35.

Taylor, J.B. (2009). *Getting Off Track: How Government Actions and Interventions Caused, Prolonged, and Worsened the Financial Crisis*. Hoover Institution Press.

Timney Bailey, M. (1992). Do Physicists Use Case Studies? Thoughts on Public Administration Research. *Public Administration Review*, *52*(1), 47–54.

van de Walle, S. (2007). The State of the World's Bureaucracies. *Journal of Comparative Policy Analysis: Research and Practice*, *8*(4), 437–48.

Van Gunsteren, H.R. (1998). *A Theory of Citizenship: Organizing Plurality in Contemporary Democracies*. Boulder: Westview Press.

Van Hulst, M. (2008). Quite an Experience: Using Ethnography to Study Local Governance. *Critical Policy Studies*, *2*(2), 143–59.

Van Strien, P.J. (1997). Towards a Methodology of Psychological Practice – The Regulative Cycle. *Theory & Psychology*, *7*(5), 683–700.

Van Thiel, S. (2001). *Quangos: Trends, Causes and Consequences*. Aldershot: Ashgate Publishing Ltd.

Verhoest, K., van Thiel, S., Bouckaert, G., & Laegreid, P. (Eds.). (2012). *Government Agencies: Practices and Lessons from 30 Countries*. Basingstoke: Palgrave Macmillan.

Verschuren, P., & Doorewaard, H. (2010, 2nd edition). *Designing a Research Project*. Schiedam: Boom Juridische Uitgevers.

Vink, M., & Meijerink, F. (2003). Asylum Applications and Recognition Rates in EU Member States 1982–2001: A Quantitative Analysis. *Journal of Refugee Studies*, *16*(3), 297–315.

Vis, B. (2007). States of Welfare or States of Workfare? Welfare State Restructuring in 16 Capitalist Democracies, 1985–2002. *Policy & Politics*, *35*(1), 105–22.

Voogt, R.J.J., & van Kempen, H. (2002). Nonresponse Bias and Stimulus Effects in the Dutch National Election Study. *Quality and Quantity*, *36*(4), 325–45.

Webb, E.J., Campbell, D.T., Schwartz, R.D., & Sechrest, L. (1999, 2nd edition). *Unobtrusive Measures: Nonreactive Research in the Social Sciences*. London: SAGE.

Weiss, R.S. (1994). *Learning from Strangers: The Art and Method of Qualitative Interview Studies*. New York: The Free Press.

Wildavsky, A. (1979). Introduction: Analysis as Art. In A. Wildavsky, *Speaking Truth to Power: The Art and Craft of Policy Analysis* (pp. 1–19). Transaction Publishers.

Wright, K.B. (2006). Researching Internet-Based Populations: Advantages and Disadvantages of Online Survey Research, Online Questionnaire Authoring

173

Software Packages, and Web Survey Services. *Journal of Computer-Mediated Communication, 10*(3). doi: 10.1111/j.1083-6101.2005.tb00259.x (April 2006).

Yanow, D. (1996). *How Does a Policy Mean? Interpreting Policy and Organizational Actions*. Washington, DC: Georgetown University Press.

Yildiz, M. (2007). E-government Research: Reviewing the Literature, Limitations and Ways Forward. *Government Information Quarterly, 24*(3), 646–65.

Yin, R.K. (2008, 4th edition). *Case Study Research: Design and Methods*. Thousand Oaks: Sage Publications Inc.

Glossary

Action research   form of research in which the research aim gradually changes. Action research is typically geared towards solving a practical problem. On the basis of the diagnosis made, recommendations can be formulated. The researcher is also involved in implementing the suggested solution (intervention) and evaluating its effects.

Analytical framework   a schematic overview of the relations that are assumed to exist between variables. The framework can be graphically represented by means of, for example, an arrow diagram.

Analytical generalizability   refers to the application of the results of a case study to modify or extend an existing theory. The theory is tested, as it were, by studying a certain case (deductive approach).

Answering tendencies   the inclination of respondents to answer questions in a certain pattern, diverging from their 'true' answers. For example, people may always choose to answer yes or no, or never tick an extreme answer category. Answering tendencies can create problems for validity.

Artefacts   1 objects used in empirical research, for example works of art; 2 in statistical analyses: artificial effects that are a by-product of the actual analysis.

Axiom   theoretical statement based on empirical research, derived by means of induction, which ultimately leads to the development of new theories.

Bivariate   a term used for forms of statistical analysis in which the relation between (no more than) two variables are studied.

Body of knowledge   the total of all existing theories in a scientific discipline.

Case study   research strategy in which the researcher concentrates on one or two cases of the research subject, which are studied in their everyday setting.

Case study protocol   an overview of the choices made and steps taken in a case study – for example, how the case was selected, which data sources were used, and what methods and analytical techniques were applied.

Causality   two things or events are causally connected if there is a cause-effect relation between the two. In research, causality refers to the effect of the independent variable on the dependent variable.

Code book   an overview of the variables included in the study, and the values they can assume in the data matrix.

Coding   the process of assigning a (theoretically relevant) code to empirical data during the analysis. Coding creates the possibility to compare and merge research data, and discover certain patterns. These patterns can lead to conclusions.

Cohort   a homogeneous group of units of study who share a certain characteristic. An example of a cohort is a group of people who were all born in the same year.

Conditions   the circumstances under which an effect can be observed of the independent variable on the dependent variable.

Construct   a theoretical concept or phenomenon that is intangible itself and cannot be measured directly. Examples are the concepts of intelligence and ministerial responsibility. Constructs consist of dimensions that can be operationalized and measured.

Content analysis   method for gathering and analysing the content of existing data sources, for example documents. The idea is to filter the texts for facts and opinions, or to reconstruct the arguments used in the text.

Control group   the units of study who are not subjected to the experimental condition or stimulus in an experiment. By comparing the measurements taken in the control group with those of the experimental group, the pure effect of the experimental stimulus can be established.

Control items   questions or statements in a questionnaire that are included to counter answering tendencies.

Control variables   variables that are included in the analysis to limit their potential interfering influence. By including control variables in the analysis, the estimated effects will become purer.

Correlation   a statistically provable relation between two or more variables.

Cross-sectional design   a form of research in which the units of study in the sample are divided into groups who share a certain characteristic (for example age). The cross-sectional design allows for drawing conclusions about the different groups of respondents.

Data inspection   checking the dataset for: 1 errors made during the phase of data entry; 2 statistical features, such as mean and spread; or 3 the representativeness of the sample.

Data matrix a format for storing quantitative research data. The rows give the data or scores per unit of study (respondent); the columns of the matrix show the variables. The contents of the data matrix are described in the code book. The data stored in the data matrix can serve as input for diverse forms of statistical analysis.

Data sources person, documents, or other sources of information that can be used for research. Sometimes the data sources are the units of study.

Deduction the process of deriving suppositions or hypotheses from the theory. These theoretical expectations can subsequently be tested.

Delphi method multi-stage interviewing technique in which experts (respondents) react to questions posed by the researcher or their fellow experts. After each round of questions, the researcher draws up a report, which is used as input for the next round. The study ends with a plenary group discussion.

Dependent variable a variable that shows a change or effect as a result of a change in the independent variable. An example is the increasing frequency with which people fall ill (the dependent variable) with age (the independent variable).

Description research aimed at describing the subject of study. Usually, the description answers research questions of the 'how', 'what', or 'which' type.

Design research aimed at arriving at a solution to a practical problem, or to formulate recommendations on how a situation can be improved. (See *research design* for a different definition.)

Diagnosis research aimed at pinpointing the practical stumbling block in a certain situation. The diagnosis can be used to suggest possible solutions to the problem.

Dichotomy refers to answers that can only assume two shapes, such as: 'yes/no', 'left/right', or 'male/female'. Dichotomous variables are also called dummy variables.

Discourse analysis the analysis of the contents of a text, in particular the language that is used. A discourse is a shared way of thinking and talking about a certain subject.

Double hermeneutics refers to the risk of the researcher reinterpreting the subject of study, which leads to a layering of interpretations, and lower reliability and validity.

Elite interview interview with respondents who occupy a prominent position in the research situation, and are knowledgeable on the subject of study.

Empirical refers to reality and real life. Empirical research information consists of data that have been gathered in the real, everyday setting.

177

Empirical-analytical approach a view on science and doing research that stresses the testing of theoretical laws and the falsification of hypotheses. Tries to match the methodological ideal of physical science. Empirical-analytical scientists conduct research in as objective a manner as possible; they take a quantitative approach, and pay close attention to validity and reliability.

Empirical cycle describes the different stages of doing research. Taken together, the inductive and the deductive phases form a complete research cycle.

Endogenous variables variables that form part of the research situation.

Epistemology philosophy of knowledge, which revolves around the question of whether it is possible to gain objective knowledge of reality.

Estimation error every statistical analysis leaves a certain amount of variance in the scores unexplained. This unexplained variance is called the estimation error. Usually the estimation error consists of random deviations in the scores, but the researcher always has to check whether this is indeed the case.

Evaluation research form of research aimed at establishing whether a certain policy target has been reached. Evaluations can be done before (*ex ante*) or after (*ex post*) a policy is implemented. An evaluation study can be summative and concentrate on what results have been achieved, or it can be of the formative type, which means to say that the process of developing and implementing a policy is studied.

Existing data sources data sources that have been produced by others. Such sources can comprise primary material which has not been used for research purposes before, for example a company's annual reports. Existing sources can also contain secondary data, such as the research findings from previous studies which have already been published.

Exogenous variables variables that do not form part of the research situation but which can or do exert an influence on the (dependent) variable or variables.

Experiment research strategy in which the units of study (subjects) are divided into two groups. The experimental group is subjected to a certain stimulus; the control group does not receive the stimulus. By comparing the pre-test and post-test measurements of both groups, the effect of the stimulus can be established; the emphasis lies on causality. There are different types of experiment, such as the classic experiment, the field experiment, or the quasi-experiment.

Expert someone who can give advice on the selection of cases or documents, or who can be interviewed for consultancy purposes. Experts are not actually involved in the research situation.

Exploration   research that is carried out when only little or nothing is known on the subject of study. Exploratory research results in a description (not to be confused with descriptive research).

External validity   refers to the generalizability of the research findings to other units of study, or different periods and locations (think of countries).

Factor analysis   form of statistical analysis used for distilling the joint relation between several variables, which together constitute a factor. Usually, the factor itself cannot be captured in one single measurement, because it concerns an intangible construct.

Falsification   the process of rejecting theoretical predictions or hypotheses by proving them false. As long as a hypothesis cannot be refuted, it holds true. Popper developed the principle of falsification as a more efficient approach to science than trying to seek verification for hypotheses.

Field experiment   an experiment that is conducted outside the laboratory, in an everyday setting. For example, in a policy experiment the effect of a certain experimental condition (such as a policy measure) can be studied. The researcher has to adapt to the limitations and possibilities of the real world, and does not benefit from the advantages and controlled conditions of the classic laboratory experiment.

Focus groups   an interviewing technique with a group of respondents who have an open discussion led by a moderator. The respondents are usually people with similar experiences, or from a similar background.

Fundamental research   research aimed at testing existing theories or formulating new theories. The societal relevance of this kind of research is usually not immediately or directly clear.

Hidden observation   observation technique in which the researcher does not get involved in the research situation.

Holism   an approach that tries to regard the subject of study as one whole, with all relevant contextual features. Closely fits in with the interpretative approach to science.

Hypothesis   testable prediction in the form of a statement on the change that, under certain conditions, will be observed in the dependent variable as a result of a change in the independent variable. The change in the dependent variable may be caused by a mechanism.

Independent variable   the variable that causes the effect or the change in which the researcher is interested.

Induction   deriving theoretical suppositions (axioms) from empirical research data with the aim of formulating new theories. Part of the empirical cycle.

Informants   people who are not or are no longer involved in the research situation, but who can provide relevant information to the researcher. An example is a former employee of an organization.

Interdisciplinary   a label to indicate that a researcher or a piece of research integrates knowledge derived from different disciplines. Not to be confused with 'multidisciplinary', which refers to research where knowledge from various disciplines is applied without this knowledge really being integrated.

Internal validity   the soundness and effectiveness of a piece of research. Has the researcher really measured what he or she intended to measure, and can the effect observed in the dependent variable be attributed to a change in the independent variable?

Interpretative approach   philosophy of science which takes the subjectivity of observation as a starting point. Everybody is said to perceive reality in their own particular way. Researchers will have to strive after understanding (*Verstehen*) people's perceptions, and study the research situation in its entirety.

Inter-researcher reliability   the degree to which measurements or observations of the same phenomenon by different researchers concur with each other. The higher the concurrence, the more reliable the findings are.

Inter-subjectivity   a term used to indicate that knowledge is only valid if it is based on criteria set and agreed upon by a group of people. The validity of knowledge is shared or supported by the group, but not based on objective criteria.

Intervening variables   variables that influence the effect of the independent variable on the dependent variable. Intervening variables can cause the effects that are found in a study to be distorted.

Interview   a conversation in which the researcher poses questions to one or more respondents in order to gather information on the subject of study.

Interview manual   list of topics or questions for discussion in a semi-structured interview.

Intra-researcher reliability   the degree to which several measurements taken by the same researcher of several or comparable research phenomena concur with each other.

Items   questions or statements in a written questionnaire.

Key figure   someone who holds a position in the research situation that enables them to inform the researcher about which respondents or documents would be suitable for inclusion in the study.

Level of measurement   refers to the kind of values a variable can assume. There are four levels of measurement: nominal (no order), ordinal (values are ordered, but not set at regular intervals), interval (ordered values at regular intervals), and ratio (equally distant and ordered values, plus a reference point). The level of measurement determines what options there are for statistical analysis.

Literature review overview of the knowledge that already exists on a subject ('status quaestionis'). The literature review can serve as a basis for formulating a relevant research problem, and to determine what the scientific and societal relevance of the study will be.

Log notes made by the researcher on the decisions made and the events that occurred in the course of the study. The log can be used later to reconstruct what happened during the research, and to motivate the methodological decisions made.

Longitudinal research study with a wider time frame, in which several measurements are taken at different moments in time.

Manipulating variables a term used to indicate that in certain research situations, such as experiments or simulations, the researcher fully determines which variables will and which variables will not play a role.

Matching 1 in an experiment: dividing the test population into an experimental group and a control group on the basis of an equal division of certain characteristics; 2 in an analysis of qualitative data: *pattern matching* refers to the process of distilling certain patterns from the data.

Mechanism in a theory or model, the mechanism shows the relation between variables, given certain conditions. For example, because people will fall ill more frequently as they grow older (the mechanism), population ageing will cause higher healthcare costs.

Member check presenting research results (acquired by, for example, interviews or observation) to the units of study. A member check can be done to see whether the researcher has made any mistakes, or to create support with the sponsor for the conclusions drawn from the study.

Meta-analysis method for gathering and analysing existing data from several previously conducted studies are brought together. The resulting dataset can be used to test new hypotheses, or to generate new research questions.

Methodological individualism refers to research conclusions based on individual measurements, which are aggregated to a macro-level unit, such as organizations or countries. The researcher has to indicate how aggregation takes place. The representativeness of the units of study can be of crucial importance here.

Multi-disciplinary a term used to indicate that knowledge from several disciplines is applied in conjunction. Not to be confused with the term 'interdisciplinary', a term that refers to the integration of knowledge derived from several disciplines.

Multivariate analysis   statistical analysis with several independent variables. Compare with bivariate analysis, which focuses on the relation between no more than two variables. In regression analysis, the word 'multiple' is used, instead of multivariate.

Narrative analysis   form of textual analysis (content analysis) in which the information obtained is used to construct a story, with certain features such as a particular plot or certain genre characteristics.

Non-probability sample   sample in which the units of study are selected consciously and purposively. The term non-probability sample is also used when the total population consists of only one or just a few units of study which are all included in the research.

Non-response   the failure of respondents to participate in a study (by not completing a questionnaire, for example). Non-response can cause research results to be distorted, as it may reduce the representativeness of the sample.

Normative   refers to a research conclusion or theory that is prescriptive ('it should be like this'), instead of descriptive (factual, neutral, objective).

Object of knowledge   the central object of study in a discipline. Public Administration concentrates on acquiring knowledge on the management, operation and functioning of government bodies and organizations in the public sector.

Observation   research method in which the researcher draws conclusions on the basis of observing people's behaviour. Observation can take place in a more or a less open manner; in an open observation format, the researcher participates in the research situation. In a structured format, an observation scheme is used.

Observation scheme or protocol   an instrument for noting down observations. The observation scheme has a number of categories (for example, types of behaviour shown by the units of study). These categories are either derived deductively from the theory, or developed inductively in the course of research. The observation scheme or protocol is used to structure the observation process.

Observer effect   if subjects or respondents are aware of being studied or tested (due to, for example, the presence of a researcher), they can modify their behaviour accordingly. The observer effect can decrease the reliability and validity of the research findings.

Ontology   philosophy of 'being', which revolves around the question of whether reality truly does exist. To what extent is a certain subject of study real? Also, is the subject of study similar or the same to everyone, or does reality rather depend on individual perception? Different scientists or researchers will answer these questions differently, depending on their philosophy of science.

Open interview   interview technique in which the opening question is the only fixed item. Also referred to as a qualitative or free-attitude interview.

Open observation   observation technique where the researcher is present in the research situation but does not interact with the units of study. The people who are observed will not always be aware that they are being studied.

Operationalization   the process of translating theoretical concepts into variables that can be observed or measured in everyday life and reality.

Outlier   a score or result that deviates strongly from other observations or measurements. For example, in a study on young people an elderly person will be an outlier, as his or her age will deviate strongly from the mean.

Panel study   a form of longitudinal research, in which the same units of study (the panel) are measured at several points in time.

Paradigm   a theoretical tradition or accepted way of thinking in a certain discipline, which expresses itself in a concrete research agenda and research approach, which is shared by a group of researchers. The term paradigm was first introduced by Kuhn. Paradigms tend to shift over time. In this book, two paradigms have been discussed, namely, the empirical-analytical approach, and the interpretative approach.

Participant observation   observation method in which the researcher is involved or participates in the research situation. The degree of involvement varies: the researcher can be merely present, or take an active part in activities and events.

Philosophy of science   the view a researcher holds on what science is, how scientific research should be carried out, and what contribution science should make to society.

Pilot   a preliminary or test study to see whether the chosen method (for example, a questionnaire) is clear and user-friendly enough. Another option is studying just one case in the pilot, to establish how meaningful the study will be, and whether the chosen method can actually be applied in the research situation. A pilot helps to gain insight into how the study should best be carried out.

Population   the total of all possible units of study, from which the researcher draws a sample. Only the sample will be included in the research.

Prescription   prescriptive research aims to arrive at recommendations on how to improve the situation that has been studied.

Probability sample   sample created by selecting the units of study (persons, documents, cases) from the total population on the basis of chance (at random). In a probability sample, every potential unit of study has an equally large chance of being selected.

Problematizing   the process of arriving at an adequate research problem by determining which particular aspects of a subject will be studied. Problematizing results from, amongst others, the preparatory research stage (what is already known on the subject?), and sometimes by asking a sponsor what exactly the problem is for which a solution is sought.

Programme theory   the suppositions and assumptions on which a certain policy is founded. A programme theory is practical rather than scientific in character, and focuses on problems and solutions.

Qualitative data   qualitative data are non-numerical research data (nominal or ordinal level). Qualitative data cannot be used in statistical calculations but must be analysed by other methods, such as coding or interpretation.

Quantitative data   quantitative data are numerical research data. Quantitative data can be used in statistical calculations.

Quasi-experiment   variant of the research strategy of the experiment, in which not all conditions for the classic experiment are met. For example, randomization may not have taken place, there may be no control group, or no pre-test measurement was taken.

Questionnaire   list with a large number of standardized or closed-ended questions on different variables, often in written form or online. The respondent fills in the questionnaire.

Quota sample   sample of an equal number of respondents or subjects in the various strata or groups specified by the researcher. For example, a researcher may want to conduct a survey of 50 men and 50 women: selection will continue until these quotas have been reached.

Randomization   using a random procedure. For example, dividing a number of subjects into an experimental group and a control group on the basis of chance, or putting the questions in a questionnaire in a random order. Randomization is used to reduce the influence of factors that can harm validity and reliability.

Regression analysis   form of statistical analysis which presupposes a linear relation between two or more variables. The relation between the variables is expressed in an equation: $Y = a + bX + e$. Y is the dependent variable; X is the independent variable.

Regulative cycle   practical or applied research has its own logic. The stages that the researcher has to go through are the following: formulating the research problem, diagnosis, planning, intervention and evaluation. The regulative cycle was designed as an alternative to the empirical cycle, for applied research.

Reliability   the accuracy and consistency of measurements. A measurement instrument is reliable if – under similar conditions – it shows the same results every time it is used (repeatability).

Replication   repeating a previously conducted study (for example, with a different sample, or at a different moment in time) to test its reliability. Replication increases reliability, and makes it possible to standardize measurement instruments.

Research aim   specifies why the study will be carried out, and what its purpose is. Constitutes part of the research problem. Possible research aims are trying to find an explanation for a certain phenomenon, testing something, or designing a solution.

Research design   the research design specifies all the choices that have been made on how the study will be implemented. The research design consists of eight elements: the research problem; the theoretical framework; the sampling frame; the research strategy, method and technique; a note on reliability and validity; the intended research method; planning; and reporting.

Research problem   describes what is being studied (the research question) and why (research aim). The research problem reflects the existing knowledge on the subject of study, the researcher's own interests, the scientific and societal relevance of the subject of study, and the preferences of any sponsors.

Research question   part of the research problem. The research question states what exactly will be studied. Usually it consists of a main or overarching question and a set of sub-questions.

Research strategy   the overarching design or logic of the study. Within a certain chosen strategy, different methods (and various techniques) can be applied.

Respondents   term used for the units of study (persons) in methods such as interviews or questionnaires. Not to be confused with informants, subjects, or key figures.

Respondents report   report on the results of the study, usually a questionnaire, which is given to respondents who have expressed an interest in reading such a report.

Retrospective study   study of events that took place in the past.

Review study a meta-analysis of existing sources, in which findings from earlier research are gathered together to arrive at new insights and conclusions. In their turn, review studies provide material for the literature review. (Not to be confused with peer review, which is a review procedure of scientific publications.)

Rhetorical analysis textual analysis (content analysis) for tracing the rhetorical techniques used by the producer of the text or speech to convey a certain message. An example is the use of metaphors.

Sampling selection of units of study, cases or data sources from the total population.

Sampling frame description and motivation of the way in which a sample is drawn, describing the chosen sample size, the selection method applied and how non-response is dealt with.

Scale construction form of research in which respondents' answers are measured by means of a scale (for example, people are asked whether they agree or disagree with a certain statement). A statistical analysis of the answers can provide insight into the extent to which certain questions (statements or items) are interrelated, and to see whether they constitute one scale that can be used to measure the phenomenon under study.

Scenario research can result in the formulation of one or more future scenarios, for example, on the expected impact of current trends for future policymaking. Policymakers can use scenarios to develop new policies or to facilitate the decision making on existing plans.

Scientific relevance refers to the degree to which the knowledge to be acquired will contribute to the existing body of knowledge.

Secondary analysis a new (statistical) analysis of existing data which have been gathered for a different purpose. (Note: 'analysing secondary material' is not necessarily the same.)

Semi-structured interview interviewing technique in which the researcher formulates a few open questions or subjects for discussion beforehand, and writes these down in the interview manual. The interview manual is used to guide the conversation in a certain direction. There are no pre-structured answer categories, however.

Simulation a situation (game) in which reality is imitated in an environment controlled by the researcher. A simulation or game can be compared to a field experiment or a quasi-experiment. The researcher can use them to study how and why certain events take place.

Snowball sample form of sampling in which the first respondent is asked to provide the names of other suitable respondents, who are asked the same question in their turn, and so forth. This method is often applied in situations where respondents may be difficult to access directly (for example, criminals), or when studying taboo subjects.

Social desirability the inclination of respondents not to answer questions truthfully, but reply in a manner that they think is expected of them, or which seems politically correct. Socially desirable answers can decrease the internal validity of a study.

Societal relevance refers to the extent to which a study is expected to contribute to the solution of social problems and questions.

Statistical significance a statistically significant effect means to say that the effect that has been measured cannot be ascribed to chance, but is caused by the independent variables in the study. Statistical significance is expressed by the p-value. In the ideal case, p is less than 5%; the chance that the effect is random after all is less than 5%.

Stratification dividing the research population into different strata by creating groups in terms of characteristics such as age, gender, background, or educational level. Stratification can help to arrive at a sample that is representative of the entire population.

Stratified sample sample drawn by taking certain characteristics of the respondents into account (such as age or educational level). These characteristics are called strata (singular: 'stratum'). Stratification is used to increase the representativeness of the sample.

String variables non-numerical variables in a data matrix.

Structured interview interview in which the researcher asks closed-ended questions, with matching answer categories. Comparable to the oral application of a written questionnaire.

Subjects the participants in an experiment.

Sub-questions questions derived from the main research question specified in the research problem. Sub-questions divide the research into practically feasible parts. The sum of the answers to all sub-questions taken together constitutes the answer to the main research question.

Survey research strategy in which standardized measurements are taken on a large scale (the study comprises a large number of units of study and a large number of variables). Surveys are often used to do research on attitudes. The most frequently chosen survey method is the written questionnaire.

Testing testing research aims to establish whether one or more theoretical predictions (usually in the form of hypotheses) are accurate.

Theoretical framework   a conceptual outline of the answer provided by one or more theories to the research question. The theoretical framework is not a summary or literature overview: the researcher builds an independent argument on the basis of existing or new theoretical notions. A well-developed theoretical framework is consistent, relevant to the subject of study, testable and empirically applicable.

Theoretical generalizability   using the results of research to formulate new axioms for the development of new theories (inductive research).

Theory   a scientific theory is an interrelated set of statements to describe, explain or predict a phenomenon. A theory consists of assumptions, a model and hypotheses.

Trend studies   research in which measurements are taken at different points in time for comparable groups (for example, people aged 50–59 in the 1970s, people aged 50–59 in the 1980s, and people aged 50–59 in the 1990s). In this manner, a certain trend or development can be studied.

Triangulation   using several operationalizations, sources, methods, researchers, or techniques to enhance the validity of the research conclusions. Information obtained via various channels can serve for mutual confirmation.

T-test   the t-test calculates whether a difference between two groups, variables or measurements is systematic, and cannot be ascribed to factors such as circumstance, interfering variables, or a wrongly drawn sample.

Two-step sampling   step-by-step or phased sampling method. The ultimate sample is drawn by sampling several times over: the sample of the previous round constitutes the population from which the smaller sample of the next round is drawn. Different techniques can be used in each consecutive phase. To give an example, first a selection of regions can be made, from which subsequently a number of municipalities are drawn.

Unit of study   a unit of what or who is being studied. The unit of study can be a person, an organization, a country, but also something such as a law or a policy document.

Validation   refers to the standardization of a test or questionnaire. By using a validated questionnaire in a representative sample, conclusions can be drawn that apply to the entire population. The IQ test is an example of a validated test: an individual score can be compared directly to the population mean.

Variable   a characteristic or aspect of a unit of study, such as someone's age.

Variance analysis   statistical technique that analyses the difference between the scores of two groups or the scores of one individual at two different points in time. Ideally, the difference measured is caused by the independent variable.

Verification   striving after confirmation of a certain expectation or prediction (hypothesis). The opposite of falsification, in which the researcher aims to gain new knowledge by the process of refuting hypotheses.

Index

9/11 events 5

action research 16–17, 28, 33, 67, 86, 140, 156, 159
analytical generalization 92
ANOVA (analysis of variance) 132
answering tendencies 82, 84–85, 95
applied research 15
arithmetic mean 123
ATLAS.ti software 142
axioms 25, 28, 41, 55, 85, 92, 110, 114, 146, 149, 162

bibliography 169–74
book summary 10–11

Canadian Vote Compass 80
Care Quality Commission, UK 103
case study: choices 91; interviews 93–100; reliability and validity 91–92; research 86–88; research in public administration 87–89; selection 89–91
case study – interviews: Delphi method 97–98; interview manual 96; open 93–94; reliability and validity 100; report 99; respondents selection 96–97, 100; rule of thumb 98; semi-structured 94–96; summary 93
case study protocol 91–92
choices in designing case studies 91
citizenship 38
classic experiment 61–64
co-production (politicians/civil servants and citizens) 2–3

COBRA network (research into semi-autonomous agencies) 77
code book 121–22, 126
coding 70, 114, 125–26, 136, 139, 143, 144–46, 147–48, 150, 162–63
cohorts 56
construct (theoretical framework) 25–26, 28–30, 37, 38
content analysis 104, 107, 108–10, 111, 115–16
cost-benefit analyses (CBA) 108
crisis management 3
Cronbach's alpha (scales) 134
cross-section 57
Cuban Missile Crisis 37

data inspection 122–25, 127, 136
data matrix 121–22, 125–26
deduction 26–27, 32, 36, 38, 110, 119
deductive research 43, 54–55, 57, 70, 162
Delphi method 93, 97–98
democracy (quantitative data) 134
dependent variable (DV) 22, 29–30, 34, 44, 49
desk research: content analysis in public administration 111; healthcare research data sources 103–4; meta-analysis in public administration/ management research 114–15; secondary analysis in public administration 112–13; summary 102; textual analysis 108–10; three methods for gathering/analysing existing data 107–16; using/re-using existing data 102–7

desk research (three methods for gathering/analysing existing data): conclusions 116; content analysis 108–10; meta-analysis 113–14; methods comparison 115–16; secondary analysis 111–12

desk research (using/re-using existing data): description 102–5; making a selection 105–6; public administration and public management 106–7

discourse analysis 58, 109

double hermeneutics 35, 99

Dutch National Voters Study (*Nationale Kiezersonderzock*) 83

Economic Development Administration (EDA) 87–88

education experiments 67

Eigenvalues 133

empirical cycle 24–28, 41–42, 57

empirical-analytical approach 31, 32–34, 35–36, 154

Environmental Protection Agency 89

ethical rules of research: beneficence 154; confidentiality 154–55; informed consent 154–55; privacy 154–55; veracity 154–55

ethnography (qualitative research) 140

European Union (EU): codes 154; constitution 110–11; content analysis in public administration 111; environmental policies 141; exogenous/intervening variables 63–64; experiment example 62–63, 69; globalization 3; international comparative data 104; online databases 103; regulatory agencies 89; subject for publication 156

Europeanization 3

evaluation 5–6, 8–9, 163, 165, 166

exogenous variables and intervening variables 63–64

experiment: classic 61–64; exogenous variables and interviewing variables 63–64; field 67–69; observation 70–72; observation study 71; policy experiments 67–68; reliability and validity 68–70; simulation game design 65–66; simulations and gaming 64–67

experiment (observation): introduction 70; participants 71–72; public administration research 71; reliability and validity 72

factor analysis 128, 132, 133–34, 135

falsification 26–27, 32, 36, 40, 133, 140, 151

field experiment 67–68

focus groups 97

fundamental research 15

fuzzy set qualitative comparative analysis (QCA) 143, 149–50

glossary 175–89

Government Effective indicators 105

grid-group culture (GGC) theory 37–38

grounded theory (qualitative research) 139

Group Decision Room (GDR) 66

Growth Competitive Index 105

'Hawthorne effect' (awareness of being studied) 31, 64

healthcare: experiments 68; research data sources 103–4

Hurricane Katrina 89

hypothesis 22, 27, 129, 132–33

Implementation: How Great Expectations in Washington … 87

independent variable (IV) 29, 34, 44, 63, 81

induction 25–27, 35–36, 110, 119, 140, 151

international comparative data 104

International Institute for Management Development (IMD) 105

international refereed journals in public administration/management 157

international security 88–89

interpretative approach 31, 34–35, 87

interviews; manual 96; rule of thumb for conduct 98–99; report 99; reliability and validity 100; respondent selection 96–97

interviews (types): elite 97; open 93–94; semi-structured 94–96; structured 93

IQ tests 50

Kennedy, President 37

leadership 3

level of measurement 112, 128, 135

Likert scales 76, 79–80

literature skills 39

log 66, 92, 123, 143, 147, 150, 165

longitudinal research 37, 56, 91, 107

managers (observation study) 71
MANOVA (multivariate ANOVA) 132
matching 64, 69
member check 99, 150–51
meta-analysis 58–59, 92, 105, 107,
    113–14, 116
methodological individualism 33
methods comparison (desk research):
    performance indicators in hospitals
    115–16; school segregation 116;
    women in top positions 116
mistakes in research question:
    incompleteness 21–22; incorrect
    suppositions (prejudice) 22;
    insufficiently precise wording 21;
    wrong level of abstraction 21
multi-level governance 3

narrative analysis 109
National Archives 104
National Institute for Health and Care
    Excellence (NICE), UK 68
Netherlands Court of Audit 106
New Public Management (NPM) 2, 5, 8,
    88, 109, 114
non-governmental organizations (NGOs)
    1–2
non-response 76, 82–83, 124, 136
normal distribution 124
North Atlantic Treaty Organization
    (NATO) 3
NVivo software 142

observation: description 70; reliability
    and validity 72; scheme or protocol 71
observation (types): hidden 70; open 70;
    participant 71–72
observer effect 69
ontology 32–36
open (qualitative) interview 93–96
operationalization: reliability and validity
    48–50; sampling 45–48; scales of
    measurement 44–45;
    three steps 43–45; triangulation
    52–53; validating/standardizing
    measurement instruments 50–51;
    validity and reliability – interference
    51–52
operationalization (data analysis):
    qualitative 143,145, 146; quantitative
    120, 125
operationalization (reliability and validity):
    reliability 48–49; validity 49–50

operationalization (sampling):
    introduction 45–46; non-probability
    sampling 46–47; probability sampling
    47; sample representativeness 47–48
operationalization (validity and
    reliability – interference): measurement
    instruments as interference 52;
    researcher as interference 51; units of
    study as interference 52
operationalization problem 106–7, 112
Organisation for Economic
    Co-operation and Development
    (OECD) 104
outliers 123, 136, 151

panel studies 56, 60
paradigm 31
philosophies of science: description 31;
    epistemology 32; methodological
    position 32; model of man 32;
    ontology 32; public administration
    research 36
pilot studies 47, 50, 75, 78, 80, 82,
    90–91, 96, 98, 100
policy experiments: education 67;
    healthcare sector 68; water
    management 68
population 45–47, 50
prescription 16, 28, 34, 56, 164–66
press releases 157–58
'problematizing' process 12–13
programme theory 110
public administration/management
    research: applied nature 4–5;
    co-production 2; crisis management 3;
    financial crisis 2–3; globalization 3;
    leadership 3; multi-level governance 3;
    New Public Management 2–3;
    qualitative data 141; quantitative data
    134–35; security 3
Public Service Motivation (PSM) 76–77

Q-sorting 135
qualitative comparative analysis (QCA)
    143, 149–50
qualitative data: analysis 143–50; coding
    an interview 144–45; collection and
    ordering 142–43; description 138–40;
    forms of research 139–40; fuzzy set
    qualitative comparative analysis
    149–50; literature 139; public
    administration/management research
    141; reliability and validity 150–51

qualitative data (analysis): axial coding 147; codes 142–44, 145–46, 146–47; interpretation and theory development 147–49

qualitative data analysis (QDA) computer programs 142

qualitative interview *see* open interview

qualitative research (forms): ethnography 140; grounded theory 139; thick description 140

quantitative data: analysis 126; collection and ordering 119–26; description 118–19; descriptive statistics 127–28; inferential statistics 128–35; public administration/management 134–35; reliability and validity 135–36; statistical analyses results 129–30

quantitative data (collection and ordering): code book 121; data inspection 122–25; data matrix 121–22; description 119–21; recoding, categorizing and processing 125–26

quantitative data (descriptive statistics): correlation 127–28; cross-tabulation 127

quantitative data (inferential statistics): constructing scales 134; factor analysis 133; other forms of analysis 135; regression analysis 130–32; t-test 128–30; variance analysis 132–33

questionnaires: characteristics and types 74–75; design 77–82; non-response 83; reliability and validity 82–83; research 76–77; scales 79–80; written 75–82

questionnaires (written): control variables 80–81; criteria 78–79; design 77–78; layout 81–82; pilot study 82; process 75–76

randomization 47, 136

reconstruction of programme theories 6–7

regional governments, Italy 37

regression analysis 128, 130–32 134, 135

regulative cycle 28, 34, 66, 164

reliability (operationalization): accuracy 48; consistency 48–49; interference 51–52; measurement instruments 50; triangulation 52–53;

reliability (strategy and methods): case study 91–92; desk research 103,105, 107, 112, 113, 114; experiments 68–70; interviews 100; observation 72; questionnaires 82–83

reliability (types): inter/intra-researcher 49, 51, 52

replication: 49, 50, 90–92

research aim: 12–13, 14, 15–16, 17, 19

research design: elements 54–56; strategy, method and technique 57–60; time dimension 56–57

research design (elements): data analysis 55–56; material costs, staffing and time schedule 56; problem 54; reliability and validity 55; results reporting 56; sampling framework 55; strategy 55; theoretical framework 54–55; time dimension 56–57

research problem: action research 16–17; aim 15–17; choosing/formulating 12–15; hypotheses 22; question 17–22; sub-questions 20–21

research problem (aims): description 15; design 16; diagnosis 16; evaluation 16; explanation 15; exploration 15; testing 16

research problem (choice and formulation): introduction 12–14; mistakes 14–15

research problem (question): criteria 19–20; mistakes 21–22; sub-questions 20–21

research problem (question formulation): description 18; design 18; diagnosis 18; evaluation 18; explanation 18; exploration 18; testing 18

research in public administration (case studies): implementation theory 87–88; international security 88–89; public management reform 88

research in public administration (introduction): book aim/outline 10–11; evaluation and evidence-based policy making 8–9; prevalent topics 2–3; public administration and policy 5–10; reconstruction of programme theories 6–7; unique features 1–5

research in public administration (policy): feeding into policy 7–9; policy as outcome 10; policy as research subject 6–7

research with questionnaires: COBRA network 77; Public Service Motivation 76–77
respondents: case study 93–95, 96–98, 99–100; survey 75–76, 77–82, 83–84
respondents' report 154, 156
results reporting: ethical rules 154–55; formats 155–57; forums 153–55; international refereed journals in public administration/management 157; model 161–62; prescription 164–67; press releases 157–58; purpose 158–59; *Unwelcome Tidings* 166; writing 159–64
results reporting (prescription): functions 164–65; public administration/management impact 167; recommendations 165–66
results reporting (writing): academic writing style 162–63; general guidelines 159–61; practical purposes 163–64; review procedure for scientific publication 163; scientific 161–62
review study 116
rhetorical analysis 109–10

sampling: definition 45; improving representativeness 57–58
sampling (types): non-probability 46–47; probability 47; quota 46; snowball 46–47; stratification 57; two-step 46, 47
sampling frame 46, 48, 55, 60, 100, 106, 161
SARS (Severe Acute Respiratory Syndrome) 3
scales: construction 134; Likert 79–80; measurement 44–45
scattergram 131
scenarios 8, 67, 98, 111, 165
Scientific School of Management 29
secondary analysis 58–59, 67, 111–13, 115–16, 120, 125
semi-structured interviews 94–96
simulation (gaming) 61, 64–67, 70
social desirability 83–84, 107
standard deviation (SD) 123–24
statistical analyses results 129–30
sub-questions 15, 19, 20–21
subjects (selection) 69
survey: characteristics and types 74–75; non-response 83; reliability and validity of questionnaires 82–83; research with questionnaires 76–77;

scales 79–80; statistical analysis 128; written questionnaire 75–82
survey (criteria): answer categories 79; clear-cut and unambiguous items 78–79; leading questions/statements 79
survey (layout): accompanying letter 82; introductory section 81; inviting and clear 81–82; order of questions 81
survey (written questionnaire): control variables 80–81; criteria 78–79; design 77–78; layout 81–82; pilot study 82; process 75–76

TEDx online seminars 157
Texas schools (quantitative data) 134
textual analysis 108–10; discourse analysis 109; narrative analysis 109; rhetorical analysis 109–10
theoretical framework: empirical cycle 24–28; philosophies of science 31–36; theory in public administration research 36–42; research design 54–55; what is theory? 28–30
theoretical framework (philosophies of science): empirical-analytical approach 32–34; interpretative approach 34–36; introduction 31–32
theoretical framework (public administration research): conclusions 41–42; criteria 40–41; deductive research and theory 38–40; examples 37–38; falsification and verification 26–27, 32; inductive research and theory 41; introduction 36–37; literature skills 39; regulative cycle 28
theoretical framework (reporting results): deductive research 162; model 161; title 160; writing for practical purposes 163
theoretical generalization 35, 71, 92
theory: definition 28; scientific theory 28; what is theory? 28–30
theory (examples in public administration research): citizenship 38; Cuban Missile Crisis 37; *grip-group* culture theory 37–38; regional governments, Italy 37
thick description (qualitative research) 140
time dimension in research: both 'sides' of an event 56; cohort studies 56; cross-sectional studies 57; panel

studies 56–57; past events 57; trend studies 57
trend studies: 57, 111
triangulation 52–53, 86, 91, 92, 95, 100
t-test 128–30, 133

United Nations (UN): globalization 3; HCR (refugee agency) 104, 113; regulatory agencies 89
Unwelcome Tidings 166

validating/standardizing measurement instruments 50–51
validation 50
validity (strategies and methods):case studies 87, 90–91, 92–93; desk research 102, 105, 107, 112, 113, 116; experiments 68–70; interviews 95, 100; observation 72; questionnaires 75, 79–80, 82–84
validity: (types): internal 49; external 49–50
variables: operationalization 44–45, 48, 49; theoretical framework 29–30, 33–35, 40
variables (types): control 64, 80–81, 132; dependent 22, 29–30, 34, 44, 49;

endogenous 63; exogenous 63–64; independent 29, 34, 44, 63, 81; intervening 63–64, 148
variance analysis 130, 132–33, 136
verification 26–27, 123

water management experiments 68
Why It's Amazing that Federal Programs Work at All 87
World Bank 105
World Economic Forum 105
World Health Organization (WHO) 103, 104
World Values Survey: description 51; power distance measure (hierarchy in society) 135
written formats for results: case study report 156; popular science publication 156–57; professional publication for practitioners 156; research report/policy advice 156; respondents' report 156; scientific book 156; scientific, international refereed journal 156